Youth Cultures in the Age of Global Media

Studies in Childhood and Youth
Series Editors: **Allison James**, University of Sheffield, UK, and **Adrian L. James**, University of Sheffield, UK.

Titles include:

Kate Bacon
TWINS IN SOCIETY
Parents, Bodies, Space and Talk

David Buckingham, Sara Bragg and Mary Jane Kehily
YOUTH CULTURES IN THE AGE OF GLOBAL MEDIA

David Buckingham and Vebjørg Tingstad (*editors*)
CHILDHOOD AND CONSUMER CULTURE

Tom Cockburn
RETHINKING CHILDREN'S CITIZENSHIP

Sam Frankel
CHILDREN, MORALITY AND SOCIETY

Allison James
SOCIALISING CHILDREN

Allison James, Anne-Trine Kjørholt and Vebjørg Tingstad (*editors*)
CHILDREN, FOOD AND IDENTITY IN EVERYDAY LIFE

Nicholas Lee
CHILDHOOD AND BIOPOLITICS
Climate Change, Life Processes and Human Futures

Manfred Liebel, Karl Hanson, Iven Saadi and Wouter Vandenhole (*editors*)
CHILDREN'S RIGHTS FROM BELOW
Cross-Cultural Perspectives

Helen Stapleton
SURVIVING TEENAGE MOTHERHOOD
Myths and Realities

Afua Twum-Danso Imoh and Robert Ame
CHILDHOODS AT THE INTERSECTION OF THE LOCAL AND THE GLOBAL

Hanne Warming
PARTICIPATION, CITIZENSHIP AND TRUST IN CHILDREN'S LIVES

Rebekah Willett, Chris Richards, Jackie Marsh, Andrew Burn and Julia Bishop (*editors*)
CHILDREN, MEDIA AND PLAYGROUND CULTURES
Ethnographic Studies of School Playtimes

Studies in Childhood and Youth
Series Standing Order ISBN 978–0–230–21686–0 hardback
(*outside North America only*)

You can receive future titles in this series as they are published by placing a standing order. Please contact your bookseller or, in case of difficulty, write to us at the address below with your name and address, the title of the series and the ISBN quoted above.

Customer Services Department, Macmillan Distribution Ltd, Houndmills, Basingstoke, Hampshire RG21 6XS, England

Youth Cultures in the Age of Global Media

Edited by

David Buckingham
Professor of Communications and Media Studies, Loughborough University, UK

Sara Bragg
Senior Research Fellow, University of Brighton, UK

and

Mary Jane Kehily
Professor of Childhood and Youth Studies, The Open University, UK

First published 2014 by
PALGRAVE MACMILLAN

Palgrave Macmillan in the UK is an imprint of Macmillan Publishers Limited, registered in England, company number 785998, of Houndmills, Basingstoke, Hampshire RG21 6XS.

Palgrave Macmillan in the US is a division of St Martin's Press LLC, 175 Fifth Avenue, New York, NY 10010.

Palgrave Macmillan is the global academic imprint of the above companies and has companies and representatives throughout the world.

Palgrave® and Macmillan® are registered trademarks in the United States, the United Kingdom, Europe and other countries.

ISBN 978–1–137–00814–5

This book is printed on paper suitable for recycling and made from fully managed and sustained forest sources. Logging, pulping and manufacturing processes are expected to conform to the environmental regulations of the country of origin.

A catalogue record for this book is available from the British Library.

A catalog record for this book is available from the Library of Congress.

Typeset by MPS Ltd, Chennai, India.

Contents

v

Acknowledgements

Most of the chapters in this book were originally presented as papers at a series of seminars entitled 'Rethinking Youth Cultures in the Age of Global Media', which ran between 2009 and 2011. We gratefully acknowledge the funding provided by the UK Economic and Social Research Council. We would also like to recognize the contributions of the many other academics and practitioners who presented papers or acted as 'discussants' at these seminars, including Shaku Banaji, Barbie Clarke, John Clarke, Liesbeth de Block, Francesco d'Orazio, Alan France, DK of Mediasnackers, Sian Lincoln, Rob MacDonald, Bill Osgerby, David Oswell and Karen Wells.

Notes on Contributors

Patrick Alexander is College Lecturer in Social Anthropology at St Hugh's College, Oxford, and a Research Fellow in the School of Education at Oxford Brookes University. Patrick received his doctorate in 2010 from the Department of Education at the University of Oxford, where his research focused on the negotiation of age as an aspect of social identity for teachers and students in an English secondary school. Since then he has been involved in research exploring young people's perspectives of university, and is currently involved in research looking at how experiences of university frame contemporary transitions into adulthood.

Sara Bragg is Senior Research Fellow in the Education Research Centre at the University of Brighton, UK. Her doctoral research focused on 'violent' media genres, youth audiences and media education in the United Kingdom; she has also researched debates about the 'sexualization' of childhood; youth 'voice' and participation in schools; school ethos and 'creative' research methods. She is the co-author of *Young People, Sex and the Media* (with David Buckingham, 2004); co-editor of *Children and Young People's Cultural Worlds* (with Mary Jane Kehily, 2013) and has published in journals including *Feminist Media Studies, Gender and Education, Children and Society*, and edited collections including *Researching Creative Learning: Methods and Issues* (2011) and *The Routledge Companion to Media and Gender* (2013).

David Buckingham is Professor of Communications and Media Studies at Loughborough University, UK, and a Visiting Professor at the Norwegian Centre for Child Research, NTNU Trondheim. His research focuses on children's and young people's interactions with electronic media, and on media education. David is the author, co-author or editor of numerous books, including most recently *Beyond Technology: Children's Learning in the Age of Digital Culture* (2007), *Youth, Identity and Digital Media* (2008), *Video Cultures: Media Technology and Amateur Creativity* (2009) and *The Material Child: Growing Up in Consumer Culture* (2011).

Elisabeth El Rafaie is Senior Lecturer in The Centre for Language and Communication Research at Cardiff University. Her main research interests are in visual and multimodal communication, with a particular focus on newspaper cartoons, autobiographical comics (or 'graphic memoirs'), and the use of visual storytelling in health campaigns. Much of her work has explored the differences between verbal and visual/multimodal forms of metaphor, irony and humour. Her publications include 'Heterosemiosis: Mixing sign systems in graphic narrative texts' (*Semiotica*, 2012) and *Autobiographical Comics: Life Writing in Pictures*.

Carles Feixa is Professor of Social Anthropology at the University of Lleida (Catalonia, Spain). Former VP for Europe of ISA RC34 (Sociology of Youth), he is author of several books: *De Jovenes bandas y tribus* (1998), *Jovens na America Latina* (with S. Caccia-Bava and Y. Gonlezalez, 2004) and *Global Youth? Hybrid Identities and Plural Worlds* (with Pam Nilan, 2006).

Rosalind Gill is Professor of Social and Cultural Analysis at King's College London. She is interested in questions of power, inequality and social justice as they relate to culture, subjectivity, technology, representation and labour. She is the author of *Gender and the Media* (2007), and the co-editor of *Secrecy and Silence in the Research Process* (with Roisin Ryan-Flood, 2010); *New Femininities* (with Christina Scharff, 2011) and *Theorising Cultural Work* (with Mark Banks and Stephanie Taylor, 2013).

Christine Griffin is Professor of Social Psychology at the University of Bath. She has been involved in a wide variety of research projects on aspects of young people's lives, often working in multi-disciplinary teams. Much of her recent work explores the relationship between identities and consumption for young people, with a long-standing interest in gender relations and young women's negotiation of contemporary femininity. Her publications include *Standpoints and Differences: Essays in Practice of Feminist Psychology* (with Karen Henwood and Ann Phoenix, 1998), *Typical Girls? Young Women from School to the Job Market* (1985) and *Representations of Youth* (1993).

Rupa Huq is Senior Lecturer in Sociology at Kingston University, UK. She has also taught on Media and Cultural Studies courses at Kingston University. Research interests largely cluster around youth culture and pop music, which were the subject of her first book *Beyond Subculture* (2006), which was shortlisted for the Philip Abrams Memorial Prize of the British Sociological Association; and around cultures of suburbia, the subject of two further books: *On the Edge: The Contested Cultures of English Suburbia* (2013) and *Making Sense of Suburbia Through Popular Culture* (2013).

Kathrin Hörschelmann is Senior Lecturer in Human Geography at the University of Durham and currently a Visiting Research Fellow at the Leibniz Institute for Regional Studies in Leipzig, Germany. Her research interests include the political geographies of youth; visual and media culture; globalization, youth culture and social inequalities; feminist theory and the cultural politics of post-socialist transformation. She is the co-author of *Children, Youth and the City* (2011), co-editor of *Contested Bodies of Childhood and Youth* (2010) and *Spaces of Masculinities* (2004) and author of several articles in international journals such as *Transactions of the Institute of British Geographers, Antipode, Political Geography, Social and Cultural Geography*, and *Environment and Planning A*.

Mary Celeste Kearney is Associate Professor of Film, Television, and Theatre at the University of Notre Dame, Indiana. She earned her PhD from the University of Southern California's School of Cinematic Arts, and has taught in the Department of Radio–Television–Film at the University of Texas at Austin the past 14 years. Mary's research to date has focused primarily on gender, youth and media culture. She is the author of *Girls Make Media* (2006) and the editor of *Mediated Girlhoods: New Explorations of Girls' Media Culture* (2011) and *The Gender and Media Reader* (2011). She is Founding Director of Cinemakids, a programme for inspiring young media producers.

Mary Jane Kehily is Professor of Childhood and Youth Studies at the Open University, UK. She has a background in cultural studies and education and research interests in gender and sexuality, narrative and identity and popular culture. Recent work explores changing conceptualizations of Western childhood and new motherhood as a site of identity change. Books include *Gender, Sexuality and Schooling: Shifting Agendas in Social Learning* (2002), *An Introduction to Childhood Studies* (2009), *Understanding Youth: Perspectives, Identities and Practices* (2007), *Gender, Youth and Culture: Young Masculinities and Femininities* (with Anoop Nayak, 2008), *Making Modern Mothers* (co-authored with Rachel Thomson, Lucy Hadfield and Sue Sharpe, 2011) and *Understanding Childhood* (2013).

Ofra Koffman has recently completed a Leverhulme Postdoctoral Fellowship at the Department for Culture, Media and Creative Industries, King's College London, and is currently on maternity leave. Her postdoctoral research examined the recent focus on adolescent girls within development policy, particularly the work of DFID, the Nike Foundation and the World Bank. She has previously researched 'adolescence', 'girlhood' and 'teenage pregnancy' policy in Britain.

Ritty A. Lukose is Associate Professor at The Gallatin School of New York University. Her research and writing focus on the cultural and political dimensions of globalization within India. She is currently focused on the transformations of feminist political imaginaries within this context. She is the author of *Liberalization's Children: Gender, Youth and Consumer Citizenship in Globalizing India* (2009/2010) and the co-editor of *South Asian Feminisms* (with Ania Loomba, 2012).

Sunaina Maira is Professor of Asian American Studies at the University of California, Davis. She is the author of *Desis in the House: Indian American Youth Culture in New York City* (2002). She co-edited *Youthscapes: The Popular, the National, the Global and Contours of the Heart: South Asians Map North America*, which won the American Book Award in 1997. Her most recent book is *Missing: Youth, Citizenship, and Empire after 9/11* (2009).

Angela McFarlane is Director of Public Engagement and Learning at Kew Gardens and Visiting Professor at Kings College London. Until 2008, she was Professor of Education at Bristol University. She is responsible for the public programme at Kew, including the visitor experience of the gardens, visitor services, marketing, PR, publishing, digital media and education.

Anoop Nayak is Professor of Social and Cultural Geography at Newcastle University. His research interests are in race and ethnicity, youth cultural identities, class cultures, and masculinities and social change. He is the author of an ethnographic study *Race, Place and Globalization: Youth Cultures in a Changing World* (2003), *Gender, Youth and Culture: Young Masculinities and Femininities* (with Mary Jane Kehily, 2008) and *Geographical Thought: An Introduction to Ideas in Human Geography* (with Alex Jeffries, 2011).

Hilary Pilkington is Professor of Sociology at the University of Manchester. She has researched and published widely on late and post-Soviet Russian youth practices. Publications include *Russia's Youth and Its Culture* (1994), *Looking West? Cultural Globalization and Russian Youth Cultures* (with E. Omel'chenko, M. Flynn and E. Starkova, 2002) and *Russia's Skinheads: Exploring and Rethinking Subcultural Lives* (with E.Omel'chenko and A. Garifzianova, 2010). She is currently coordinating the AHRC-funded project *Post-socialist Punk: Beyond the Double Irony* *of Self-abasement* (2009–2013) and the EC-funded FP7 'MYPLACE' project on youth and civic engagement (2011–15).

Oriol Romaní is Professor of Social Anthropology at the University Rovira i Virgili of Tarragona and President of the interdisciplinary association on Drugs and Health Group, Igia. He specializes in medical and urban anthropology, biographical methodology, use of drugs, youth and marginalization. He has published widely on these themes.

Elisabeth Soep is Senior Producer and Research Director at Youth Radio, the Oakland, California-based youth-driven production company that serves as National Public Radio's official youth desk. With a PhD from Stanford, Lissa has written about digital media and learning for academic journals (*Harvard Educational Review, National Civic Review, Comunicar*); popular outlets (Boing Boing, NPR, Edutopia) and books including *Drop that Knowledge* (with V. Chávez, 2010) and *Youthscapes* (with S. Maira, 2004). In 2011, Lissa became one of the six members of the MacArthur Foundation's Youth and Participatory Politics Research Network, which explores how young people use digital and social media to express voice and exert influence in public spheres.

Helen Thornham is Research Fellow in the Institute of Communication Studies, University of Leeds. She is the author of *Ethnographies of the Videogame* (2011) and the co-editor of *Renewing Feminisms* (with Elke Weissmann, 2013) and *Content Cultures* (with Simon Popple, 2013). She currently leads an RCUK Digital Economy Network+ investigating the digital transformations of communities and culture, and is interested in issues of gender, technology, youth, mediations and identity.

Kyong Yoon is Assistant Professor in Cultural Studies at the University of British Columbia's Okanagan Campus where he teaches new media culture. He has recently researched new media audiences, mediated tourism and reputation on the Internet. His ongoing research project entitled 'Being Digital, Migratory and Narrative: The Diaspora of Korean "Digital Native" Immigrants in Canada' explores how digital technologies engage with migratory processes and transform Canada's landscape of immigration.

Introduction: Rethinking Youth Cultures in the Age of Global Media

David Buckingham and Mary Jane Kehily

Most of the chapters in this book were originally presented during a two-year seminar series funded by the UK Economic and Social Research Council. Under the title 'Rethinking youth cultures in the age of global media', our discussions ranged across a set of key themes, including the history of research on youth culture, the impact of globalization, youth participation, the role of digital media and the place of youth in the commercial market. By way of an introduction, we would like to explore some of the challenges that are implicitly posed by our title. Do we need to rethink youth cultures in the age of global media – and if so, why?

Youth cultures

The category of 'youth' has been a focus of attention for academic researchers since the psychologist G. Stanley Hall's groundbreaking work on adolescence at the beginning of the twentieth century (Hall, 1906); while the term 'youth culture' was first coined by the sociologist Talcott Parsons in 1942. Despite the many differences between them, both writers saw youth as a separate and distinctive phase of human development, and as a potentially difficult period of adjustment to social norms and expectations. Succeeding generations of sociologists and psychologists have sought to define the unique characteristics of youth and youth culture, often in starkly divergent terms. In recent years, for example, psychological research has seen the development of the 'emerging adulthood' perspective (Arnett, 2004), while sociological research in the United Kingdom has coalesced around the notion of 'youth transitions' (e.g., MacDonald and Marsh, 2005).

However, at least in the English-speaking world, research on youth *culture* – or, as we would prefer, youth *cultures* in the plural – has

1

been massively influenced by the pioneering work of the University of Birmingham Centre for Contemporary Cultural Studies (CCCS). Building to some extent on the 'Chicago School' of sociology that had preceded it, the CCCS established the study of youth culture as an important dimension of the emerging academic discipline of Cultural Studies (e.g., Hall and Jefferson, 1976; Hebdige, 1979). Through ethnographic research and semiotic textual analysis of key groups such as the teds, the mods and rockers, the skinheads and the punks, this work situated young people's cultural practices – including their consumption and use of media and popular culture – within a broader account of the social and historical context of post-war Britain. The Centre's analysis of youth culture was part of its wider political project, which was centrally informed by varieties of Marxist and post-Marxist theory: youth culture was implicitly seen, in the terms of the Italian Marxist Antonio Gramsci, as a site of struggle, in which the hegemony of the dominant classes might be challenged and contested.

The CCCS researchers analysed youth subcultures as expressions of resistance, in which young people made connections between their everyday experience and the wider social inequalities inscribed in class relations (Hall and Jefferson, 1976). The CCCS analysis suggested that engaging in subcultural activity involved young people in acts of 'double articulation', firstly with the parental generation and secondly with political formations and agents of post-war social change. In the process, the CCCS provided an account of working-class youth culture that effectively challenged the pathological views of 'deviance' and 'delinquency' that dominated both public debate and a good deal of mainstream academic research. To view youth subcultures merely as manifestations of adolescent rebellion underestimates young people's collective investment in change through intergenerational conversations and creative forms of protest. By contrast, the CCCS approach sought to provide a generative way of interpreting youth subcultures as purposeful inventions, imbued with meaning.

The story of the Birmingham Centre has taken on almost mythological proportions, and in recent years its legacy has been widely questioned. Subsequent authors – not least exponents of 'post-subcultural' research (e.g., Muggleton and Weinzierl, 2003) – have extensively challenged what they see as the limitations and absences of the CCCS approach. The 'Birmingham School' is now routinely dismissed for its narrow preoccupation with social class, and its neglect of gender, 'race', and sexuality. It is accused of 'over-politicizing' youth culture, and merely celebrating youthful resistance to adult authority. And it is criticized for adopting a romantic notion of authenticity – as though youth culture arises 'from the streets', somehow expressing a pristine and spontaneous rebellion against the established social order. For examples of such criticisms, see Bennett (1999), Muggleton (2000); and Thornton (1995).

The paradox, as Christine Griffin points out in her contribution to this book, is that many of these same criticisms were being made by members of the 'Birmingham School' at the time; and if we follow this tradition from its origins in the mid-1970s into the 1980s, we can find plenty of examples of research addressing precisely these absences and concerns. Indeed, if we look back to the 'canonical' texts of the CCCS, such as Hall and Jefferson's *Resistance Through Rituals* (1976) or Willis's *Learning to Labour* (1977), it is hard to see much evidence of the 'celebratory' approach to youth culture of which they are often accused: if anything, they seem rather gloomily preoccupied with the limited and self-defeating nature of much youthful 'resistance'.

Yet if recent researchers have perhaps been unduly inclined to caricature the CCCS approach, and to proclaim that we are in the age of the 'post', a careful reappraisal of this tradition is certainly necessary. Critiques of the 'Birmingham School' have commonly focused on a small selection of early studies and tended to ignore its wider body of work. CCCS has been set up as the 'straw man' to be knocked down in order to make way for the post-subcultural new order. This compressed reading overlooks the diversity of interests and methods within the Centre. Collections such as *Policing the Crisis* (Hall et al., 1978), *Off Centre* (Franklin et al., 1991) and *Border Patrols* (Steinberg et al., 1997) bear testimony to the range of work exploring 'race', gender and sexuality, respectively, while also offering insights into the politics and pedagogy of collaborative work (see Kehily, 2010). CCCS can be seen as part of a broader project of knowledge production that was also radical in educational terms, blending new ways of looking with new ways of working together. The CCCS experience entailed working collectively towards shared goals, developing new ways of understanding the interplay between individual and society, for instance through autobiography, memory work and narrative approaches. Distinctive features of work from the Centre such as the concern with the aesthetics of writing, historically informed accounts, and the early recognition of intersectionality remain under-acknowledged in subsequent critical accounts.

Meanwhile, the 'classic' Birmingham studies of the 1970s also need to be understood in their historical context, as a contingent response to a particular set of cultural and political circumstances. Read today, they speak of a society beginning to fragment, with the collapse of an industrial economy, the rise of global migration and the challenges of new forms of 'identity politics'. It would indeed be surprising if the insights and analytical concepts developed at this time were sufficient to encompass the vastly changed circumstances of the twenty-first century. Yet ultimately, the CCCS offered a theory and an analysis of youth *sub*cultures, and not of youth cultures more broadly: not least for political reasons, it was self-consciously concerned with an important but limited range of cultural practices. As authors such as Gary Clarke (1981) pointed out at the time, there was a bias in favour of the spectacular – a bias that inevitably led to a neglect of the complexity and diversity of most young people's experience. The cultural practices of the 'ordinary' young people of the 1970s – the teenyboppers, the glam rockers, the disco dancers – barely make an appearance in the CCCS texts of the time (although there are couple of notable exceptions to this: McRobbie and Garber, 1975; Taylor and Wall, 1976). One suspects that such apparently conformist, consumerist tastes would have proven hard to mobilize in the interests of the Centre's broader political project.

Recent authors have attempted to reconceptualize the concept of 'subculture' – or alternatively to replace it with different metaphors (see Bennett, 1999; Hesmondhalgh, 2005) – although such attempts have been less than conclusive. In a manner that directly echoes Clarke's argument from 1981, they have suggested that contemporary youth cultures are generally more diverse, more fluid and more provisional than the 'classic' subcultures of the CCCS research of the 1970s. Card-carrying members of subcultures are, they argue, few and far between; and contemporary youth cultural practices are more commercialized, and more politically ambivalent. While some groups – such as goths or 'emo kids' – can perhaps still be accounted for in terms of subcultural theory, the range of cultural practices that followed in the wake of the 'club cultures' of the late 1980s and 1990s are much harder to explain in terms of resistance and hegemony.

This post-subcultural moment has resulted in a stronger emphasis on the mercurial character of youth formations. Soaking up the impact of late modern 'choice biographies' and processes of globalization, post-subcultural studies have drawn attention to plurality, fragmentation and the proliferation of multiple cultures of youth, with shifting 'scenes' and changeable alliances based on notions of style and taste (Muggleton and Weinzierl, 2003; Redhead et al., 1997; Thornton, 1995). The investments of these second- and third-generation youth researchers appear to cohere in the sphere of leisure. Going out, drinking, clubbing and group participation in city centre nightlife have become the focus of studies that portray youth as the hedonistic occupants of 'cool places' (Skelton and Valentine, 1998). The interpretative shift from reading young people's practices as meaningful social commentary to an exploration of pleasure-seeking individualism can be seen as a reflection of changing times, as well as the changing political and emotional investments of researchers themselves.

The post-subculturalists in their turn have been rightly criticized for their neglect of the continuing relevance of class (Blackman, 2005; Shildrick and MacDonald, 2005). The latter argument has to some extent been reinforced by the recent emergence of a new working-class 'folk devil' in the figure of the 'chav' – a figure that, as Mary Jane Kehily and Anoop Nayak explain in their chapter, has become the vehicle of a contemporary form of class disgust. In practice, the work of the 'post-subculturalists' also appears oddly preoccupied with spectacular manifestations of youth cultural style: there are many cultural practices that are engaged in by 'ordinary' young people that continue to fall well outside the remit of such research. Academic researchers still appear strangely reluctant to look at the relatively mundane, conservative things that the majority of young people do in their leisure time – and indeed to consider the possibility that in such respects, young people may actually be rather more like adults than we might be prepared to admit.

The rethinking that is taking place here is thus a necessary, ongoing process: it reflects changes in academic fashions as well as youthful ones, and it relates to much broader social, cultural and political changes. Yet in reassessing academic traditions, it is important to avoid a kind of 'presentism' – a tendency to reread the past in light of the very different circumstances of the present. Like youth culture itself, academic research in this field needs to be understood historically, in terms of the imperatives of its time.

Youth

A further reason for rethinking relates to the category of 'youth' itself. Like 'childhood', youth can of course be seen as a social construct. The ways in which societies divide up the life course vary significantly across different time periods and cultural contexts. Historical studies of youth (e.g., Gillis, 1981; Mitterauer, 1992) and 'classic' anthropological accounts (e.g., van Gennep, 1909; Mead, 1928) illustrate something of the diversity here; and these differences have also been increasingly apparent in recent studies of youth culture (see, among many others, Austin and Willard, 1998; Nilan and Feixa, 2006; Nayak and Kehily, 2007). Yet even within contemporary Western societies, many of the meanings that are associated with youth are undoubtedly changing; and the period that is encompassed by the term 'youth' itself seems to have become ever-more elastic.

Thus, on the one hand, it can be argued that childhood seems to be blurring into youth – or at least that public perceptions and anxieties about such a prospect appear to be growing. The recent debate in the United Kingdom (and in many other English-speaking countries) about the 'sexualization' of childhood provides an especially controversial case in point here (see Bragg and Buckingham, 2013). Campaigners in this area are crucially preoccupied with policing the boundary between childhood and youth, in relation not only to sexual experience but also to sexual *knowledge*; yet in a period when sexual representations have become much more widely available through digital media, such attempts at regulation appear increasingly impossible to sustain. This example of course reflects a wider anxiety about the 'disappearance' of childhood, in which the media and popular culture are frequently seen as the destroyers of children's innocence. While this argument has been around for many years, it appears to have taken on a renewed force in recent years, not least in response to children's growing access to consumer culture (see Buckingham, 2011).

Yet on the other hand, we are also witnessing an extension of youth, or a blurring of the boundary between youth and adulthood. If youth is, as Erikson (1968) argued, a kind of 'moratorium' – a liminal, in-between state – then it is arguably one that appears to be lasting much longer and ending much later than it used to do. Young people are leaving the family home at an older age, and 'settling down' in terms of stable jobs and relationships at a later point. Indeed, the lack of stable jobs or affordable independent housing means that 'settling down' is hardly a prospect for many young people. Some psychologists argue that this period of 'emerging adulthood' is now continuing well into the thirties (e.g., Arnett, 2004); while in a different way, sociologists confirm that the 'transition to adulthood' has become a significantly more unstable, precarious process (e.g., Blatterer, 2007). Indeed, one might well ask what kind of state young people are transitioning towards: what is the stable condition of adult maturity which young people are apparently taking longer to achieve? It could be argued that, for all sorts of reasons, the values of achieved 'adulthood' are less easily obtainable than they used to be, but also, for many, less desirable in the first place.

Media and marketing undoubtedly play a key role in this process, but it is a difficult and ambivalent one. The marketing of computer games or rock music, for example, increasingly seems to reflect a broadening of the youth demographic – a sense that 'youthfulness' is something that can be invoked, packaged and sold to people who are not by any stretch of the imagination any longer youthful. As Andy Bennett (2007) has pointed out, forms of popular music that were once identified as exclusive to youth are now increasingly attracting multigenerational audiences: this applies not just to well-established styles (like punk and metal) that have established, 'die-hard' fans, but also to newer electronic dance styles. Similar phenomena can arguably be identified in areas such as fashion and the fitness industry. As Bennett suggests, contemporary marketing often implies that you are 'as young as you feel'. However, there may also be a contrary process of reaction here. Young people may come to resent older people trespassing on 'their' territory, and seek to defend it by deploying ever-more arcane and inaccessible forms of cultural capital. Meanwhile, marketers and media producers may find themselves trapped in an ever-moving spiral of credibility, where broadening one's audience comes to be seen as a form of 'sell-out' and a betrayal of authenticity (see Buckingham's chapter in this volume).

'Youth' is, of course, a matter of lived experience; but its cultural meanings are socially and historically defined. At present – at least in Western societies – it appears that these meanings have become more problematic, and more contested. While it has always been seen as a state of transition, the status of youth seems to have become ever-more provisional and uncertain. In this context, we might well ask whether it still makes sense to think of 'youth culture' as something that is specific to young people at all.

The global and the local

Much of the discussion thus far requires further qualification and rethinking once we begin to include a global perspective. For several years, one of the present authors (DB) taught a masters' course about youth culture to a very diverse group of international students. The course often began with an autobiographical 'icebreaker', in which the students were invited to describe their own relationship with youth culture, and specifically with the role of media. The exercise was designed to raise broader questions – for example, about what it means to be a 'member' of a youth culture – but it also very clearly demonstrated a range of cultural differences. In terms of media, what the students recalled from their own youth was often a complex mixture of the global and the local. They talked about mainstream British or US pop music or Hollywood teen movies, but also about Brazilian funk, Danish death metal, Japanese anime and cosplay, or French ska. Furthermore, it was clear from the comparisons between them that 'youth' as a specific life stage, and 'youth culture' as an aspect of that stage, was not a universal experience. For many of them, youth was not about resistance, subversion and subculture at all: it was a period of relative conformity, of remaining close to their parents and their parents' values, and of doing what was expected of them. While some described themselves as members of specific 'subcultural' groups, this was not a common experience: most were aware of such groups, but felt ambivalent and uncertain about the possibility of identifying with them.

Teaching these students – and indeed younger, but equally diverse, groups of undergraduates – about the canonical texts of youth culture research ('Birmingham and beyond') reinforced a sense that the academic debate about youth culture is highly culturally and historically specific, indeed, almost parochial in its limited scope. As we have suggested, the CCCS approach arises from a particular moment in the history of postwar Britain, and from a particular *interpretation* of that history. Its cultural specificity – or even its parochialism – is not simply about the specific phenomena it explored (the skinheads, the teddy boys or the punks), but also about the theories that were used to explain them.

As teachers and researchers, we have become increasingly aware of the potential mismatch here, between the experiences of our global students and the kind of research and theory that they can use to help them understand those experiences. It remains important for students to read 'canonical' texts – although we can certainly have a debate about which texts are in or out. But the abiding question is whether that canon of texts any longer equips us with the theoretical concepts and tools that we need in a context of increasing global diversity and mobility. As Ritty Lukose argues in her chapter – and as several other contributors to this book amply demonstrate – we need to understand the various manifestations of global youth culture not just in relation to broad theories of globalization but also in the context of specific local histories and circumstances. This 'globalizing turn' in youth culture research has been manifested in many other recent texts (e.g., Huq, 2005; Maira and Soep, 2005; Nayak, 2003; Nilan and Feixa, 2006), and represents a much-needed opening out of the field.

Meanwhile, of course, the media play a crucial role in these changing relationships between the global and the local. Young people are now growing up with significantly greater access to globalized media: media companies are increasingly constructing and targeting global markets, and young people are using new media to form and sustain transnational connections. Growing numbers of them have also experienced global migration, and inhabit communities in which a wide range of global cultures mix and cross-fertilize (see de Block and Buckingham, 2007). New media technologies offer new possibilities for transnational connectedness and dialogue; and yet the media market is increasingly dominated by a small number of global corporations. These developments are manifested in youth culture in specific ways, through the emergence of a global *lingua franca* (e.g., in the form of MTV or celebrity culture) and through the development of new 'hybrid' forms (as in the case of hip-hop or bhangra).

However, this is not simply a matter of changing relations between 'centre' and 'periphery': on the contrary, youth cultures typically display a complex and uneven negotiation between the global and the local. For some young people, the 'flows' of global capital can be enjoyed and embraced in ways that increase the repertoire of expressive youth cultures and styles. For others who are geographically displaced and living transitional lives, their relationship to global cultures may seem distant and remote; and there remain significant inequalities in access to media, both within nations and at a global level. The study of youth culture in this wider global context thus challenges the limitations of place-based research, and necessitates a less parochial approach; and it also requires innovative methodologies for accessing the cultural worlds of young people.

Media

Media have always occupied a rather awkward position in research on youth culture. In much of the early CCCS work, media were implicitly identified with mainstream adult society and with the operation of hegemonic power. They were seen as purveyors of misrepresentations (as in 'moral panics') or of 'the dominant ideology', a mysterious force that was seen to impose consensus and obedience to the social order, even among those whose interests it did not serve. Following the theory of 'repressive tolerance', the media's attempts to respond to youth culture were judged to merely recuperate and commodify its resistant potential (Hebdige, 1979). Over time, however, that narrative came to be challenged: it was recognized that youth culture was always mediated (or 'mediatized'), and that the protagonists of youth subcultures often used the media in very deliberate ways for their own purposes. Academic accounts emerging in the wake of the 'club cultures' of the early 1990s (e.g., McRobbie, 1994; Thornton, 1995) moved significantly beyond the conspiratorial views of the early CCCS approach.

The emergence of digital media, and especially of so-called 'participatory' or 'social' media, marks a further shift, and indicates a further need for rethinking. Clearly, it is important to avoid the kind of idealistic celebration that has often characterized both academic and popular accounts of these developments. Nevertheless, these new media do offer significant opportunities for communication and self-representation, and young people are often in the vanguard of such practices. To date, however, there has been relatively little cross-fertilization or dialogue between youth culture research and the growing body of academic work on young people and new media. There is often passing mention of youth culture in new media research – for example, in the large-scale MacArthur Foundation studies (e.g., Ito et al., 2010) or the monumental European surveys on young people and Internet safety (e.g., Livingstone et al., 2011) – but in general the topic seems conspicuous by its absence. Meanwhile, publications on youth culture tend to include only token chapters on digital media, as though authentic youth culture is still seen to be happening offline.

The popular conception of young people as 'digital natives' or as a 'digital generation' has rightfully come in for considerable criticism (e.g., Buckingham, 2006; Herring, 2008; Thomas, 2011). Such arguments typically rest on a combination of technological determinism and an essentializing or exoticizing view of young people. Here again, it is important to insist that much of what young people (and indeed adults) are doing online or with mobile technologies is not spectacular or glamorous or revolutionary, but fairly mundane and banal. Yet the fact remains that most young people today have grown up with relatively instant access to digital technology – and here it is important to include those in the developing world, for whom that technology most frequently takes a mobile form. It may well be that much of what they are doing online is simply a displacement or an extension of what previous generations were doing offline; and it may well be that the distinction between online and offline is rapidly becoming meaningless. However, a principled scepticism and a longer-term historical approach should not lead us to ignore what is genuinely new.

Here again, the analysis of online youth culture needs to extend beyond the spectacular *sub*cultures of fan communities, hackers and dedicated gamers that have already been disproportionately heavily researched. The more mundane processes of self-representation on social networking sites, the routine exchanging of photographs on mobile phones, and the commenting on video clips on sharing sites are everyday aspects of contemporary youth culture that are in need of more sustained and systematic research. Meanwhile, it is important to recognize the consequences of a culture of constant connectivity, in which the imperatives of self-advertisement are so critical and so intense. In this new situation, the forms of identity and relationship that are central to how we think about youth culture may well be changing in some quite profound and unpredictable ways.

Who's rethinking?

Finally, it would be worth asking about who is involved in this rethinking. We have already raised several questions about *them* – about how we identify and analyse the youth we select to study. But what about *us* – the researchers, academics, and perhaps public commentators who are doing this? And how do *we* relate to *them*? These are issues we take up in greater detail in our concluding chapter, but they are worth flagging up at this point.

There has been some useful discussion in recent years about the relationship between 'insider' and 'outsider' research on youth culture (e.g., Best, 2007; Hodkinson, 2005; MacRae, 2007). However, we would argue that the large majority of youth culture researchers are *by definition* outsiders: they are people who were formerly young. This does not invalidate the whole enterprise, but it does point to the need for rather more critical reflexivity than has often been the case. Youth culture researchers are by no means immune from the tendency to exoticize, to romanticize or to vicariously identify with those whom they study. Like many public commentators, and indeed many other adults, they can easily fall prey to the pleasures of nostalgia or wish fulfilment. Alternatively, they can implicitly judge present-day youth cultures with the 'wisdom' of hindsight, and indeed with a kind of historical condescension: young people weren't like that in *our* day.

In research and in many other fields of practice – education, marketing, welfare, politics, media – the figure of 'youth' is variously imagined, represented, invoked, deployed and addressed; and in the process, its reference point acquires a somewhat elusive quality. Research, like media, is a form of representation; and while this is unavoidable, it needs to be acknowledged. Perhaps we should be most suspicious of it when it purports – as youth culture research often does – to speak *on behalf of* those whom it claims to represent. As we discuss in our concluding chapter, this often creates difficulties when we seek to respond to the growing demand for 'youth voice': ethically, methodologically and politically, 'giving voice' to young people, or enabling them to 'find' and use their own voices – while a laudable aim – is unlikely to be a straightforward matter.

Overview of the book

This book is organized in five parts, each containing three chapters. The first looks at broad theoretical and disciplinary issues in youth culture research. Subsequent parts consider the changing relations between the global and the local; media and consumption; youth participation; and political activity.

In Chapter 1, Christine Griffin explores the legacy of the Birmingham CCCS work on youth subcultures, briefly considered above. She engages with recent critiques, reasserting the value of the CCCS's focus on the mediated cultural practices through which young people constitute themselves and their gendered, classed and racialized identities. However, she also points to the need to draw on more contemporary social theory, not least in order to understand the changing nature of young people's identity construction, for example, in relation to their uses of social media.

Ritty Lukose's chapter re-evaluates frameworks for cultural studies of youth, drawing on the author's own work on globalization, youth and gender in India. Tracking changing understandings of 'culture' at the intersection between British Cultural Studies and American Anthropology, the chapter draws out the specific problems and possibilities of a distinctly cultural approach to the study of youth, and to the politics of youth identity. Lukose describes how she needed to rethink these existing frameworks in her efforts to make sense of the cultural politics of globalization, youth and gender in contemporary India.

The final chapter in this part, by Mary Celeste Kearney, makes the case for a historical approach to the study of youth cultures, both in general and specifically in relation to the author's own work on girls' media-making. Challenging a narrow preoccupation with new media technologies, the chapter draws attention to the continuities as well as the discontinuities in girls' media practices across generations. Kearney argues that this historical approach is very much in line with Cultural Studies' legacy of contextualized analysis; and that the study of previous generations of girls' media-making can help us better understand the media practices of today's female youth – and vice versa.

In Part II, 'The Global and the Local', the emphasis shifts to more detailed empirical studies. Hilary Pilkington presents some themes from her ongoing ethnographic research with skinheads in the far north of Russia. She traces the individual trajectories of some of her respondents in, through, and out of the 'skinhead' identity, discussing core elements of skinhead subculture – style, ideology and violence – as well as their family lives, friendships, the city they lived in and their educational, work and leisure contexts. In this way, the chapter develops an understanding of 'subculture' not as separate from but as deeply embedded in everyday lives and the structures and agencies that shape them.

In Chapter 5, Carles Feixa and Oriol Romaní look at a youth cultural phenomenon that articulates the global and the local in quite particular ways: the Latin Kings and Queens Nation in the Catalan city of Barcelona. Beginning from an incident of inter-gang violence, they trace the ways in which the phenomenon of 'Latin American street gangs' was represented in the mainstream media, and the meanings of 'nationhood' for the participants themselves. They look behind the headlines to explore how migrant youth are creating new forms of community and sociability that cut across borders of time and geography, reflecting new forms of globalized and nomadic identity.

In the final chapter in this part, Sunaina Maira takes us to another, very different context, presenting material from her ethnographic study of South Asian Muslim immigrant youth in the United States. Her research addresses issues of national belonging in the post-9/11 moment, exploring the impact of the 'War on Terror' on the everyday lives of working-class youth from communities targeted as suspect citizens or un-American aliens. The research focuses on a group of high school students who did not belong to formal 'activist' groups; and it interrogates the meaning of politics, citizenship and dissent in a climate of political repression, taking the argument beyond the binary of resistance and complicity.

Part III contains three chapters focusing on another of our key themes: media and consumption. Kyong Yoon explores how young people in East Asia are appropriating cultural commodities from other East Asian countries. Drawing on ethnographic inquiries into young South Koreans' engagements with Japanese media commodities, the chapter examines how these intra-Asian youth cultural practices make use of new digital technology and confront the complex mix of nationalizing, localizing and globalizing forces. The emergence of this intra-Asian youth culture usefully challenges received notions of global youth culture, which are predominantly focused on the non-Western localization of Western youth cultural forms.

In Chapter 8, Patrick Alexander explores how age is negotiated as an aspect of social identity by students and teachers at an English secondary school. The chapter proposes the idea of 'age imaginaries' as a means of conceptualizing the multiple discourses, practices and processes of meaning-making that combine to shape notions of age-based identity. Alexander explores how ideas about 'childhood' and 'growing up' are mediated through exchanges and interactions related to Internet use and mobile phone technology, in the context of lessons and in the 'illicit' media consumption and discussion that takes place on the margins of formal schooling.

Finally in this part, Mary Jane Kehily and Anoop Nayak explore how young people on the margins of social exclusion respond to the pejorative ways in which they are typically represented in mainstream media. They develop two parallel case studies, of 'pram face' teenage mothers, often seen as incompetent and unable to lift themselves out of the 'cycle of poverty', and 'chav lads' from unemployed families, who are frequently condemned for their criminal activity and for 'inappropriate' consumption practices. Drawing on their own long-term ethnographic research, Kehily and Nayak explore how these young people negotiate, displace and resist the affective power of these representations.

In Part IV, contributors address the theme of participation in a range of contrasting ways. Lissa Soep presents some experiences from her research at a community-based youth media organization in San Francisco. She analyses the production and the longer-term reception of two youth-generated radio stories about Kosovo and Northern Ireland that sparked tensions at the intersection of local, national and global youth cultures. Unlike much youth media research, the account here extends well beyond the production process by tracking the 'digital afterlife' of these stories, as they were linked to, commented upon, embedded, and otherwise reproduced online, in ways the authors themselves could neither predict nor control.

Helen Thornham and Angela McFarlane consider debates about media participation by means of a critical case study of the BBC 'user-generated content' project *Blast*. This now defunct online resource for teenagers aimed to inspire and equip its users to become creative content producers. The authors challenge the fantasies of creativity, learning and participation embedded in the project, arguing that they effaced significant questions around authorship and power. They propose that this form of user-generated work may merely represent a form of 'interpassivity', in which ideas of creative self-expression may actively prevent meaningful participation.

In Chapter 12, David Buckingham considers participation in a much more commercial context, that of contemporary marketing to young people. Beginning with a brief look at the history of youth marketing – and at academic responses to it – he moves on to consider a range of new participatory marketing practices, including peer-to-peer marketing, social networking, and 'co-creation'. Buckingham explores how these new practices are legitimated through new forms of market research discourse that represent young people not as 'passive consumers' but as active agents and participants; and he concludes by considering some of the troubling similarities between these arguments and those of some contemporary academics.

The final part of the book looks at politics, in both the narrow and broader senses. Kathrin Hörschelmann and Elisabeth El Refaie address the theme of citizenship, looking specifically at young people's interpretations of the medium of political cartoons. Drawing on qualitative research with school and college students in Bradford, UK, the chapter draws attention to the diverse, transnational character of young people's political concerns and identifications, and makes the case for an 'agonistic' conception of politics that moves beyond the rather worthy and consensual notions of citizenship that currently tend to dominate discussions of young people's civic participation and citizenship.

Chapter 14, by Ofra Koffman and Ros Gill, explores the emphasis on adolescent girls that has recently emerged within global health and development initiatives. They analyse the discourses of 'the girl effect' that have been promulgated by an alliance of corporate bodies, charitable foundations and NGOs, which see girls as holding the key to ending world poverty and improving well-being in the developing world. Examining media outputs and offline events, they interrogate the notions of girlhood, 'sisterhood' and the North/South divide that are being articulated in these initiatives, arguing that they work to efface continuing global inequalities.

Finally in this part, Rupa Huq's chapter moves away from the traditional focus on urban youth to address the experiences of suburban young people from different ethnic minority groups in two contrasting areas in the north and south of the United Kingdom. She explores the consequences of different histories of migration and settlement, experiences of 'fundamentalism' and anti-Muslim prejudice, and changing patterns of social mobility and political affiliation. In the process, Huq complicates familiar narratives of both 'radicalization' and 'assimilation', pointing to the emergence among second-generation migrants of a unique suburban British–Asian 'habitus' that transcends geographical location.

As the diverse contributions to this book suggest, 'youth' has been variously imagined, represented, invoked, deployed, researched and addressed. Yet in the process, its reference point tends to be somewhat elusive. By contrast, in fields such as education, politics, research and governance, there is a growing movement to promote, engage and listen to 'youth voice'. In these contexts, the category of youth is once more stabilized, and assigned attributes of obviousness and authenticity; and the participatory dimensions of new media are frequently celebrated as the transparent means by which youth can be accessed – and indeed 'empowered'. In the concluding chapter, Sara Bragg and David Buckingham look back over the volume as a whole, and seek to draw out some of these contrasts and connections with practice. In particular, the chapter explores how the kinds of critical, reflexive research discussed in this volume might help us respond theoretically, politically and methodologically to the demand for 'youth voice'. While offering suggestions for future research and practice, it also seeks to respect the elusiveness of youth for which our contributors have, collectively, argued.

In suggesting the need for some rethinking, then, we hope that this collection also demonstrates the need to maintain some continuities with the established traditions of research on youth culture. Youth cultures are undoubtedly protean and ever-changing, especially in an age of global media; and youth culture research needs to change with them. Yet it should also learn from and build upon the achievements of the past. We hope that the diversity and quality of the contributions we have gathered here illustrates the continuing vibrancy of this tradition of research, and its relevance to the present and the future of youth cultures.

References

Arnett, J.J. (2004). *Emerging adulthood.* Oxford: Oxford University Press.

Austin, J. and Willard, M. (eds) (1998). *Generations of youth: Youth cultures and history in twentieth-century America.* New York: New York University Press.

Bennett, A. (1999). Sub cultures or neo tribes? Rethinking the relationship between youth, style and musical taste. *Sociology, 33*(3), 599–617.

Bennett, A. (2007). As young as you feel: Youth as a discursive construct. In P. Hodkinson and W. Deicke (eds). *Youth cultures: Scenes, subcultures and tribes.* London: Routledge.

Best, A.L. (ed.) (2007). *Representing youth: Methodological issues in critical youth studies.* New York: NYU Press.

Blackman, S. (2005). Youth subcultural theory: A critical engagement with the concept, its origins and politics, from the Chicago School to postmodernism. *Journal of Youth Studies, 8*(1), 1–20.

Blatterer, H. (2007). *Coming of age in times of uncertainty.* New York: Berghahn.
Bragg, S. and Buckingham, D. (2013). Global concerns, local negotiations and moral selves: contemporary parenting and the "sexualisation of childhood" debate. *Feminist Media Studies* online, DOI: 10.1080/14680777.2012.700523
Buckingham, D. (2006). Is there a digital generation? In D. Buckingham and R. Willett (eds). *Digital generations: Children, young people and new media.* Mahwah, NJ: Erlbaum.
Buckingham, D. (2011). *The material child: Growing up in consumer culture.* Cambridge: Polity.
Clarke, G. (1981/2005). Defending ski-jumpers: A critique of theories of youth subculture. In K. Gelder (ed.). *The subcultures reader.* London: Routledge.
de Block, L. and Buckingham, D. (2007). *Global children, global media: Migration, media and childhood.* London: Palgrave Macmillan.
Erikson, E. (1968). *Identity: Youth and crisis.* New York: Norton.
Franklin, S., Lury, C. and Stacey, J. (eds) (1991). *Off centre: Feminism and cultural studies.* London: Routledge.
Gillis, J. (1981). *Youth and history.* New York: Academic Press.
Hall, G.S. (1906). *Youth: Its education, regimen and hygiene.* New York: Appleton.
Hall, S. and Jefferson, T. (1976). Resistance through rituals, youth subcultures in postwar Britain. London: Hutchinson.
Hall, S., Critcher, C., Jefferson, T., Clarke, J and Roberts, B. (1978). *Policing the crisis: Mugging, the state and law and order.* London: Palgrave Macmillan.
Hebdige, D. (1979). *Subculture: The meaning of style.* London: Methuen.
Herring, S. (2008). Questioning the generational divide: Technological exoticism and adult constructions of online youth identity. In D. Buckingham (ed.). *Youth, identity and digital media.* Cambridge, MA: MIT Press.
Hesmondhalgh, D. (2005). Subcultures, scenes or tribes? None of the above. *Journal of Youth Studies, 8*(1), 21–40.
Hodkinson, P. (2005). Insider research in the study of youth cultures. *Journal of Youth Studies, 18*(2), 131–149.
Huq, R. (2005), *Beyond subculture: Pop, youth and identity in a postcolonial world.* London: Routledge.
Ito, M. et al. (2010). *Hanging out, messing around and geeking out.* Cambridge, MA: MIT Press.
Livingstone, S., Haddon, L., Görzig, A. and Ólafsson, K. (2011). *Risks and safety on the Internet: The perspective of European children.* London: London School of Economics.
Kehily, M.J. (2010). Traditions of collective work: Cultural studies and the Birmingham school. In *Collaboration and duration: A celebration of the work and research practices of Janet Holland.* London: South Bank University, Families and Social Capital Research Group.
MacDonald, R. and Marsh, J. (2005). *Disconnected youth? Growing up in Britain's poor neighbourhoods.* London: Palgrave Macmillan.
MacRae, R. (2007). "Insider" and "outsider" issues in youth research. In P. Hodkinson and W. Deicke (eds). *Youth cultures: Scenes, subcultures and tribes.* London: Routledge.
McRobbie, A. (1994). *Postmodernism and popular culture.* London: Routledge.
McRobbie, A. and Garber, J. (1975). Girls and subcultures. In S. Hall and T. Jefferson (eds). *Resistance through rituals: Youth subcultures in postwar Britain.* London: Hutchinson.

Maira, S. and Soep, E. (eds) (2005). *Youthscapes: The popular, the national, the global.* Philadelphia: University of Pennsylvania Press.

Mead, M. (2001 [1928]). *Coming of age in Samoa.* New York: William Morrow.

Mitterauer, M. (1992). *A history of youth.* Oxford: Blackwell.

Muggleton, D. (2000). *Inside subculture: The postmodern meaning of style.* Oxford: Berg.

Muggleton, D. and Weinzierl, R. (eds) (2003). *The post-subcultures reader.* Oxford: Berg.

Nayak, A. (2003). *Race, place and globalisation: Youth culture in a changing world.* Oxford: Berg.

Nayak, A. and Kehily, M.J. (2007). *Gender, youth and culture.* London: Palgrave Macmillan.

Nilan, P. and Feixa, C. (eds) (2006). *Global youth? Hybrid identities, plural worlds.* London: Routledge.

Parsons, T. (1942). Age and sex in the social structure of the United States. *American Sociological Review, 7*(2), 604–616.

Redhead, S. et al. (eds) (1997). *The club cultures reader: Readings in popular cultural studies.* Oxford: Blackwell.

Shildrick, T. and MacDonald, R. (2006). In defence of subculture: Young people, leisure and social divisions. *Journal of Youth Studies, 9*(2), 125–140.

Skelton, T. and Valentine, G. (eds) (1998). *Cool places: Geographies of youth culture.* London: Routledge.

Steinberg, D.L., Epstein, D. and Johnson, R. (eds) (1997). *Border patrols: Policing the boundaries of heterosexuality.* London: Continuum.

Taylor, I. and Wall, D. (1976). Beyond the skinheads: Comments on the emergence and significance of the glamrock cult. In G. Mungham and G. Pearson (eds). *Working class youth culture.* London: Routledge and Kegan Paul.

Thomas, M. (ed.) (2011). *Deconstructing digital natives: Young people, technology and the new literacies.* London: Routledge.

Thornton, S. (1995). *Club cultures: Music, media and subcultural capital.* Cambridge: Polity.

van Gennep, A. (2010 [1909]). *The rites of passage.* New York: Routledge.

Willis, P. (1977). *Learning to labour.* Farnborough: Saxon House.

Part I
Theorizing Youth Cultures

1
'What Time Is Now?': Researching Youth and Culture beyond the 'Birmingham School'

Christine Griffin

Introduction

In the second half of the 1970s, the Centre for Contemporary Cultural Studies (hereafter CCCS)[1] at Birmingham University produced a series of highly influential texts on the relationship between (predominantly white, male, working class, heterosexual, British) youth and popular culture. Texts by Hall and Jefferson (1975), Hebdige (1979), Willis (1978) and McRobbie (1978) were to prove formative for what became the new field of youth sub/cultural studies. Work linked to 'the Birmingham School' attempted to represent youth sub/cultures 'from the inside', employing ethnographic methods and drawing on versions of New Left/Marxist and feminist theory. This work took young people's cultural practices seriously, in opposition to the then contemporary academic and popular orthodoxy that viewed working class youth in overwhelmingly negative terms.

As someone who worked at CCCS in the early 1980s, I have always been surprised by the speed with which this diverse and profoundly oppositional body of work came to be constituted as a uniform approach and even as an orthodoxy.[2] The 'CCCS approach' was never a unified set of ideas or a common framework: it was forged in and through contestation, although only some debates were reflected in published texts (e.g. Clarke, 1981; Frith, 1983; McRobbie, 1980; McRobbie and Garber, 1975; Mungham and Pearson, 1976; Powell and Clarke, 1975). These could be heated disputes, but they reflected a passionate engagement with theory, research and politics. Despite their differences, many of those involved in the early youth sub/cultures project were grappling with a common set of politically informed theoretical debates, which contributed to a sense of coherence, as did the collective working practices from which much of this work emerged.

Resistance through Rituals: The youth sub/cultures project and post-war Britain

The youth sub/cultures project[3] was formed at a particular historical, cultural and political conjuncture, as referenced in the sub-title of *Resistance through Rituals: Youth Subcultures in Post-War Britain* (Hall and Jefferson, 1975; hereafter 'RTR'). This period was characterized by the emergence of 'teenagers' as an increasingly visible social group with more disposable income, a growing market geared to youth consumption and an expanding media culture industry focussed around this distinctive 'youth' market (Griffin, 1993). Its wider context was the loss of Empire amid the post-war era of apparent affluence, embourgeoisement and consensus. The youth sub/cultures project treated (primarily white, male, heterosexual, British) working class youth cultural practices as potentially creative, imbued with meaning and political significance and as worthy of study in their own terms. The work also aimed to understand working class youth sub/cultures via a mediated view that explored the cultural and political significance of youth styles, music and popular culture. Youth sub/cultural theory politicized (working class) youth style.

The youth sub/cultures project also aimed to document what John Clarke and colleagues termed 'the *stubborn refusal of class to disappear* as a major dimension and dynamic of the social structure' in post-war Britain (Clarke et al., 1975, p. 25, original emphasis). 'RTR' put class at the centre in theorizing the lives of young people, viewing working class youth cultures through a lens of power and challenging the predominant generational perspective of the period (Clarke et al., 1975). The youth sub/cultures project aimed to understand how young working class people reproduce, negotiate and transform their material conditions through signifying cultural practices, but (to paraphrase Marx) not in circumstances of their own making (Clarke, 2009). Working class youth subcultures were therefore viewed both as *responses* to the 'material and situated experience' of (primarily white, male, heterosexual) working class young people and as *attempted solutions* to those problems, or 'magical resolutions' as Phil Cohen put it (Cohen, 1972). 'RTR' did not dismiss such 'magical resolutions' as forms of 'false consciousness' (like traditional Marxists), or 'juvenile delinquency' (like those working in the sociology of deviance), nor did it valorize them as the key to revolutionary change as some subsequent critics have argued.

One of the most valuable contributions of the youth sub/cultures project was the recognition that such sub/cultural 'magical resolutions' could never deliver on what they appeared to offer working class young people. The 'magical resolutions' offered by youth sub/cultural practices could operate (in part) as forms of creative cultural resistance with radical political significance (Hall and Jefferson, 1975), but the tragedy for working class youth was that these sub/cultural practices also operated as a trap, locking them into the very conditions from which they strove so hard to escape (Willis, 1977, 1978). Youth sub/cultural styles appeared to promise a route out of the boring drudgery of poor education, low-paid work, unemployment, limited money, and for young women, a lifetime of unpaid housework and childcare. Early contributions to the youth sub/cultures project drew attention to the grim conditions in which many young working class people were growing up in 1970s' Britain, *and* demonstrated how such promises of escape could constrain them into an obsession with fashion and the rapidly changing market for youth-oriented consumer goods (e.g. Hebdige, 1979; McRobbie, 1978).

The youth sub/cultures project has tended to be judged (and found wanting) according to the values of subsequent political moments, especially where the intersections of 'race', gender and sexuality are concerned. Its (neo-)Marxist foundations tended to overlook gender, 'race' and sexuality; according class a primary that eclipsed the potential impact of other important sets of social relations. However, this was the focus of sustained critique from the start (Amos and Parmar, 1981; Jones, 1988; McRobbie and Garber, 1975; Race and Politics Group, 1982), and the force of more recent critiques sometimes obscures the battles of those who were involved in the youth sub/cultures project during this formative period.

Following 'RTR': Post- and anti-subcultural critiques of 'the Birmingham School'

By the 1990s, the work of 'the Birmingham school' had become the focus of more sustained critique. This was partly a consequence of postmodernist debates about representation, politics and resistance (e.g. Baudrillard, 1983; Maffesoli, 1986), but also a reflection of the shifting terrain of youth sub/cultures in the UK and elsewhere (Sharma et al., 1996; Blackman, 2005). Postmodern theorists challenged the notion that people's political, social and psychological perspectives could be read off from their structural locations in any straightforward way, and subsequent work criticized the overly simplistic, even romanticized perspective of the 'CCCS approach' (Bennett and Kahn-Harris, 2004;

Hodkinson and Diecke, 2007). Critics also addressed the apparent reluctance of CCCS researchers to recognize that many sub/cultural forms involved young people from a range of class locations and trajectories, incorporating considerable internal diversity and contradiction (e.g. Clarke, 1981; Jenkins, 1983). Recent critiques of the youth sub/cultures project prefer to designate their approach as 'post-subcultural' – or even 'anti-subcultural' (Hodkinson and Deicke, 2007). However, much of this 'post-subcultural' work has failed to engage with the complex shifting terrain of class in British society during and after the 1980s (although see Brown, 2003, 2007, for one exception). As I have argued elsewhere, many 'post-Birmingham' youth sub/cultural researchers have had a difficult relationship with the theorization of class (Griffin, 2011).

Youth sub/cultures in the UK undoubtedly changed and dissolved as the rave and party scenes expanded into a global phenomenon during the 1980s and '90s (Blackman, 2005; Malbon, 1999). Aspects of feminist and gay/lesbian culture were incorporated into mainstream popular culture (McRobbie, 2009; Bell and Valentine, 1995), and urban youth became increasingly diverse in terms of race, ethnicity, nationality and culture (Sharma et al., 1996). The 1990s brought a shift towards more complex constellations of youth cultures that bore little resemblance to the more clearly demarcated, classed, gendered and racialized youth sub/cultural groups of the immediate post-war period. These were 'Thatcher's children', partying on the other side of what Hall and Jefferson termed 'the fault line of the 1980s' (2006, p. xxix). Youth culture had also become increasingly commercialized, and the yellow smiley face trope of early acid house music became a ubiquitous symbol in mainstream popular culture, much to the horror of its early adherents (Thornton, 1995). The growth of electronic dance music culture and emerging technologies forged faster and more complex relationships between popular youth cultural production and consumption (Riley et al., 2010; Wilson, 2006). The 'CCCS approach' began to appear increasingly outmoded.

Sarah Thornton's *Club Cultures* (Thornton, 1995) was a particularly influential attempt to explore the cultural and political significance of electronic dance music culture, engaging with postmodern theory via a critique of youth sub/cultural theory (see also Malbon, 1999). She identified 'the Birmingham school' as being of minimal value for understanding club cultures, positioning her work as 'post-Birmingham' on several grounds. Thornton drew on Bourdieu's work on distinction and cultural capital (Bourdieu, 1984) to develop the alternative concept of 'subcultural capital', in which sub/cultures were reconceptualized as 'taste cultures'. She argued that 'subcultural capital is not as class-bound as cultural capital', since class 'does not correlate in any one-to-one way with levels of youthful subcultural capital' (Thornton, 1995, p. 12). Thornton interpreted this as evidence of the *lessening* relevance of class in the lives of clubbers, although as I have argued elsewhere, her work could equally be viewed as reflecting the *heightened* significance of class in post-Thatcherite Britain (Griffin, 2011).

Thornton's work shifted youth sub/cultural studies towards a fuller engagement with rave and dance culture and the economic, political and cultural changes of the late 1980s and '90s. Her exploration of 'subcultural capital' emphasized the significance of diversity *within* youth sub/cultures, in contrast to some earlier work in the CCCS mould. *Club Cultures* also explored the implications of late modernity for youth culture, especially the expanding role of the media culture industries and the increasing importance of consumption. Much subsequent work in the arena of 'post-subcultural' youth research engaged in detailed debates about the most appropriate way of conceptualizing youth's relationship to culture: via notions of '(neo-) tribe' (following Maffesoli, 1986; see Bennett, 1999); 'scene' (Redhead, 1993); 'lifestyle' (Jenkins, 1983; Miles, 2000); 'taste cultures' (Lewis, 1992; Thornton, 1995) or 'none of the above' (Hesmondhalgh, 2005). I have not engaged with this work in any detail here, partly because it has been discussed at length in a range of other texts (e.g. Bennett and Kahn-Harris, 2004; Hodkinson and Deicke, 2007; Pilkington et al., 2010).

'Symptomatic readings' and 'conjunctural analyses': The core of the youth sub/cultures project

A key basis for critiques of the youth sub/cultures project rested on objections to the 'theory-driven' Marxist perspective that dominated early work at CCCS. Critics argued that such arguments would be unsettled or even dissolve when working class youth sub/cultures were subject to the close rigorous scrutiny involved in more in-depth ethnographic research (see Hodkinson, 2012, for recent review). However, the youth sub/cultures project was not primarily concerned with the specific experiential aspects of sub/cultural practice for young people themselves: it set out to explore a much broader terrain.

As Hall and Jefferson pointed out in their introduction to the new edition of 'RTR' thirty years after its initial publication, the identification of particular youth sub/cultural forms was never the primary aim of the youth sub/cultures project. Rather, it aimed to develop a 'symptomatic reading' within the frame of a 'conjunctural analysis' (Hall and Jefferson, 2006). As Hall and Jefferson indicate, a conjunctural analysis would lead us to ask 'why now?', and to understand youth sub/cultural phenomena in relation to the 'political, economic and socio-cultural changes of their respective times' (p. xiv). Hall and Jefferson suggest that a 'symptomatic reading' of contemporary developments would mean asking 'what is the postmodernism in [contemporary youth] sub-cultures symptomatic of?' (p. xxi), rather than (as Thornton and others have done) representing the shift from class-based youth sub/cultures to taste-based club culture as an indication of the redundancy of the CCCS approach.

What CCCS did next: The legacy of the 'Birmingham School'

Furthermore, the CCCS work on youth culture did not end with the class-based analysis of 'RTR'. The texts discussed below share the empha-sis on conjunctural analysis, and while several of them come from what might be called the 'second generation' of CCCS, not all of them would immediately be associated with the youth sub/cultures project. These lesser known texts reflect the legacy of the youth sub/cultures project according to the definition offered by Hall and Jefferson above.[4] Some of this work emerged in a spirit of critique and dialogue with 'RTR' and early youth subcultural studies; some attempted to understand the nexus of youth, culture and class (and gender, 'race' and sexuality) fol-lowing the faultlines of the 1980s in the UK and elsewhere; and some did both. Many of these texts moved beyond examinations of young people's music-based leisure and style groupings to explore the forma-tion and significance of youth sub/cultural practices in the domains of education, the labour market, family life and the domestic sphere.[5]

One important strand of work linked to the 'Birmingham School' attempted to trace new formations of 'race' and ethnicity as these intersected with class and gender in 1970s and '80s Britain, some-times via a focus on black youth. *The Empire Strikes Back*, edited by the Race and Politics Group at CCCS, was an influential contribution to these debates (Race and Politics Group, 1982). Emerging shortly after the CCCS text *Policing the Crisis* (Hall et al., 1978), the core argument of the book was that 'the construction of an authoritarian state in Britain is fundamentally intertwined with the elaboration of popular racism in the 1970s' (Solomos et al., 1982, p. 9). *The Empire Strikes Back* did not explore the lives of Afro-Caribbean and Asian youth[6] in Britain in terms of their involvement in specific youth sub/cultures, but examined how 'new' racist ideologies were shaping the representation and treatment of black youth in education, the labour market, family life, policing and the criminal justice system. The primary focus was therefore on white society, 'new' racist ideologies and the role of the state, rather than the sub/cultural styles of black youth.

This work examined the significance of the uprisings[7] that took place during the early 1980s in cities across the UK in the context of dominant representations of black (i.e. Afro-Caribbean male) youth as 'criminal', black families as 'inadequate' and black cultures as 'deprived', all of which formed part of a new racism based around the mobilization of racist ideology as 'just common sense' (Lawrence, 1982). This work continued the focus of the youth sub/cultures project on understanding dominant representations of 'youth' (and particular groups of young people) as reflecting wider social formations and economic conditions (Griffin, 1993). This examination of the wider representational context in which (working class) young people were growing up is also found in Paul Gilroy's chapter on 'the popular culture and politics of Britons of Afro-Caribbean descent' (1982, p. 289). Gilroy explored the political, ideological and cultural significance of 'Rastafarianism', as it was represented in the dominant ideology of the time (see also Gilroy, 1981/82, 1987). Examining the formation of Rastafari and Rasta discourse in the lyrics of key songs, interviews with reggae musicians, Rasta style and socio-cultural practices, Gilroy represented reggae (and dub) as a prime site of cultural and political struggle by African-Caribbean youth in 1970s Britain.

Gilroy's work was not based on in-depth ethnographic research on the meaning of Rasta, reggae and dub for Afro-Caribbean youth themselves. To this extent it was not a study of a specific youth sub/culture. However, I would argue that the scale of Gilroy's ambitions and his approach locate this work more firmly within the youth sub/cultures project than many contributions to standard texts on youth sub/cultural studies (e.g. Gelder and Thornton, 1997). A similar argument could be made about other texts which were attempting to map the changing terrain of 'race', class and gender in post-war Britain, especially in the period after Margaret Thatcher came to power in 1979. These would include Phil Cohen and Harwant Bains's edited collection *Multiracist Britain* (Cohen and Bains, 1988) and Mairtin Mac an Ghaill's more traditional ethnographic study of young Afro-Caribbean and Asian youth groups in an English secondary school, *Young, Gifted and Black*

(Mac an Ghaill, 1988). Simon Jones's *Black Culture, White Youth*, based around an ethnographic study in inner city Birmingham during the 1980s, aimed to explore 'the impact of Jamaican popular culture and music on the lives of young white people' (Jones, 1988, p. xv). A member of the editorial group on *The Empire Strikes Back*, Jones employed a focus on youth subcultural music and style as a lens through which to trace a history of social relations around race and class in urban Britain.[8] Jones's book is closer to a study of a specific youth sub/culture explored through a focus on music, but this is used as the basis for a broader examination of the changing formations of 'race' and class in 1970s and '80s Britain.[9]

A second strand of work to emerge from the youth sub/cultures project grew out of feminist explorations of intersecting social relations around gender, sexuality, 'race' and class as these shaped contemporary femininity and the conditions of young women's lives. The overwhelming focus of early youth sub/cultures research on the lives of primarily white, working class and heterosexual young men reflected a more widespread lack of interest in the lives of girls and young women in the youth research of the 1960s and '70s (Griffin, 1987). Academic theorizing about young people's lives was based on a pervasive 'male norm' that cut across the social sciences, which was profoundly unsettled by feminist work in the 1980s. In the youth sub/cultures project, the kernel of this shift spread from heated debates within CCCS and elsewhere about the relationship between gender and class, feminism and Marxism, patriarchy and capitalism (Women's Studies Group, 1978; Race and Politics Group, 1982). Influential early texts include Angela McRobbie and Jenny Garber's contribution to 'RTR' and McRobbie's chapter in '*Women Take Issue*', edited by the Women's Studies Group at CCCS (McRobbie and Garber, 1975; McRobbie, 1978).

This work 'took issue' with the boys' own blinkers that dominated 'RTR' and most youth research of the period, focussing instead on the lives of young white working class women and girls. McRobbie and Garber argued that young women were positioned differently in relation to pervasive youth sub/cultural forms compared to their male peers. Their sub/cultures revolved around smaller female friendship groups, often based in the private domestic sphere of the bedroom rather than on the street corner (McRobbie and Garber, 1975). McRobbie went on to argue that gender intersected with class in important ways, shaping a 'culture of femininity' based on female solidarity, in which working class young women negotiated the restricted opportunities available to them in the education system and the job market, as well as likely futures in heterosexual relationships and family life (McRobbie, 1978). McRobbie's key arguments were that young working class women 'are both saved by and locked within the culture of femininity', and that their lives are shaped by 'the material limitations imposed on them as a result of their class position, but also as an index of, and response to their sexual oppression as women' (1978, p. 108).

It is possible to question the accuracy of these conclusions, based as they were on a relatively brief six-month period of ethnographic work in a Birmingham youth club, but this text was an important influence on feminist youth research during the 1980s (e.g. Griffin, 1985; Mirza, 1992; Phoenix, 1991; Weiner, 1985). Much of this work challenged dominant representations of young working class women as feckless, immoral, stupid and/or insignificant in popular culture, academic research and Marxist/Left politics. Influenced by the active Women's Liberation Movement of the period and by feminist youth work, these texts placed greater emphasis on young women's accounts and perspectives, displaying less abstract and distanced interpretations of the significance of their sub/cultural practices (e.g. Hemmings, 1982; McRobbie and McCabe, 1981).

The influence of feminist interpretations of the youth sub/cultures project can still be found in recent texts such as Sian Lincoln's study of young women's (and men's) bedrooms, shaped in part by early CCCS work on cultures of femininity and young women's use of private domestic space (Lincoln, 2012). There are resonances here too with Valerie Hey's ethnographic study of girls' friendships in school, which represented this secret(ive) dimension of the culture of femininity as a protective response to the intensive surveillance of patriarchal culture (Hey, 1997). Carried out some ten years later, Lincoln's project reflects the highly mediated world inhabited by many young people in affluent Western societies (boyd, 2007).

In different ways, all these texts reflect the continuing legacy of the youth sub/cultures project. The authors were not simply presenting accounts of how young people in the UK mobilized creative collective cultural practices to negotiate a passage through schooling, the labour market and/or family life: many also called for radical reconsideration of the intersection between social relations around class, gender, race and sexuality. They also examined the ways in which the cultural practices of white, Asian and African Caribbean working class young people were forged in specific historical and political moments in relation to oppressive material, economic and ideological conditions.

What time is now? Reconfiguring youth and culture in the neoliberal social order

What are the implications of the legacy of the youth sub/cultures project for contemporary youth research? For Hall and Jefferson, the shift from relatively distinctive class-based youth subcultures to more diffused club cultures of the 1980s and '90s reflected an important cultural and political move in British society – and indeed in global capitalism as a whole. Hall and Jefferson understand this youth cultural shift as both a response to and an attempt at 'magical resolution' of major changes that have taken place in late capitalism. The latter include globalization, the commercialization of culture, the development of mass consumption, the de-industrialization of the Anglo-American world, post-feminism and the emergence of the new Right, all of which characterize the neoliberal social order (Rose, 1989; Hall, 2011; Gill, 2007). According to this perspective, an important legacy of the youth sub/cultures project is reflected in attempts to identify the representational importance of 'youth' and the significance of youth cultural practices in the context of neoliberalism.

Theorists of neoliberalism argue that its emphasis on the 'biographical project of the self' carries with it powerful new forms of governance (Rose, 1989). That is, contemporary discourses of individual freedom, self-expression and authenticity demand that we live our lives *as if* this was part of a biographical project of self-realization in a society in which we all have 'free' choice to consume whatever we want and to become whoever we want to be. This authentic and fully-realized self should be subject to continual (self-)surveillance, transformation and improvement, in a process that has long formed a central element of normative femininity, but is now being intensified and extended to affect masculinity as well (Walkerdine, 2003).

There is growing evidence that the distinctive pressures of neoliberalism are taking a considerable toll on the mental health of young people in many parts of the affluent 'First World' (Forbrig, 2005). This operates through a perceived imperative on individual subjects to construct and display themselves as distinctive, authentic and discerning selves through consumption, and as ethical, responsible moral subjects. If young people behave or appear in ways that are taken to be excessive, unhealthy, irresponsible or undisciplined, then this is constituted as a *moral* failure of the self (Croghan et al., 2006; Griffin et al., 2009). Given that there is not a 'level playing field' (Skeggs, 2005, p. 974), some simply do not have access to the 'right' cultural resources and techniques to construct and display themselves in appropriate ways, with the result that many poor and working class young people can only display a 'lack' of possession of culturally valued resources.

Neoliberalism operates in a globalized culture of celebrity, self-commodification and excess which has particular resonances for young people (Duits and van Romondt Vis, 2009). The obsession with identity, image and celebrity as well as constant innovation and change requires that the reflexive project of the self involves continual (re)creation and maintenance, an ongoing cycle of self-invention (Hearn, 2008). Such highly stylized self-construction can be seen across several commercially mediated cultural forms where individuals celebrate and celebritize the self and, in doing so, construct their identities (Griffin, 2011). This crafting of an 'authentic' subjectivity (or performing one's own celebrity brand) is highly contradictory, particularly in a neoliberal social order in which people are supposed to have a stable, resilient core identity (Walkerdine, 2003). These developments have been enthusiastically endorsed and catalysed by the discipline and practice of marketing (Goodwin, 2011). They herald a new age of selling in which relationships and identity are central, with commerce using personalized marketing that tailors (online) advertising to individuals' co-created needs (McCreanor et al., 2005). However, the legacy of the youth sub/cultures project tells us that young people are likely to be engaged in a variety of collective creative sub/cultural practices that undermine, challenge, unsettle and reproduce the dominant social order.

The main legacy of the youth sub/cultural project, for me, is that it urges youth researchers to seek to understand and critique the processes of the global neoliberal order as this is lived and struggled with by young people in relation to dominant representations of youth. As Stuart Hall has argued, neoliberalism is a model, a narrative and an ideology which is diverse, constantly evolving and growing in influence (Hall, 2011). As he points out:

> Ideology is always contradictory. There is no single ruling ideology ... Ideology works best by suturing together contradictory lines of argument and emotional investments ... Contradiction is its metier (2011, p. 18).

Youth research can enable us to understand the ways in which different groups of young people live with and survive multiple subordination in the neoliberal order and to interrogate the continuing representational force of that desired and feared category – youth – as a means of understanding broader social formations around class, race, sexuality and gender.

Acknowledgements

I am grateful to Andy Brown for his comments on an earlier draft of this chapter, which is a revised version of talks presented at the Youth 2010 conference at the University of Surrey on 6–9 July 2010, and at the ESRC Research Seminar series on 'Rethinking Youth Cultures in the Age of Global Media' at the Institute of Education, University of London, 18 February 2009. I am also grateful to John Clarke for discussions relating to his paper at the same ESRC seminar (Clarke, 2009) and to two anonymous reviewers of an earlier draft of this chapter.

Notes

1. CCCS (or what it became – the Department of Cultural Studies and Sociology) was summarily closed by the University of Birmingham during the summer of 2003 despite an international campaign objecting to this decision.
2. The author was a researcher at CCCS from 1979 to 1982, working on a Social Science Research Council funded project on 'Young Women and Work', later published as '*Typical Girls?*' (Griffin, 1985).
3. I have used the term 'youth sub/cultures project' throughout this text, following the terminology adopted by Stuart Hall and Tony Jefferson in the Introduction to the second edition of *Resistance through Rituals* (Hall and Jefferson, 2006).
4. It is not possible to separate different texts into neat categories, so what follows is a necessarily brief consideration of a limited number of exemplars that aims to map the legacy of the youth sub/cultures project into the 1980s and beyond. It is not possible to do justice to the range and diversity of this work here, and I have had to omit major strands of work on the position of working class youth in education (Education Group, 1981), training (Finn, 1987) and the 'transition from school to work' (Hollands, 1990), as well as important discussions of the creative potential of working class young people's cultural engagement with consumption (Willis et al., 1990).
5. Paul Willis' influential text *Learning to Labour* was an early example of this trend (Willis, 1977), followed by my work on the move from school to the job market for young working class women (Griffin, 1985).
6. I have employed the terminology used by these authors here to refer to different groups of young black people.
7. These events were represented as 'riots' in the dominant ideology of the period.
8. Like many CCCS texts, the British location of this study did not reflect a parochial local story, since the analysis identified the emergence of particular social, cultural, political and economic changes as consequences of the ending(s) of Empire(s) during the mid-20th century (Clarke, 2009; Gilroy, 1982, 1987).

9. I have limited space to do justice to the diverse legacy of the youth sub/
cultures project outside the UK, especially as this has reflected the recent
growth of consumer culture, digital technologies and neoliberalism (e.g.
Harris, 2008; Pilkington et al., 2010).

References

Amos, V. and Parmar, P. (1981). Resistances and responses: The experiences of
Black girls in Britain. In A. McRobbie and T. McCabe (eds). *Feminism: An adven-
ture story for girls* (pp. 129–148). London: Routledge.

Baudrillard, J. (1983). *Simulation*. New York: Semiotext(e).

Bell, D. and Valentine, G. (1995). *Mapping desire: Geographies of sexualities*.
London: Routledge.

Bennett, A., (1999). Subcultures or neo-tribes? Rethinking the relationship
between youth, style and musical taste. *Sociology*, 33 (3), 599–617.

Bennett, A. and Kahn-Harris, K. (eds). (2004). *After subculture: Critical studies in
contemporary youth culture*. London: Palgrave Macmillan.

Blackman, S. (2005). Youth subcultural theory: A critical engagement with the
concept, its origins and politics, from the Chicago School to Postmodernism,
Journal of Youth Studies, 8 (1), 1–20.

Bourdieu, P. (1984). *Distinction: A social critique of the judgement of taste*. London:
Routledge.

boyd, d. (2007). Why youth (heart) social network sites: The role of nerworked
publics in teenage social life. In D. Buckinhgam (ed.) Digital learning: Youth,
identity and digital media. Cambridge: MIT Press.

Brown, A.R. (2003). Heavy metal and subcultural theory: A paradigmatic case
of neglect. In D. Muggleton and R. Weinzierl (eds) *The post-subcultures reader*
(pp. 209–222). Oxford and New York: Berg.

Brown, A.R. (2007). Rethinking the subcultural commodity: The case of heavy
metal t-short culture(s). In P. Hodkinson and W. Deicke (eds) *Youth cultures:
Scenes, subcultures and tribes* (pp. 63–78). London: Routledge.

Clarke, G. (1981). *Defending ski-jumpers*. CCCS, University of Birmingham: CCCS
Working Paper.

Clarke, J. (2009). No regrets? Reflections on the study of youth (sub) cultures.
Paper presented at ESRC Research Seminar, 'Rethinking Youth Cultures in the
Age of Global Media', Institute of Education, University of London, 18 February.

Clarke, J., Hall, S., Jefferson, T. and Roberts, B. (1975) Subcultures, cultures and
class. In S. Hall and T. Jefferson (eds) *Resistance through rituals* (pp. 9–74).
London: Hutchinson.

Cohen, P. (1972). *Subcultural conflict and working class community*. Working papers
in Cultural Studies 2. Centre for Contemporary Cultural Studies, University of
Birmingham.

Cohen P. and Bains, H. (eds) (1988). *Multi-racist Britain*. London: Macmillan.

Croghan, R., Griffin, C., Hunter, J. and Phoenix, A. (2006). Style failure: Consumption,
identity and social exclusion. *Journal of Youth Studies*, 9 (4), 463–478.

Duits, L. and van Romondt Vis, P. (2009). Girls make sense: Girls, celebrities and
identities. *European Journal of Cultural Studies*, 12 (1), 41–58.

Education Group, CCCS. (eds) (1981). *Unpopular education*. London: Hutchinson.

Finn, D. (1987). *Training without jobs.* London: Macmillan.

Forbrig, J. (ed.). (2005). *Revisiting youth political participation: Challenges for research and democratic practice in Europe.* Strasbourg: Council of Europe.

Frith, S. (1983). *Sound effects: Youth, leisure and the politics of rock 'n' roll.* London: Constable.

Gelder, K. and Thornton, S. (eds) (1997). *The subcultures reader.* London: Routledge.

Gill, R. (2007). Postfeminist media culture: Elements of a sensibility. *European Journal of Cultural Studies*, 10 (2), 147–166.

Gilroy, P. (1981/82). You can't fool the youths ... race and class formation in the 1980s. *Race and Class*, XXIII (2/3), 207–222.

Gilroy, P. (1982). Steppin' out of Babylon – race, class and autonomy. In Race and Politics Group, *The Empire strikes back: Race and racism in 1970s Britain* (pp. 276–314). London: Hutchinson.

Gilroy, P. (1987). *There ain't no black in the Union Jack.* London: Routledge.

Goodwin, I. (2011). Power to the people? Web 2.0, Facebook, and DIY cultural citizenship in Aotearoa New Zealand. *New Zealand Journal of Media Studies*, 12 (2), 110–134.

Griffin, C. (1985). *Typical girls? Young women from school to the job market.* London: Routledge and Kegan Paul.

Griffin, C. (1987). Youth research: Young women and the 'gang of lads' model. In J. Hazekamp, W. Meeus and Y. te Poel (eds) *European contributions to youth research.* Amsterdam: Free University Press.

Griffin, C. (1993). *Representations of youth: The study of youth and adolescence in Britain and America.* Oxford: Polity Press.

Griffin, C. (2011). 'The trouble with class: Researching youth, class and culture beyond the "Birmingham school"'. *Journal of Youth Studies*, 14 (3), 245–260.

Griffin, C., Szmigin, I.T., Hackley, C., Mistral, M. and Bengry Howell, A. (2009). 'Every time I do it I absolutely annihilate myself': Loss of (self)-consciousness and loss of memory in young people's drinking narratives. *Sociology*, 43 (3), 457–476.

Hall, S. (2011). The neoliberal revolution. *Soundings*, 48, 9–17.

Hall, S. and Jefferson, T. (eds). (1975). *Resistance through rituals: Youth cultures in post-war Britain.* London: Hutchinson.

Hall, S. and Jefferson, T. (2006). Once more around 'Resistance through Rituals'. In S. Hall and T. Jefferson (eds). *Resistance through rituals* (2nd edition, pp. vii–xxxii). London: Routledge.

Hall, S., Critcher, C., Jefferson, T., Clarke, J. and Roberts, B. (1978). *Policing the crisis: Mugging, the state, and law and order.* London and Basingstoke: Macmillan.

Harris, A. (ed.). (2008). *Next wave cultures: Feminism, subcultures, activism.* New York: Routledge.

Hearn, A. (2008). 'Meat, mask, burden': Probing the contours of the branded self. *Journal of Consumer Culture*, 8 (2), 197–217.

Hebdige, D. (1979). *Subculture: The meaning of style.* London: Methuen.

Hemmings, S. (ed.) (1982). *Girls are powerful: Young women's writings from Spare Rib.* London: Sheba Feminist.

Hesmondhalgh, D. (2005). Subcultures, scenes or tribes? None of the above. *Journal of Youth Studies*, 8 (1), 21–40.

Hey, V. (1997). *The company she keeps: An ethnography of girls' friendships.* Buckingham: Open University Press.

particular. Nevertheless, I hope that this chapter adds something to ongoing conversations.

The anthropology of youth and youth cultural studies

My interest in anthropology, fuelled by questions of cultural change and social transformation, came before my interest in youth, and when I entered the discipline in the early 1990s, it was at a crossroads. While the question of how societies change has always been a fundamental one within many strands of anthropological thinking, there was much debate about how the discipline had come to produce static images of unchanging societies, frozen in time and place. Within my own specific focus, the anthropology of South Asia, this took the form of rethinking the ways in which the anthropology of village life or of caste neglected the role of history and power, particularly colonialism and the workings of the colonial state, in producing stereotyped images of unchanging village life or a 'traditional' caste system. The influence of Edward Said's critique of Orientalism and the work of pioneering scholars at the intersection of History and Anthropology, such as my teachers Bernard Cohn, Arjun Appadurai and several others, problematized the image of a hermetically sealed culture, divorced from history and power.

This was part of a wider ferment within American Anthropology. Perhaps epitomized by what is sometimes, either disparagingly or positively, referred to as the 'Writing Culture' moment (referring to the seminal volume edited by James Clifford and George Marcus, published in 1986), Anthropology underwent what is often called a 'disciplinary crisis' in which its central theoretical concept, culture, its methodology, fieldwork and its dominant genre of writing, the ethnographic monograph, were subjected to contest and critical scrutiny. This moment of critique within Anthropology occurred against the backdrop of a broad-based 'cultural turn' within the interpretive social sciences, something that is, more often than not, linked to the seminal influence of Clifford Geertz and his holistic and semiotic conception of culture as meaning. The critique of the concept within Anthropology emerged through questioning what was seen to be an evasion of questions of power in anthropological analysis, tied to a semiotic concept of culture – a questioning that must be understood in relation to the rise of Cultural Studies, cultural Marxism, the influence of postmodernism and post-structuralism, and to a certain extent postcolonial theory. In a seminal 1999 article tracking the conceptual architecture of an anthropological concept of culture as it contributed to a broadly based 'cultural turn' within the human sciences, William Sewell commented that 'it is paradoxical that as a discourse about culture becomes ever more pervasive and multifarious, anthropology, the discipline that invented the concept – or at least shaped it into something like its present form – is somewhat ambivalently backing away from its long-standing identification with culture as its keyword and central symbol' (1999, p. 37).

It is important to note that this questioning does not displace the concept of culture at all. Rather, it seeks to draw on a semiotic understanding of culture, of which Geertz was the most eloquent proponent, in order to render it contested. Culture moved from being a 'thing', a noun, to being an adjective. Over the course of the 1990s, we became more comfortable using the term 'cultural' than 'culture' – where the 'cultural' became an aspect, a dimension of struggle and contestation in and through which meaning and power are produced and reproduced.

Today, this cross-fertilization between Anthropology and Cultural Studies has created a situation in which the relationship between culture and power is taken as axiomatic. The critical intervention of Cultural Studies – namely, to politicize culture, render it contested and a worthy terrain of political struggle – was absorbed into Anthropology. Rather than the demise of the culture concept, we might follow David Scott in noting how culture recedes into the background and becomes the grounds of analysis rather than an object of analysis. As he argues, culture as constructed meaning becomes the basis on which we study a variety of objects – something he has called 'the Geertz effect' (Scott, 2003).

Within this contested conversation about how culture should be conceptualized, I quickly became interested in youth. Given my interest in social and cultural transformation and change, intergenerational relations seemed a good place to start. And once again, what might count as an anthropology of youth seemed less than helpful given its inattention to questions of power. From Van Gennep's *The Rites of Passage* to Margaret Mead's focus on socialization into cultural personality types, anthropological approaches to the study of young people constructed the category as a transitory stage within a developmental and maturational life cycle. The naturalization of socialization into family and kinship norms and the inattention to dynamics of power within trajectories of youth all became problematic as holistic understandings of culture gave way to more dynamic understandings of meaning-making within contexts of power.

In line with the broader influence of Cultural Studies within Anthropology, cultural studies of youth proved especially productive.

For all its problems, the early work of the Birmingham School wrested youth research away from naturalized, teleological approaches to life stages and contributed greatly to a renewed focus within Anthropology on the situatedness and embeddedness of young people's life experiences. In this sense, if Anthropology too quickly folded the experiences and dynamics of youth into naturalized temporal logics, Cultural Studies approaches seemed to locate youth within their own spatio-temporal matrices. While these early Cultural Studies approaches might have read too much into the semiotic texts they fashioned youth to be (among other problems), the desire to focus on youth within their cultural and political contexts influenced a new generation of anthropologists to take the specific contexts of youth – their own time and place – as significant contexts for ethnographic exploration, contexts that could speak to larger questions about cultural, social and political transformation that anthropologists were becoming increasingly interested in exploring.

In these ways, my specific ethnographic focus on emblematic 'youth cultural practices' – especially the everyday ways of doing fashion and romance within the public spaces of college student life in South India – owes much to the cross-fertilization between Anthropology and Cultural Studies and more specifically to the analyses of youth culture that emerged within the British Cultural Studies literature. My attention to bodily practices, style and self-fashioning, mass-mediated texts such as films and novels and the dynamics of consumer spaces such as the staging of beauty pageants were greatly inspired by the ways in which Cultural Studies approaches to youth drew our attention to these semiotic mediations as significant sites for understanding cultural politics. What has, by now, consolidated into a vibrant anthropology of youth owes much to this early cross-fertilization.

Globalization, culture and youth

Influenced by a cultural studies largely located in the West, the approach to youth I have been outlining revitalized the anthropology of youth by focusing analytical attention on the lived contexts and practices of youth and by opening up to questions of class, dominance and hegemony. However, my research on youth during the early 1990s was not geared towards expanding the scope of cultural studies of youth per se. Rather, research on youth became a way to explore the impact of globalization and the new forms of cultural politics that it was generating within India. As the liberalization of the Indian economy, which began in the late 1980s, expanded, deepened and intensified, dominant and scholarly discussions about cultural, economic and political change in the country focused on what came to be widely called 'liberalization' and its effects. In the realms of advertising, policymaking, politics, academia, and everyday talk, as must be self-evident now, 'globalization' references the sense that we are now living in a deeply and ever-increasingly interconnected, mobile, and speeded-up world that is fuelled by technological innovations, circulations of mass media and geopolitical and economic transformations. As a way to name our contemporary moment, the term globalization entered popular media and advertising discourse in the early 1990s (Tsing, 2000). After the fall of the Berlin Wall and the break-up of the Soviet Union, enthusiasm for increasing international trade, deregulating national economies, privatizing the state, structurally adjusting third world economies and the increasing transnationalization of corporations were all signalled in the use of 'globalization' as a new term to capture the triumph of the capitalist market.

The significance of youth to the discourse of globalization in India (and arguably other parts of the world, especially the Global South) became clear as the promise of India as a new global power seemed significantly to rest on its youthful population. Media discussions of liberalization often point to statistics showing that 54 per cent of Indians are below the age of twenty-five, making India one of the youngest nations in the world. People between the ages of fifteen and twenty-five are said to make up 45 per cent of the total population in Kerala. The construction of this demographic hinges on considering youth as a potent new market in the urban, consumer-driven middle class.

Emblematic of journalistic coverage on India's globalizing youth, one major publication (Lukose, 2009) has labelled those who fall into this age category 'liberalization's children': a play on the so-called generation of 'midnight's children' – named after Salman Rushdie's novel of post-independence India, which focused on those born during the first hour of the year 1947, when India gained its independence from British colonial rule. Rushdie's novel intertwines the lives of those born in the immediate aftermath of independence with the life of the nation, a nation shaped by the socialist-inspired understanding of national development represented by Jawaharlal Nehru, India's first prime minister. The contemporary reworking of generational sensibilities posits 'midnight's children' as being mired in the ideological baggage of Nehruvian nationalist development, with its focus on the rural poor and service to the nation as lacking in ambition and being risk-averse, 'uncool', and fearful. On the other hand, 'liberalization's children', embodying India's newly found confidence and ambition on the global stage, are urban, hip, and cool.

My research sought to understand how the experiences of young women and men, within a marginal college in a marginal town in Kerala articulated with (or not) these broader, large-scale processes of cultural, political and economic transformation. And here, the Cultural Studies approaches to youth that been inspiring and productive proved less than helpful. Critiques of the subcultures framework that was dominant in early cultural studies of youth have been produced and discussed by many (see Griffin, this volume). While this framework was helpful in linking youth experience to questions of class, generation, dominance and hegemony, the deterministic and static ways in which it did so have been well scrutinized. I certainly was interested in questions of dominance and hierarchy. The generational narrative I outlined above is an elite, urban discourse in which 'liberalization's children' are understood to be middle class, globally oriented and metropolitan. I took inspiration from the Cultural Studies literature as I struggled to articulate the experiences and aspirations of non-elite, largely low-caste/class students with the contemporary narratives of globalizing Indian youth. Yet a static focus on dominant and subordinate cultures and a singular focus on class could not capture the complex articulations of caste, class and gender, or region, nation and globe, of the rural–small town–metropole continuum that marked the locations of the young people I was working with.

In this regard, my developing work on youth drew inspiration from an emergent anthropology of globalization. Dominant theories of globalization are, more often than not, macrosociological, emphasizing large-scale economic, political, and cultural transformations that are understood to either fuel or result from globalization. One of the key contributions of the anthropology of globalization has been to emphasize the interconnection between what is called the 'local' and the 'global', emphasizing the interplay between large-scale global transformations and the realities of long-standing social and cultural worlds. An attention to this interplay has led to a focus on mapping and naming the large-scale shifts in culture and political economy that constitute globalization, but also a focus on people's everyday lived experiences and their transformations under globalized conditions. My work on the everyday experiences of young women and men was situated within this anthropological framework, emphasizing the importance of such contexts for understanding the mediations of large-scale global transformations.

Contextualizing the local within the global was a key way that Anthropology began to shift its own frameworks for understanding the productions of culture and meaning within the contemporary world. In this sense, my interest in understanding the shifting contours of youth experience within the expanding commodity markets of the 1990s entailed an attention to local experience and context but one that understood those contexts to be complexly intertwined with circulations of money, commodities, labour and capital as the Indian economy liberalized. In this sense, the anthropology of globalization prodded me to think critically about the situated and embedded nature of local youth contexts but within new and transformative processes that were profoundly deterritorializing.

This perspective also enabled me to challenge clichéd, simple-minded and triumphalist notions of the impact of global consumer culture on youth within non-Western contexts. Dominant theories of globalization often render it as a primarily economic and political process and if these theories do pay attention to the cultural dimensions of globalization, it is often to argue that the economic and political transformations that underlie globalization lead to cultural homogenization, often understood as 'Americanization'. As I have indicated, this thesis is often rendered in terms of the cultural consequences of dominant American commodity exports such as McDonald's and American television programmes. The anthropology of globalization, for example, the work of Arjun Appadurai (1996), has argued that globalization is not a monolithic American export, but rather a 'disjunctive', heterogeneous process with multiple centres of influence and interaction. Further, culture is not simply derivative of economy and politics. The emphasis on people's experiences, lived realities and what Appadurai calls the 'social imaginary', which characterizes large-scale global processes and transformations, suggests that cultural worlds are not simply derivative of dominant capital and labour 'flows'. This has led to an emphasis on heterogeneous, multiple and varied cultural responses to globalization, ones that emphasize the production of meaning within localized contexts. This framework became productive for helping me situate 'youth' as an analytic concept that I tried to render as complex, multidimensional and fluid.

My interest in youth and globalization did not only seek to track the changing cultural politics of globalization within India, but also wanted to hold at bay the triumphalism of the new discourse of globalization – which is a ubiquitous dimension of generational narratives that herald the new. The discourse of 'India Rising' proclaims that the nation has transcended its colonial and postcolonial histories. I was interested in examining globalization as a complex encounter between such legacies and their transformations under liberalization. In this sense, I was not simply interested in a more mobile, fluid, ambiguous sense of youth versus the more rigid and static one that subcultural theory provided. It seemed to me that the category had to be opened up to deal with the kinds of contexts I was addressing, but also situated in ways that helped to show how the category of youth was invested with meaning within colonial and postcolonial trajectories and their contemporary transformations. While it seemed important to emphasize the deterritorializing dimensions of globalization, it seemed equally important to pay attention to how 'globalization' as discourse, a contested object within youth cultural life, intersected with multiple and overlapping struggles for social membership and collective belonging at the intersection of region and nation. In these ways, it seemed important to use some of the insights and perspectives of postcolonial scholarship to address critically the claims being made about globalization's effects and triumphs.

It is in this sense that the subcultural framework became problematic in other ways. One of the great difficulties I had with the translation of this framework to the work that I was trying to do involved how the framework naturalized the very terrain of consumption itself and assumed the given-ness of commodity markets. Within this framework, consumption and the popular cultures it generates are marked by arguments about high and low culture within Euro-American scholarship, whereas in the Indian context, it was highly gendered debates about Westernization, tradition and modernity generated out of the problematic of anti-colonial and nationalist cultural projects that shaped the dynamics of consumption and debates about consumerism. Of course, these had their class dynamics, which I was very interested in. But this difference forced me to contextualize debates about fashion and romance, for example, through the categories of colonial modernity that were generated out of postcolonial scholarship. For example, the wearing of a pair of jeans on the part of a young man or woman was not simply the imposition of a global commodity that was resisted or agentively appropriated; it was part of a long-standing struggle about the meanings of fashion that were intimately tied to the reworkings of caste and gendered bodies within colonial modernity within the region. It was insufficient, from my point of view, to simply contextualize the local within the global. The global circulations of mass media and commodities needed to be contextualized within the changing dynamics of the cultural politics of belonging within Kerala that had their own ongoing histories – particularly around gender and caste. In this sense, there was nothing simple about the local. It had a history in which youth, gender, caste and class relations were profoundly shaped by colonial modernity and the consolidations of the postcolonial development state.

In the process, the very category of youth also needed to be reoriented and recontextualized. One of Anthropology's enduring elements is scepticism about how categories that Western social sciences and intellectual traditions might take for granted get defined. Certainly, Anthropology is part of those traditions and it has struggled with its own conceptual indebtedness to those traditions in the face of other traditions, practices and experiences. But this is a productive tension to which Anthropology remains open: an anthropological approach can capture the ways social and cultural categories are dynamically produced at the intersection of culture, history, economy and politics while attending to how they are mediated within multiple lifeworlds. 'Youth' is such a category. One can understand it in many ways; for example, as a stage of life, a marketing term or a generation within the unfolding narrative of different kinds of nationalisms – and there are many discourses and institutions that do just that. There are interesting ways in which such conceptions collide, collude and overlap. Instead of beginning with some *a priori* definition of the term, Anthropology can and does attend to how the category is invested with meaning through powerful social processes and institutions, rather than taking it for granted. This is an important way in which one can analytically capture the 'slipperiness' of the social category and make that part of the analysis itself.

In Kerala, the lack of job prospects and extremely high rates of education have transformed life for a large group of young men and women. Instead of moving quickly into marriage and employment, they spend an extended period pursuing one educational degree or course after another, all the while negotiating jobs and marriage at home or abroad – Kerala is in important respects a remittance economy with transnational migration, especially to the Persian Gulf, and this is an important component of the way the state functions. This has created a consumer-driven social and cultural world in which one could situate emblematic youth cultural practices such as fashion and romance. However, I could not simply render this as a subculture. In order to apprehend figurations of youth and the ways young people inhabit them, I reconceptualized youth as a social category that sits at the crossroads between familial and educational contexts, a category that is structured by job, marriage and consumer markets. It is a category that closely links education and the possibilities of migration. Importantly, it is also a product of the postcolonial development state, which seeks to produce citizens through its educational and labour infrastructure.

In the end, it is the intersection of the historical legacies of colonial and postcolonial cultural projects, the postcolonial development state and the circulations of labour, commodities and money through transnational migration and liberalization of the Indian economy that was being mediated within the lifeworlds of the young women and men I worked with. So, the category of youth had to be critically apprehended in this way. The spatio-temporal matrix of the 'local–global' could not simply be about young people's resilience and agency or resistance to essentialized understandings of culture and place. Categories like 'youth' and 'consumption' – so central to cultural studies of youth – had to be contextualized with colonial and postcolonial trajectories and cultural and state projects that gave these categories different inflections and meanings. In these ways, the anthropology of globalization and postcolonial understandings of colonialism and nationalism transformed how I took the insights of Cultural Studies developed within a Euro-American context into the research on youth, culture and globalization I conducted within India.

Culture, politics and citizenship

The ways in which youth cultural studies drew attention to consumption as a significant site of culture and politics was very productive for me. However, as I have argued, how one situates consumption within cultural–ideological fields requires attention to the specificities of colonialism and nationalism within a postcolonial context such as India. As I sought to contextualize and understand the experiences, discourses and practices of consumption that I saw among the young people I worked with, I became somewhat frustrated with the focus on identity/agency/resistance that the literature seemed to adopt. In the critical and salutary desire to render youth cultural practices politically significant, much of this literature began with spectacular forms of youth consumption and self-fashioning, drew out the dynamics of the youth identities associated with various youth styles and then moved out further to say something about their cultural–political significance by analysing how a given youth identity implicitly resisted dominant norms. Certainly, this is an approach that has yielded much.

However, perhaps because of my feminist scepticism about the self-evidently spectacular and public as well as the fact that expanding commodity markets had not quite, at that time anyway, produced hyper-commoditized youth styles that were fragmented and differentiated in the ways assumed by the subculture framework, my approach to youth style and self-fashioning did not begin and end with style itself. I was more interested in how young people navigated, both literally and figuratively, public spaces of consumption, education and sociality. In this way, the idea of private and public became crucial to my analysis. I was not interested in deploying this binary to demonstrate its universality, as was prominent in the early writings on this distinction in feminist anthropology. Rather than understand it to be a feature of social organization that somehow 'explains' the universal subordination of women, I focused on its emergence in the context of colonial modernity and of a modern patriarchy that underwrites anti-colonial nationalism. I drew out the significance of this history in terms of the gendered legacies of colonial modernity that shape fashion and romance within the region and the nation, as well as its implications for understanding youth politics and education. Importantly, I linked these different inflections of private and public to debates about the privatization of education and the impact of youth politics, demonstrating how liberalization is transforming understandings of the state and citizenship. One can see in my interest and focus on what I came to call 'consumer citizenship' an interest in taking studies of youth consumption away from an exclusive focus on identity/resistance/ agency and pushing my analysis to understand the implications of youth self-fashioning for public politics and a broader cultural politics of belonging.

Here again, it was anthropological approaches to the study of citizenship that enabled me to draw attention to the dynamics of cultural belonging and social membership within the modern public sphere – one that is being transformed by contemporary discourses and practices of consumption within liberalizing markets. Through a focus on fashion, romance, politics and education, I argued that the breakdown of the Nehruvian vision of the Indian nation in the context of globalization connects with ongoing struggles over the meanings of public life, lower-caste cultural–political assertion, the ascendancy of Hindu nationalism, reconfigurations of upper-caste/class aspirations and attempts by the middle class to reconfigure understandings of citizenship through a critique of the postcolonial state that demands the state ensure the rights of newly articulated citizen-consumers.

Using this anthropological conception of 'citizenship', then, was one way in which my work has tried to move beyond the framing of culture and politics that was embedded in earlier attempts to politicize the concept of culture; where in some sense the critical desire seemed to be to conflate the two terms. The impetus of the early Cultural Studies approaches (in general and with respect to youth) as well as cultural Marxist approaches was to demonstrate that culture was a form of politics and that the consuming habits and bodily matrices of youth were sites where one could demonstrate this. As this approach got absorbed into Anthropology, as I have already discussed, much critical energy was spent arguing for the link between culture and power. However, now that the cultural turn has given way to a broad-based social and cultural constructionism in which the relationship between culture and power becomes axiomatic, there remains a need to investigate broader processes of cultural and political struggle and transformation.

For me, the framework of citizenship and careful attention to struggles over cultural belonging and social membership within and outside the spaces (literal and figurative) of democratic citizenship (consumption and education) became a way to engage with the question of the state and public politics, and their inclusions and exclusions. Rather than collapse the two terms, I became interested in understanding the dynamics between them. I became interested in how domains and practices that might be understood to be 'cultural' (in Anthropology and Cultural Studies) – mass-mediated practices of masculinity and femininity tied to fashion and romance – have implications for the politics of social membership in publics that are constitutive of citizenship formation within modern nation states – and specifically in higher education. I charted the ways in which consumption becomes a new axis of belonging in and through which claims on public life are rendered in ways that mediate social membership and what is narrowly called politics. So, the cultural practices of masculinity and femininity, I argue, have implications for the 'politics of citizenship formation'. In this way, I was not simply interested in asserting the power-laden nature of youth self-fashioning, but also interested in how that self-fashioning enabled and constrained claims on collective political life.

If this line of inquiry suggests the politicization of the cultural, my approach to the study of 'politics' culturalizes the political. Here, I explored how student politics, as a self-conscious demarcation of a zone and set of practices that exist within the ambit of the state, is tied to gender and generational practices of fun, masculinity and femininity in ways that demonstrate the gendering and class/caste inflections of this demarcated zone. Here, politics is rendered as an everyday practice, in a somewhat nominalist fashion, to de-ontologize it and turn it into a kind of 'cultural practice' much like fashion or romance. In this way, rather than collapse culture and politics, I found it productive to hold the terms slightly apart and try and understand their dynamic interactions. Contextualizing youth practices within a feminist apprehension of the public/private distinction in this way helped me link the everyday cultural politics of youth to changing discourses of citizenship and politics.

The cultural and the political in youth Cultural Studies

Today, we live in a self-evidently global world in which our understandings of culture are axiomatically political. Given this, how can we understand youth cultural formations in ways that illuminate our contemporary world? One of the important insights of the early Cultural Studies frameworks on youth was that young people are significant cultural and political agents in their own right. This is an enduring contribution, well worth remembering. As I have suggested, we are now living in a moment when a view of youth as self-consciously political agents rather than cultural ones has come to the foreground. I would like to suggest that there are some lessons to be drawn from the short history I have been charting as studies of youth and globalization move forward to engage this new situation.

As with consumption, it would be wrong for us to assume that there is some transhistorical understanding of 'politics' that we can map onto young people. Politics emerges as a distinct zone of engagement, much like consumption, through the conjunctural intersection between long-standing histories of local, national and regional politics tied to histories of colonialism and nationalism and new circulations of ideas of democracy and freedom, transformed by new social media and the like. Further, it would be wrong for us to focus simply on youth as political actors without contextualizing their political engagements within the multiple and fluid institutions (of state, market, family, education) that structure their lifeworlds. More than ever, a dynamic understanding of the intersections between culture and politics will enable critical apprehension of the emergence of youth as self-consciously political, as generational transformations alter the culture and politics of many societies in the Global South at a time of great economic and political uncertainty. If cultural studies of youth are to do more than simply rehearse the Western-centric, triumphalist discourse of Internet-savvy youth fighting their elders, they must be critically attentive to the active mobilization and mass mediations of youth as a social category. Further, they must be critical of the ways that youth is often mobilized to mask other matrices of social difference.

Scholarly debates about the subcultures framework have, of course, challenged the singular focus on class, and pointed to its masculine bias. A robust intersectional analysis seems central to understanding how the category of youth functions while the experiences of a diverse array of young people, differently positioned along multiple vectors that need to be brought into the analytic frame. However, I would also suggest that the problem might not lie with scholars themselves but might inhere in the very category of youth. I have always been interested in the ways in which the category of youth, when actively mobilized, seems to persistently elide other narratives that might be more centrally focused on class, gender, race and sexuality. For example, take the ways in which the recent events of the Arab Spring in Egypt and Tunisia were represented as a media-savvy revolt of the young. I do not want to undermine the significance of young people and their involvement and role but such a discourse immediately makes me wonder about how this narrative elides urban–rural articulations and class and gender dynamics. Such generational narratives of revolutionary transformation point to the ways in which youth is an enduring and powerful site for understanding cultural and political transformation. How to apprehend these transformations critically while tracking how young people, differently located, inhabit and negotiate these transformations is the task of critical scholarship. This requires attention to the active production and circulations of images and discourses of youth as powerfully generative of globalization and the more politically fractious world that has come in its wake. It also requires careful attention to how cultural mediations of larger global forces intersect with local, regional and nationally inflected processes of change and the articulations of politics. These materializations of youth intersect with the actual lifeworlds of young women and men along diverse matrices of social difference.

References

Amit-Talai, V. and Wulff, H. (eds) (1995). *Youth cultures: A cross-cultural perspective.* London: Routledge.
Appadurai, A. (1996). *Modernity at large: Cultural dimensions of globalization.* Minneapolis, MN: University of Minnesota Press.

Barber, B. (1995). *Jihad vs. McWorld: Terrorism's challenge to democracy*. New York: Ballantine Books.

Clifford, J. and Marcus, G. (1986). *Writing culture: The poetics and politics of ethnography*. Berkeley, CA: University of California Press.

Lukose, R. (2009). *Liberalization's children: Gender, youth and consumer citizenship in globalizing India*. Durham, NC: Duke University Press.

Scott, D. (2003). Culture in political theory. *Political Theory*, 31, 92–115.

Sewell, W. (1999). The concept(s) of culture. In V. Bonnell, L. Hunt and R. Biernacki (eds) *Beyond the cultural turn: New directions in the study of society and culture*. Berkeley, CA: University of California Press.

Skelton, T. and Valentine, G. (eds) (1998). *Cool places: Geographies of youth cultures*. London: Routledge.

Tsing, A. (2000). The Global Situation. *Cultural Anthropology*, 15(3), 327–60.

Van Gennep, A. (2010 [1909]). *The rites of passage*. New York: Routledge.

3
Historicize This! Contextualism in Youth Media Studies

Mary Celeste Kearney

This chapter is part of a larger project I am undertaking to rebrand my academic identity and work. Rather than describe myself as a media and cultural studies scholar, I have decided to label my research as that of a media and cultural historian. Why? Primarily, I want to improve the accessibility of my scholarship for the public. Time and again when I tell non-academics that I study 'media', they jump to the conclusion that I mean the news. 'No, no,' I say. 'I study *girls'* media.' 'Ohhhh,' they respond, struggling to understand. 'You mean like *Twilight*?' This, in fact, is not the type of girls' media I typically analyse; my speciality is girls' media production, which, when announced, usually elicits blank stares, given the prevalent idea that female youth engage with media only as consumers. What is most intriguing to me about these interactions, however, is that the examples of girls' media offered at this point in these conversations are always current. Before *Twilight*, common guesses as to my objects of study were *Hannah Montana*, *Buffy the Vampire Slayer*, and *Clueless*, among the most popular texts within girls' media since I began research in this area. No one has ever assumed that some of the texts I analyse might have been made before 1995.

Unfortunately, this temporally limited perspective on media culture is not restricted to non-academics, which is my secondary reason for rebranding my work. Since the expansion of the Internet in the late 1990s, it seems that a large number of media scholars have been struck with a case of presentism, an infectious disease that is reaching epidemic proportions in academia today. Its chief symptoms are a myopic focus on the present moment and contemporary popular culture coupled with a blind eye to history. Such a perspective results in the lack of critical reflection on the present as a temporal location different from, yet always in an articulated relationship with, both the past and the future.

I have written elsewhere about presentism and ahistoricism within girls' media studies (Kearney, 2008). I broaden the scope of my concern here to youth media research, since these problems are not specific to those who analyse girls' culture. Thus, the primary dimension that concerns me with regard to our field's development is not one of spatiality – as with this book's theme of globalization – but of temporality. In other words, I want to strategically intervene in youth media research by encouraging scholars to engage with history as much as geography, time as much as space, and generations as much as locations. To invigorate this historical perspective in youth media research, I draw attention here to the legacy of contextualism within Cultural Studies, and explore that approach within the realm of youth media scholarship with which I am most familiar: girls' media studies. The primary questions motivating this chapter are: What is the context for the presentist/ahistorical perspective currently dominant in youth media studies? How can we facilitate more youth media research that adopts a contextualist approach, that is, research that attends to both historical specificity and historical development, similarity as well as change? And what might we learn from the cultural activities of earlier generations that can help us to understand better the media practices of today's young people and vice versa?

Coming to contextualism

I began my doctoral studies with a plan to write my dissertation on music videos featuring women rock performers. Two things happened early in my PhD coursework, however, that redirected my research interests and goals towards the fields of youth media and Cultural Studies. The first was my introduction to Riot Grrrl, a punk feminist youth culture that emerged in the early 1990s in the United States before spreading internationally. The second was my reading of Angela McRobbie and Jenny Garber's 'Girls and Subcultures' essay (1976), from the pioneering collection of Birmingham subcultural studies, *Resistance through Rituals*. While Riot Grrrl has been enormously influential on how I understand contemporary feminism, girlhood and girls' culture, I want to linger here for a moment on McRobbie and Garber's essay, since it serves well as a touchpoint for my larger discussion of contextualism in youth media studies.

As a feminist scholar, I am committed to the project McRobbie and Garber first articulated in their essay: to foreground gender in youth studies. Without a doubt, their work helped me to understand girls' collective media practices as well as girls' negotiations of male-dominated youth cultures. Nevertheless, their theories of girls' culture have also posed several challenges in terms of applicability to the objects, practices and communities I study.[1] In the first place, McRobbie and Garber's essay focuses exclusively on British subcultures from the 1950s through to the 1970s, whereas most of my work has concerned US girls' media culture from the 1990s onward. Undoubtedly, there are some continuities in girls' practices across these spaces and times (a point to which I will return). Nonetheless, different sociohistorical contexts necessarily produce different cultural phenomena; therefore, my application of their theories proved difficult. For example, although McRobbie and Garber offer an excellent analysis of why the cultural practices of female youth have been centred on the domestic sphere, their theory of 'bedroom culture' cannot fully explain developments like Riot Grrrl, a female-dominated subculture that exists largely outside girls' homes. Furthermore, while McRobbie and Garber theorized bedroom culture as offering female youth opportunities for cultural resistance, that culture, as they describe it, is grounded in the capitalist culture industries as well as heteronormative patriarchal gender politics. This formulation was virtually impossible to apply to Riot Grrrl, which opposes these ideological foundations of girls' bedroom culture even as it reaffirms the homosocial bonding and collective practices facilitated within it.

Yet the main limitation I had when attempting to apply McRobbie and Garber's work to recent iterations of US girls' culture is that they present bedroom culture as primarily consumerist. At the centre of their theory is girls' participation in mainstream popular culture via their consumption of commercial magazines and pop idols. Grounded in the gender politics of 1970s British society when writing 'Girls and Subcultures', McRobbie and Garber were somewhat incapable of envisioning an oppositional girls' culture, such as Riot Grrrl, where female youth rearticulate feminism through media production, 'girl power', and punk's anarchic politics.

Lesson learned? *Context is everything.* It impinges upon not only the cultural practices youth engage in and scholars study, but also the methods and theories by which we analyse such practices. To understand Riot Grrrl, therefore, I needed to look to the sociohistorical context of which it was part, including the dispersion of feminist ideologies and the transformation of gender norms, the growth of entrepreneurial youth cultures and the reinvigoration of the girl consumer market in the United States during the late 1980s and early 1990s. And to equip myself for that project, I relied on the theories and methods developed within Cultural Studies.

Contextualism as politicized cultural analysis

According to Lawrence Grossberg, Cultural Studies' radical claim for the significance of contextuality in cultural analysis is that '[n]o element can be isolated from its relations'. Instead, 'the identity, significance, and effects of any practice or event ... are defined only by the complex set of relations that surround, interpenetrate, and shape it, and make it what it is ... Any event can only be understood relationally, as a condensation of multiple determinations and effects' (Grossberg, 2010, p. 20). In keeping with Michel Foucault's (1977) genealogical method, Cultural Studies scholars are interested primarily in discerning how such contextualized relations are (re)produced through the operations of power. Cultural Studies' political project of contextualism, then, is to intervene in systems of oppression by drawing critical attention to relations that are productive of inequality so that those relations can be dis- and rearticulated towards progressive ends.

Academics who practice the contextualist approach owe a great deal to British Cultural Studies, especially Raymond Williams, one of the first scholars to theorize culture as a 'whole way of life' rather than as a standard of excellence (Williams, 1958). For Williams, this shift in conceptualizing culture did not mean abandoning close analyses of cultural artefacts and practices, but 'studying their modes of change to discover certain general causes or "trends" by which social and cultural developments as a whole can be better understood' (Williams, 1965, p. 47). In other words, Williams was bent on the 'study of relationships between elements in a whole way of life' (p. 63). Particularly significant to the contextualist method he developed were Antonio Gramsci's (1971) ideas about hegemony as an ongoing process – in other words, a *historical* process – involving contestations between dominant, residual and emergent cultural elements.

Since the 1970s, Cultural Studies scholars have refined the contextualist approach pioneered by Williams. In particular, Stuart Hall (e.g., 1980a) has been essential to the development of the concept, theory and method now known as articulation, which explores the construction, deconstruction and reconstruction of cultural practices and relations that collectively, albeit often contradictorily, cohere in historical conjunctures (Slack, 1996). Such an approach has significantly reconfigured the methods scholars use to examine culture. For example, Cultural Studies theorists have encouraged researchers in a variety of disciplines to rethink the usefulness of text-only scholarship. As Richard Dyer avers:

> [O]nce it is granted that all texts are social facts, then it follows that these textual assumptions must be grounded in sociological ones. You need to know what kind of thing a text is in society in order to know what kind of questions you can legitimately pose of it, what kind of knowledge you can reasonably expect for it to yield. (Dyer, 1979, pp. 1–2)

In his 'Encoding/Decoding' essay (1980b), Hall proposed a model of media culture where texts are always situated in relation to their contexts of production and consumption. Needless to say, his essay has motivated a large amount of scholarship on media audiences and reception, and, slowly but surely, studies of media producers and production. Together these two sub-areas of media research have helped to enrich our understanding of popular culture as involving more than just texts, while also reimagining media studies as involving more than just textual analysis.

Many scholars have critiqued and tweaked Hall's model over the years, including Richard Johnson, who followed Hall as Director of the University of Birmingham's Centre for Contemporary Cultural Studies.[2] Johnson's model built from Williams's theory of culture as a whole way of life and thus rounded out Hall's semicircular model by adding the dimension of 'lived cultures/social relations' while also bringing sociohistorical context to the fore (Johnson, 1986–87, p. 47). As Johnson explains in 'What is Cultural Studies Anyway?', he favoured cultural analyses that '[trace] a social form right through the circuit of its transformations and [make] some attempt to place it within the whole context of relations of hegemony within the society' (p. 72). Further defining his terms, Johnson argued: 'Context determines the meaning, transformations, or salience of a particular subjective form as much as the form itself. [It] includes ... the contexts of immediate situations ... and the larger historical context or conjuncture' (p. 67). In light of Johnson's inclusion of 'immediate situations', it is interesting to note that he saw himself as a 'historian-of-the-contemporary' (p. 42), a role that requires critical reflection on the present as a specific temporal location and thus refuses the pitfalls of both ahistoricism and presentism.

Contextualizing presentism and ahistoricism in youth media research today

By the early 1990s, it seemed contextualism had become routine in a variety of disciplines formerly focused primarily on texts, including media studies. Indeed, in his 1990 book on British Cultural Studies, Graeme Turner argued, 'since the active relationship between audiences and texts has been acknowledged, the boundary between textual and contextual work, between representation and history is breaking down' (Turner, 1990, p. 30). Interestingly, in his latest edition of that book, published thirteen years later, Turner has changed the final three words to 'has broken down', while also adding 'since the insertion of both within a historical context is regarded as fundamental' (Turner, 2003, p. 24).

While both of Turner's alterations may now be truisms within Cultural Studies, I do not believe they describe the dominant practice or perspective among media scholars today. Certainly, an increased amount of attention has been given in recent years to the spatial dynamics of media, as demonstrated by work on globalization. Yet, by comparison, few scholars consider the historical contexts of media, focusing instead on contemporary culture with a myopically presentist and ahistorical lens.

Speaking to the importance of historical contextualization, Michael Pickering argues that cultural analysis is 'weakened when it abandons such thinking, when it becomes fixated with stridently immediate concerns and insistently new issues, in a faddishness and obsession with trend-spotting that runs the danger of mimicking what it attempts to track' (Pickering, 2008, pp. 193–4). My additional concern for youth media studies specifically is that the privileging of current culture and the absence of historical contextualization not only construct the present as normative via a refusal to engage with it as a specific temporal location (the presentist perspective), but also elide the past as well as the present moment's relations to it (the ahistorical perspective). The various discourses and social forces collectively articulating this phenomenon deserve exploration, as they can reveal potential sites for intervention in the theoretical and methodological approaches used in youth media research.

The first reason for the preponderance of presentist/ahistorical perspectives in youth media studies today involves disciplinarity. Although our field has roots in Cultural Studies via subcultural research on youth-made media (e.g., Hebdige, 1979), it is largely comprised today of scholars associated with sociology, education, psychology, and communication studies, disciplines that tend to privilege analyses of contemporary society over historical research. As a result, our primary objects of study – youth media – are most often understood as *contemporary* youth media, the second reason the presentist/ahistorical perspectives dominate. Hence, some scholars assume that contextualization is not a necessary part of their analyses since, ostensibly, we all understand the present historical moment because we are living through it. In other words, the present is self-evident.

The conflation of youth media and contemporary youth media seems to be somewhat medium specific, however, which is yet a third factor to consider when attempting to understand the presentism/ahistoricism of many youth media studies. For example, film studies has a long tradition of historical analyses, while television studies is, by and large, about current TV culture. The presentist perspective seems most apparent in Internet studies, however, no doubt because of the relatively young age of the Web and thus the seeming absence of its history.

The fourth reason for the dominance of presentist/ahistorical perspectives in youth media studies involves the privileging and definition of academic innovation. Scholars are required to pursue original research. Yet 'original' seems to be defined today primarily in relation to 'a focus on the present'. In other words, what's new is now, and what's now is new. While historical scholarship can certainly be innovative, novelty and presentness have become equated to such a degree that historical work is undervalued, if not seen as irrelevant. This phenomenon seems true for research funding also, as media historians struggle to find funds for archival work while scholars studying 'new media' have a plethora of funding options. Yet as Carolyn Marvin reminds us, this privileging of newness often produces wrong-headed analyses by ignoring historical continuity and development: *'New technologies* is a historically relative term ... In a historical sense, ... all the communications inventions ... have simply been elaborations on the telegraph's original work' (Marvin, 1988, p. 3).

The fifth reason for the dominance of these perspectives is related to the fourth: publishers are often most interested in promoting work on current popular culture trends, because scholarship on those subjects produces the most revenue. What's now is hot, and what's hot is what sells. Therefore, like funding agencies, publishers award book contracts to those studying contemporary media to a far greater extent than those doing historical research. (The same can be said for academic job searches.)

The relatively young age of most media scholars is the sixth reason for the dominance of presentist/ahistorical perspectives. I am not deriding younger students and professors for being youthful: that perspective can be useful when studying youth and youth cultures. But, with little personal history, young people tend to focus far more on the present than on the past. 'Be here now' is not a philosophy foreign to youth, although they probably wonder why a perspective so second nature to them needs a mantra.

Related to this last point is the seventh and final reason: focusing on contemporary culture is easier and cheaper than historical work because much of the former is available via the Internet. Although an ever-increasing amount of archival material is accessible online, most historical research still requires additional time and money for travel to distant archives. A scholar's rank is crucial here: less experienced researchers have less access than senior scholars to the resources required for doing historical analysis.

Given the multiple factors that have converged to create and perpetuate the presentist/ahistorical perspectives in youth media research in recent years, it will take the concerted effort of many scholars to shift the dominant mindset so that historical contextualization is consistently part of our work. If we are to recreate youth media studies as the rich site of analysis it can and should be, and if we are to help others to understand better the articulated, relational nature of culture and sites for strategic intervention, then we will need to rethink the frames we use for our research.

In suggesting a revamping of our methods with context and history in mind, I am not simply suggesting that youth media scholars ask how contemporary young people's media practices relate to the current historical context. While such micro histories-of-the-present are necessary, I am also recommending that we adopt a macro, genealogical view of history that considers more than the present moment. Thus, we must ask also: in what media practices and with what media forms and technologies have youths engaged during different historical periods, and what function have those practices, forms and technologies served in young people's lives? How do those practices and functions compare, and what can we learn by attending to the continuities and discontinuities between different periods of youth media culture?

Historical approaches in the study of girls' media culture

To demonstrate the kind of historical work I advocate for future youth media studies, I draw attention here to some recent research on girls' media culture, including my own. I do not have space here to contextualize fully the development of this approach within this sub-field of youth media studies; however, some factors worth considering include the increasing involvement of scholars from disciplines in which historical approaches have been privileged, such as literary and film studies, third wave feminist scholars' critical reflections on feminist history and thus historical awareness and the growing temporal distance from the late twentieth century, the period which saw the greatest proliferation of girls' media since the mid-1960s.

Catalysed by my dissertation research on US media texts featuring female adolescents, two of my journal articles exemplify the value of the contextualist approach for youth media studies. The first, 'Recycling Judy and Corliss' (Kearney, 2004), examines the emergence of teen-girl media culture. Building from the historical work of other girl studies' scholars, especially Kelly Schrum (2004), my main goal in that piece was to examine how the related articulations of a particular context – specifically, growing public interest in teenage girlhood and media producers' increased practice of transmedia exploitation – worked together in forming the first teen-girl production trend in the United States during the 1940s and 1950s. Via archival research and historical analysis, 'Recycling Judy and Corliss' refutes the prevalent notion that girls' media first emerged in the 1990s, traces shifts in girls' representation during and after World War II and thus raises significant questions about continuity and change in girls' media culture.

The second article, 'Birds on the Wire' (Kearney, 2005), also uses the contextualist approach to explore an older iteration of an ostensibly new media phenomenon. Attending to historical transformations in technology, gender politics and nation building during this period, I examine the use and development of the image of the teenage girl on the telephone across different US media during the mid-twentieth century. Via semiotics and formal analysis, this article explores how the image of the girl on the phone operated bivalently, signifying a new form of semi-independent female subjectivity while also carrying within it the means to contain the threat that identity posed to adult heterosexual patriarchy. This article does not examine twenty-first-century images of girls on the phone. However, it inspires critical reflection on the contemporary media industries' use of similar imagery, and thus a questioning of narrative and aesthetic norms as well as the socio-cultural work at stake in such practices of signification.

Much more historical work on girls' media representation and con-sumption in different national contexts is necessary for us to have a better sense of continuities and shifts within this realm of popular culture.[3] I want to turn now, however, to some recent research on girls' media production that further exemplifies the practice and value of the contextualist approach for youth media studies. In my own scholarship on girl-made media, I have attempted not only to contextualize such texts in relation to their specific place and time, but also to draw out similarities in content, form and function across various periods of girls' media, as well as discontinuities that result from different historical contexts. Admittedly, my historical perspective in this regard was a bit slow to develop. For example, in my initial essay on girls' media-making (Kearney, 1998), I focused narrowly on the connections and disconnections between teen magazines and Riot Grrrl zines published in the 1990s without contextualizing these companion media in relation to their historical moment, not to mention the longer history of girls' written culture. I was excited by the broad array of media female youth were creating at that time, as well as by their transformations of media, feminism and youth culture, and was inspired by the prospect of the further changes these girls might make in politics and popular culture as they grew older. Yet the more girl-made zines, videos and websites I encountered over the next decade as I developed that essay into a book, the more desire I had to look not forward to the twenty-first century, but backward to the past. As I ultimately argued in *Girls Make Media*, '[I]f we hope to comprehend fully how the contemporary field of girls' media production has developed, we cannot study it apart from the larger history of girls' cultural practices and the various social factors that have both influenced its formation as well as complicated its development' (Kearney, 2006, p. 21).

Taking this to heart, the first chapter of *Girls Make Media* (Kearney, 2006) explores the prehistory of girls' media production by analysing forms of cultural production engaged in by American female youth prior to the late twentieth century, including needlework, diaries, letters and photography. As I discovered through my research, many girls from previous eras were engaged in various forms of creative expression, and, despite their use of different forms and technologies, their cultural work clearly helped to pave the way for later generations' active engagement in media production. Moreover, female youth of the nineteenth and early twentieth century seemed interested in cultural production for many of the reasons today's girls are: to record their experiences, to express themselves creatively and to explore their identities. Yet these objectives also changed over time, as girls living through different historical periods faced different challenges and opportunities with regard to literacy, resources, leisure time and cultural production.

Additionally, through the work of Jane Hunter (1992) I learned that prior to the twentieth century, girls created diaries that were semi-public documents often shared with friends and family members. While reflecting on this social networking function, it was also clear to me that it had diminished during the turn of the twentieth century, as gender norms changed and female youth were increasingly encouraged to dump their thoughts and emotions in journals, which were deemed private and meant to be tucked away safely from others. Clearly, different historical contexts impinged on the purposes of girls' diaries in different periods. Nonetheless, my knowledge that diaries once served a relational purpose inspired me to question the novelty of social media produced by female youth today, as well as to reflect on how this function remains residual today in girl-made zines and other contemporary media.

And yet it is not just the functions of girls' media that we should attend to via Cultural Studies' contextualist perspective. Further consideration of historical continuities and discontinuities in the formal properties and aesthetic strategies of girls' media is necessary also. Consider, for example, these passages from a recent academic study:

> [T]he 'choicest treasures' that girls snipped, clipped, authored, and arranged were often not what they were directed to preserve. (Greer, 2011, p. 221)

> Girls created intriguing juxtapositions by disregarding the organizational headings [suggested for them]. They arranged collages of snapshots and provided additional layers of meaning with their own original, sometimes enigmatic, captions. (p. 223)

> [The] young women seemed to view these [texts] as more fluid composing spaces where the verbal and the visual could coexist; where the material artifacts of culture and their own intangible desires could collide; and where they could resist the erasure of their experiences and compose their own ... histories. (p. 221)

> The technology ... created a flexible but bounded composing space in which young women could exercise their agency as cultural producers and commemorate their interests, practices, and friends. (p. 237)

Most people reading these passages will probably think of girls' online activities today. Yet the practices described above are over a century old, associated not with early twenty-first-century blogs and Facebook, but rather with early twentieth-century memory albums. These passages come from Jane Greer's 'Remixing Educational History: Girls and Their Memory Albums, 1913–1929' (2011). In her analysis, Greer uses Lawrence Lessig's (2008) theory of the 'remix' to explore early-twentieth-century American schoolgirls' creative appropriations from popular culture to produce memory albums. In addition to contextualizing such practices in their specific sociohistorical moment, particularly the rise of girls' education and mediated entertainment, she demonstrates that the practices we typically associate today with online media production – selecting, borrowing, editing and recombining images and text – are strikingly similar to those engaged in a century ago by girl album makers.

Greer is keen to attend to the authorship, identity work and negotiated cultural consumption facilitated by schoolgirls' engagement in these remixing practices. I would add that this method of media production is especially appealing to members of minoritarian communities, including girls, because of their limited access to resources, coupled with their desire to explore and challenge roles and experiences created for them via the culture industries. Over the past century or more, girls' remixes of media images and words have helped them to fashion and refashion identities and communities for themselves while also negotiating the normative values of their time.

Another function of memory albums and similar companion media should be considered as well. Amy Mecklenburg-Faenger demonstrates that girls' friendships were not just represented in their memory albums and scrapbooks, but also produced through the circulation of such texts among others: '[S]crapbooking often, although not always, was constructed as a communal activity. That is, scrapbooks were not understood as private documents, but as artifacts meant to be shared with others' (Mecklenburg-Faenger, 2007, p. 61). Thus, in ways quite similar to girls' early diaries, the content of girl-made scrapbooks and memory albums was not necessarily individualized, nor were their creators assumed to be their sole audience. In other words, such texts were social media: technologies for bonding with others and nurturing relationships. Moreover, as Greer notes (2011, p. 224), the production of such cultural forms helped girls to construct their own histories, both personal and collective – histories, I would add, that were rarely deemed significant enough to be documented and archived by professional historians.

Clearly, blogging software and social networking sites facilitate these functions for girls today. Yet contemporary media texts' striking similarity to scrapbooks, memory albums and other older forms – not to mention their place in the longer history of girls' cultural production – is rarely mentioned in studies of girls' digital media practices. Jacqueline Vickery's (2010) recent essay on girls' blogging is a rare exception. Three weblogs, each created by a different girl in the early 2000s, are at the heart of her study. Yet Vickery takes time to compare blogs with other forms of girls' media produced before the digital age. While she notes that blogging shares with journaling a focus on self-expression and personal narrative, she ultimately argues that girls' blogs have more in common with girls' zines, since both 'embrace the notion of the audience and construct a community based solely on the textual practices of writing' (Vickery, 2010, p. 187). Although Vickery might have drawn more attention to the visual aspects of these companion media, her research productively analyses girls' blogging as part of an evolving cultural practice that began with girls' diary-writing and developed further in girls' zine-making before the emergence of digital media.

Greer's and Vickery's research reveals an interest in exploring the continuities between different moments and forms of girls' media production, and thus provides a foundation for critical reflection on the similarities in girls' creative cultural practices over time. Unfortunately, few scholars studying girl-made media have focused in depth on instances of historical discontinuity, which is interesting given the privileging of the particular over the universal by scholars trained in poststructuralist theory. As if in response to this lacuna, Alison Piepmeier's book, *Girl Zines* (2009), provides a detailed exploration of the dissimilarities between zines and blogs, which were introduced decades apart but coexist today. Although Piepmeier argues that both forms can be understood as 'participatory media, spaces in which individuals can become creators rather than simply consumers of culture' (Piepmeier, 2009, p. 13), her primary concern in comparing blogs and zines is how variations in physical form and structure produce different meanings and affective responses for readers. In turn, through attention to changes in technology and the movement from paper to digital media over the turn of the twenty-first century, she examines discontinuities at the level of production, asserting that 'zines demand a level of aesthetic decision-making that digital media like blogs sometimes don't' (p. 65). While Piepmeier takes pains to connect contemporary girls' zines to pamphlets produced by earlier generations of (adult) feminists, she does not compare zines to companion media produced by different generations of girls, such as diaries and journals. Nevertheless, her parsing of the dissimilarities between blogs and zines helps us to understand better the particularities of older and emergent forms of girls' media and the different sociohistorical contexts that impact on their creation and consumption.

Conclusion

Elucidating the strategic interventions made possible through Cultural Studies' project of historical contextualization, Pickering argues that such an approach 'enables us to draw creatively and reflexively on what the past has bequeathed, to discover what was different then and learn from that difference while also adapting and taking forward what can be gleaned across successive waves of social and cultural change' (Pickering, 2008, p. 197). A great necessity exists today for more youth media scholars to resist presentism/ahistoricism and to adopt the historical/contextualist perspective. Those of us researching youth media must not assume that the current moment is ubiquitously self-evident, or that young people's media practices today are altogether new, radically different from or more important than those of the past. Neither should we assume that contemporary youth media are identical to those of previous generations. More historical research on previous periods of youth media is surely required; however, adopting the con-textualist approach does not mean that we should engage only with the past. We have much to learn from contemporary youth media. Yet, as Johnson suggests, those of us who study youth media culture in its present form must become historians of the contemporary. We must reflect critically on the current moment as a specific temporal location that, while unique, is necessarily shaped by, and shaping of, the past. By engaging more in these two activities – that is, historically contextualiz-ing today's youth media and exploring continuities and discontinuities across different periods – researchers in our field can help to enrich pub-lic understanding of the complexities of young people's media cultures, present and past, while also assisting in the articulation of progressive possibilities for the future.

Notes

1. For an in-depth discussion of these challenges, see Kearney (2007).
2. For an excellent analysis of the development of the circuit of media model, see D'Acci (2005).
3. More recent work in this area can be found in Kearney (2011).

References

D'Acci, J. (2005). Cultural studies, television studies, and the crisis in the humanities. In L. Spigel and J. Olsson (eds). *Television after TV: Essays on a medium in transition* (pp. 418–45). Durham: Duke University Press.

Dyer, R. (1979). *Stars.* London: BFI.

Foucault, M. (1977). Nietzsche, genealogy, history. In D. F. Bouchard (ed.). *Language, counter-memory, practice* (pp. 139–64). Ithaca: Cornell University Press.

Gramsci, A. (1971). *Selections from the prison notebooks.* New York: International Publishers.

Greer, J. (2011). Remixing Educational History: Girls and Their Memory Albums, 1913–1929. In M.C. Kearney (ed.) *Mediated girlhoods.* New York: Peter Lang.

Grossberg, L. (2010). *Cultural studies in the future tense.* Durham: Duke University Press.

Hall, S. (1980a). Cultural studies: Two paradigms. *Media, Culture and Society 2*(1), 57–72.

———— (1980b). Encoding/decoding. In S. Hall, D. Hobson, A. Lowe, and P. Willis (eds). *Culture, media, language: Working papers in cultural studies (1972–1979)* (pp. 128–38). London: Hutchinson.

Hebdige, D. (1979). *Subculture: The meaning of style.* London: Methuen.

Hunter, J. (1992). Inscribing the self in the heart of the family: Diaries and girlhood in late-Victorian America. *American Quarterly 44*(1), 51–81.

Johnson, R. (1986–87). What is cultural studies anyway? *Social Text 16,* 38–80.

Kearney, M. C. (1998). Producing girls: Rethinking the study of female youth culture. In S. A. Inness (ed.). *Delinquents and debutantes: Twentieth-century American girls' cultures* (pp. 285–310). New York: New York University Press.

———— (2004). Recycling Judy and Corliss: Transmedia exploitation and the first teen-girl production trend. *Feminist Media Studies 4*(3), 265–95.

———— (2005). Birds on the wire: Troping teenage girlhood through telephony in mid-twentieth-century US media culture. *Cultural Studies 19*(5), 568–600.

———— (2006). *Girls make media.* New York: Routledge.

———— (2007). Productive spaces: Girls' bedrooms as sites of cultural production. *Journal of Children and Media 1*(2), 126–41.

———— (2008). New directions: Girl-centered media studies for the 21st century. *Journal of Children and Media 2*(1), 82–3.

———— (ed.) (2011). *Mediated girlhoods: New explorations of girls' media culture.* New York: Peter Lang.

Lessig, L. (2008). *Remix: Making art and commerce thrive in the hybrid economy.* New York: Penguin.

Marvin, C. (1988). *When old technologies were new: Thinking about electric communication in the late nineteenth century.* New York: Oxford University Press.

McRobbie, A. and J. Garber (1976). Girls and subcultures. In S. Hall and T. Jefferson (eds). *Resistance through rituals: Youth subcultures in post-war Britain* (pp. 209–22). London: Harper Collins.

Mecklenburg-Faenger, A. L. (2007). Scissors, paste, and social change: The rhetoric of scrapbooks of women's organizations, 1875–1930. Ph.D. diss. Ohio State University.

Pickering, M. (2008). Engaging with history. In M. Pickering (ed.). *Research methods for cultural studies* (pp. 198–213). Edinburgh: Edinburgh University Press.

Piepmeier, A. (2009). *Girl zines: Making media, doing feminism.* New York: New York University Press.

Schrum, K. (2004). *Some wore bobby sox: The emergence of teenage girls' culture, 1920–1945.* New York: Palgrave.

Slack, J. D. (1996). The theory and method of articulation in cultural studies. In D. Morley and K. Chen (eds). *Stuart Hall: Critical dialogues* (pp. 112–27). New York: Routledge.

Turner, G. (1990). *British cultural studies: An introduction.* Boston: Unwin Hyman.

—— (2003). *British cultural studies: An introduction,* 3rd ed. New York: Routledge.

Vickery, J. (2010). Blogrings as virtual communities for adolescent girls. In S. R. Mazzarella (ed.). *Girl wide web 2.0: Revising girls, the Internet, and the negotiation of identity* (pp. 183–200). New York: Peter Lang.

Williams, R. (1958). Culture is ordinary. In N. Mackenzie (ed.). *Conviction* (pp. 74–92). London: MacGibbon and Kee.

—— (1965). *The Long Revolution.* Middlesex: Penguin Books.

Part II
The Global and the Local

4
'My Whole Life Is Here': Tracing Journeys through 'Skinhead'

Hilary Pilkington

Introduction

[Slava] meets us dressed in summer military uniform: camouflage, high boots, cap and water bottle attached to his belt. He marches us past what seems like a whole division of trainees waiting to go into the steam sauna (*bania*), through various dark corridors to a small room next to the changing room located right by the entrance to the sauna ... [He] thinks he will be in St Petersburg until the end of his service and plans not to go back to Vorkuta but perhaps to stay in Piter [St Petersburg] or perhaps go to Briansk ... [He is] excited by the book. [He] asks us to explain the main narrative and clearly remembers our earlier conversations when I explain that it is not about skinhead ideology but about their 'whole lives'. [He] picks out the word 'Slava' and asks us to translate things attributed to him. Apparently satisfied, he goes outside to bring one of his mates in ... to show him. From the way he talks about Andrei [another core respondent] to him, it is clear that this is not the first time he has told these stories. Finally, with a satisfied smile, he pronounces, 'my whole life is here' (*vsia moia zhizn' zdes*). (Extract from Hilary Pilkington's field diary, St Petersburg, 23 May 2010)

This field diary excerpt captures a meeting with Slava, a core respondent from an earlier ethnographic study of a skinhead group in the far northern city of Vorkuta, while he was undertaking military service in the suburbs of St Petersburg. Slava's declaration upon receiving a copy of our newly published book on the research in which he had participated, that his 'whole life' was represented in it, remained imprinted on my mind. It was at once gratifying and terrifying: terrifying because this

71

impression was based not on any real understanding of the text or our analysis, but on a brief and largely visual interaction with the book that was also emotionally charged because it evoked familiar people, places and moments from which he was currently separated. At the same time it was tempting to interpret Slava's words as evidence that we had achieved our aim of presenting respondents not as disembodied bearers of 'Nazi ideology', but as young people who drew – usually temporarily – on skinhead style, practices and ideological narratives in order to negotiate particular environments and experiences. The research had not focused on the 'spectacular' style of an 'exotic' subculture in a remote Russian context, nor on the group's ideology – both had only a marginal presence in their lives – but instead on the rudimentary domesticity, everyday talk, banter, play and fighting that structured the group's time together. What had pulled us back to this frozen field again and again was the desire to better understand the relationship between 'everyday life' and 'subcultural life' (Clarke et al., 1993, p. 16).

From subculture to whole lives

That ideological concerns may be secondary to other practices within relatively young skinhead groups is recognized in other local case studies. On the basis of research with former skinheads in Sweden, Kimmel (2007, p. 202) argues that participation in neo-Nazi skinhead groups is 'more a masculine rite of passage than evidence of a firm commitment to racialized ideologies'. Garland and Treadwell (2011, pp. 625–6) also suggest that the racist violence perpetrated by British young men they interviewed is not a direct response to particular structural conditions but mediated by a form of 'protest masculinity' (following Connell, 1995). By this they mean that tropes of hegemonic masculinity are reworked, in the context of relative deprivation and the active manipulation by organized racist groups of 'the present 'risky' status assigned to British (and particularly Muslim) Asians in the popular press', into marginal masculine identities that target ethnic and religious minority groups (Garland and Treadwell, 2011, p. 626).

Nayak's research with a small group of racist skinheads – 'The Pale Warriors' – in a white suburb of Birmingham also places masculinity centre stage. Without any secure work-based identity, he argues, 'investments in specific styles of whiteness became a substitute for the masculine-affirmative process of manual labour' (Nayak, 2005, p. 149). While the relationship between skinhead style and the symbolic reassertion of working-class identity has been well-rehearsed in theories of youth subculture, Nayak demonstrates the intersection of class with both gender and race in analysing skinhead style's articulation of 'multiple masculine fantasies of existence related to manual labour, militarism, prison identity, and "hardness"' (152). Skinhead racism, he argues, is a choreographed performance – a repetitive, hyperbolic exhibition – of whiteness that required respondents to carefully regulate desire and fantasies of the 'Other' (Nayak, 1999, pp. 82–6, 94–5).

The study of Vorkuta skinheads, discussed below, confirms the centrality to youth cultural strategies of the struggle to form workable gender and labour identities. However, it is less concerned with unpacking the intersection between class, race and gender in the production of skinhead style than with locating individual journeys through skinhead in the broader context of young people's evolving lives, structured as they are by class, race and gender. This approach moves away from rigidly differentiating between 'subcultural' and 'mainstream' youth at an analytic level, while recognizing that such distinctions remain important to narratives of authenticity for some young people. It assumes young people position themselves in some way on the youth scene whether they adopt a 'spectacular' style or not. In so doing, it switches analytic focus from the *nature* of the group – its relative closedness, fixed-ness or differentiation from 'other' groups or 'mainstream' society – to its *substance*. This is a term also used by Paul Hodkinson (2004, p. 141) who counterposes 'cultural substance' to cultural *fluidity* to illuminate the continued relative distinctiveness, shared identity, commitment and autonomy of some late modern cultural styles. Here the term 'substance' is employed rather to signify a concern with the cultural practices and affective bonds that bind a particular group of people. These practices need not be stylistic or spectacular; as Paul Corrigan (1993, p. 103) notes, the main action of subculture is, often 'doing nothing' or simply talking, 'not to communicate ideas, but to communicate the experience of talking' (ibid.). In this vein, the substance of youth cultural practices might be thought of as located not in subcultural style but in the 'communicative practices' (Frith, 2004, p. 173) or 'embodied communication' (Pilkington, 1994, pp. 236–68) that define a particular emotional community. Without denying the significance (often temporary) of particular elements (dress, music, ritual, argot) of subcultural style (Clarke et al., 1993, pp. 45–7), this shifts the object of empirical study to the ways in which 'subculture is actually "lived out"', as Cohen (2005, p. 90) puts it.

This approach also helps connect micro and macro levels of analysis, unlike CCCS conceptualizations of subcultures, which often require a leap of faith in reading macro historical and structural forces off the display of particular symbols. Embedding symbolic and style practices in the context of everyday lives allows sensitivity to the social structures that shape both. To do this, the concept of 'youth cultural strategy' (Pilkington et al., 2002, pp. 101–32) is employed to express how young people negotiate a range of cultural regimes – rooted in social divisions of (socio-economic/socio-spatial) class, gender, race/ethnicity, sexuality, (dis)ability – that enable or constrain their youth cultural possibilities. By avoiding any a priori distinction between 'ordinary' deviancy and 'subcultural' style, moreover, this approach reconnects with critical criminology or 'deviancy' literature, which has established that the perspectives of 'deviant' groups are in fact only extensions of those held by 'ordinary' members of conventional society (Becker, 1997, p. 175). This has been particularly important in the study of skinhead lives discussed here since it recognizes that there is much in common between the views of 'skinhead' respondents and the 'everyday' racism and xenophobia of 'ordinary' people (both young and old). The notion of 'youth cultural strategy' also helps locate 'skinhead' practices within longer and more varied 'street' or 'subcultural' careers that cross the boundaries of 'ordinary deviancy' (gang culture, petty crime, drug dealing) and 'subcultural' identities, and thus understand skinhead as one episode in a journey, or youth cultural trajectory. Thinking about these trajectories as 'strategies', moreover, recognizes the very real constraints that social inequalities impose on young people but also the reflexivity, agency and creativity they have in their cultural lives and the routine 'moving on' in which they engage.

Researching whole lives: method, context and introductions

The material drawn on in this chapter comes from four short periods of ethnographic research (2002–09) in the city of Vorkuta with a group of young people sharing a self-declared 'skinhead' identity. Members of the respondent group were 16–19 years old when we first met them. They became the focus of research between 2006 and 2008 when a small team of researchers (Hilary Pilkington, Elena Omel'chenko and Al'bina Garifzianova) gathered 23 audio and video taped interviews as well as photos and video images. In 2009, new interviews were conducted with two core members of the group who had remained in Vorkuta, reflecting on their participation in the research process and their own understandings of their 'journeys'. This chapter also draws on fieldwork diaries and other informal, physical and virtual, meetings and communications with participants after the completion of the research project. Respondents are referred to by pseudonym followed by the year in which the data were collected. Visual images are reproduced with the consent of respondents.

Vorkuta lies within the Arctic Circle, over 2,000 kilometres to the northeast of Moscow and with no road connections to other cities. As its territorial isolation suggests, the city did not develop organically but was established in 1932 as part of the Gulag system to exploit a major coal deposit in the Pechora basin. Over time the city's population was supplemented by friends and relatives who followed prisoners to their place of exile and, later, by young specialists attracted by the high salaries and early retirement rights offered to compensate for the harsh climatic conditions and heightened risk associated with working in the region. Today, however, Vorkuta is a rapidly deindustrializing and depopulating city. According to national and regional official data (see http://komi.gks.ru), registered unemployment is low (3.3 per cent) but educational and employment prospects are nonetheless limited. The city's economy is heavily dependent upon coal extraction, which constitutes 74 per cent of its industrial production, and further and higher educational establishments are oriented towards the training needs of this sector. However, the majority of its mines have closed since 1991 and there has been rapid outmigration; in 1995 the city's population was 181,000; by 2007 it had fallen by a third and continues to shrink rapidly, leading to whole districts (*poselki*) becoming derelict. Although extraction sector workers still receive a premium and monthly wages in the city (in 2006) remained 1.5 times higher than the Russian national average, the relative advantage of remaining in Vorkuta is declining. There is a widespread sense that the city is abandoned as well as isolated, its young people often resentful that the past symbolic and material recognition of miners' labour is denied to them (Pilkington, 2010).

This chapter follows four individual journeys through skinhead. The respondents – Andrei, Slava, Valera and Lera – were selected because they were central to the group, and because we developed long-term positive relationships with them and gained relatively open access to their everyday lives. After a brief portrait of each respondent, the chapter focuses on three moments in their youth cultural trajectories: the beginning of their journeys into skinhead, reflections on what 'being skinhead' meant to them and their movement out of, or on from, skinhead.

Andrei was one of two core respondents known to the research team since 2002, when he was 16 years old. He saw himself as the co-founder and ideological leader of the group, originally known as the 'Retribution-18' brigade, and was the only member to have had any serious engagement with radical political parties, telling us 'there is no such thing as a former skinhead'. He was the most cautious about engaging in the research; he declined to give a video interview and repeatedly reminded researchers that they posed a 'security risk' to the group. Andrei moved to Moscow in Spring 2008, has since completed military service and now returned to the same job (in a finance office of a company laying cable).

Slava first participated in the research in 2002, when he was 17 years old. He was one of the group's two acknowledged leaders until, in October 2006, a conflict with Andrei resulted in a decisive split in the group (Omel'chenko, 2010a, pp. 62–3). After leaving school he worked in the turbine room of the city's central power station until conscripted into the army in November 2009. He has always shown a great personal investment in the research, talking about himself as one of the team's 'unpaid members', remaining in regular contact and reflectively engaging in what he called 'bloody-self-criticism'.

Valera first came into the research orbit in 2006 when he was 19 years old and had only recently been released from prison. Despite participating in skinhead 'actions', he saw himself as a 'foot soldier' rather than a leader, describing himself as 'a normal lad of our times'. The research relationship with Valera became particularly close due to his willingness to share his emotions and experiences. Valera found employment with a construction company relatively quickly after release from prison and was deployed to Moscow for a while before losing his job due to drink-related absenteeism. He has remained in regular contact and, when last interviewed in 2009, remained in Vorkuta where he had resumed full-time education.

Lera was 18 when she first became involved in the research in October 2006. At that time, she lived with her parents and worked in the city's social security office, arguing 'you don't have to dress in a way that makes it obvious you are a skinhead'. She had become involved in the skinhead movement through an older male skinhead in Moscow but claimed to have led a 'brigade' of younger skinhead lads in Vorkuta. She moved to the Moscow region in 2008 at which time she re-entered education and took up karate.

Growing into skinhead: families, friends and turning points

All four respondents began their journeys into skinhead before our research with them began. Their narratives about the family and peer contexts of their entrance into the movement were often contradictory and subject to reformulation at different interview points.

The only respondent not to recount his movement into skinhead as a narrative of choice was Valera. From a large and financially struggling family, as a teenager Valera was musically and stylistically into rap. Both his older brothers were skinheads, however, and he described them as literally beating him into the movement: 'they knocked it into my head that I had to be a skinhead' (2006, age 19). Valera's home life – in particular his relationship with his mother – was volatile and the sense of inadequacy and impotence this engendered features strongly in his narration of the journey into skinhead:

> At home, I'm just a nobody. Maybe that had something to do with it. I was no fucking use to anyone, nobody paid me any attention. But on the street I had some weight. I could assert myself ... Afterwards the young skinheads fucking worshipped me ... They'd all follow wherever I led them. (2006)

The most significant turning point in Valera's life was being sent to prison for drug dealing offences as a result of a combination of material and familial circumstances. When his parents separated, both his mother and father moved out of the family flat ('they left me on my own'). At this time he was frustrated by financial dependence on his mother and, in his own words, 'uncontrollable'. At the same time, living alone in a large flat provided the material conditions to finance this 'out of control' lifestyle by selling drugs. This lifestyle move signalled a shift in youth cultural strategy too. In Valera's words, 'I just became a low-life criminal (*otmorozok*, a slang term derived from 'frost-bitten' to denote a 'hardened' criminal), who just drank. Basically I just became a normal lad of our times.' Thus although, whilst in prison, Valera had a swastika tattooed on his chest, even at the point he entered the research process, he had already begun his move out of skinhead.

Lera's journey into skinhead was also initiated by an older male, but via a process of 'grooming' rather than coercion. When she was 13 she met an inspiring, 'significantly older', male skinhead in Moscow:

> He kind of liberated me somehow. He said, 'You have a little spark in you which can be kindled into an eternal flame!' ... He explained the idea to me, that it was something to strive for, something that had to be done ... He talked so inspiringly, it was such a breath of fresh air,

> I got so into it that I didn't want to give it up. I moved here ... a year
> went by and then I became friends with these lads. (2006, aged 18)

Violence, nonetheless, marked Lera's initiation into skinhead; explaining that skinheads had to earn the right to wear 'white laces' in their boots by participating in the murder of an 'enemy', she claimed to have won her white laces by accepting the challenge of being the one to put a lighted match to the body of a 'non-Russian' policeman that her skinhead gang had beaten and doused in diesel. This story could not be corroborated by other group members since it had taken place in Moscow. However, Lera saw it as a key turning point, the moment she prioritized gaining respect from her new skinhead 'friends' over her own feelings. Remembering it continued to cause her anguish and regret.

Notwithstanding Lera's own account of having her inner 'flame' fanned by an authoritative figure on the scene, it seemed that the tinder had been well-prepared by her home life. Unlike Valera, family relations were relatively stable and secure; although Lera's father was absent for periods of time while she was growing up, this was because he was on active military service (in Afghanistan, Dagestan, Chechnia and Tajikistan). Lera insisted that her father had not made her 'think that way' but that 'gradually I developed this sense of negativity towards them [the local population]. I was kind of afraid of them, nervous [of them]' because of the way her father had treated all *khachiki* with 'contempt' after returning from military service, and expressed support for the skinhead movement (2006). (The term *khachik* is used widely in everyday racist speech to refer to those of Armenian or of undefined ethnic origin but presumed to be 'from the Caucasus' region: etymologically it derives from an Armenian first name 'Khachatur'). Perhaps even more significant in shaping Lera's prejudice was an early embedding of xenophobia in her understanding of right and wrong. For instance, she recalled episodes from her childhood such as being physically grabbed 'by the scruff of the neck' and threatened with physical violence after an incident when a little boy (a *khachik*) chased her home and her father thought she had invited him back.

Nonetheless, on one occasion, Lera related how her father returned from a tour of duty in Dagestan 'all sunburned, and with black stubble. And he had melons and watermelons too'. By resembling those she had learned to 'other', he provoked in her a similar mixture of fear and loathing towards him:

> I remember, I will never forget, I saw him and ran off in tears, crying,
> 'That's not my Dad.' Mum was going, 'It's your Dad, stop it.' And

I just looked at him, all black. 'It's not my Dad.' [I was] totally hysterical. Dad washed and shaved, but I still didn't respond. [In the end] he won me over with an apple. (2006, aged 18)

Lera's mother worked in a multicultural nursery school; however, Lera identified with her father's xenophobia rather than her mother's tolerance. Some reasons for this are considered below, in relation to the gender dimensions of Lera's cultural strategy.

Andrei too claimed that his father's views had shaped his and that he respected his father greatly 'for his constantly logical and rational manner of thinking', which he had made 'a rule for myself' (2006, aged 20). Indeed this celebration of male logic and rationality was central to Andrei's self-declared 'hard' (*brutal'nii*) masculine identity (Omel'chenko, 2010b).

In contrast, Slava's views apparently owed little to parental influence. His father had died when he was five years old and he described his relationship with his mother as 'distant'; they often communicated by leaving notes to each other in the flat (2007, aged 22). Parental absenteeism is not an unusual experience in Vorkuta, where male life expectancy at the time of our research was 58; in addition, the rapid outmigration from the city meant that parents often left older teenage children on their own while they sought better employment and living prospects elsewhere. In a 2007 conversation with a work-based friend about how parents were 'out for themselves', Slava argued that 'before their kids have reached even a decent age, their parents have given up caring about them – they're getting on with their own lives ... Here in Vorkuta, to the question, 'where are you going?' there's only ever one answer, 'things to do, here and there – stuff to do'. Your son might be away, three, four or five nights, off in Moscow somewhere ... Our parents forgot about us long ago.' In the absence of other significant influences, Slava's youth cultural strategy was formed primarily in response to peer relationships. He particularly recalled a summer youth camp trip to Bulgaria aged 14 when he had shared a chalet with a number of peers including three *khachiki*, which he experienced as ethnic bullying (2002 aged 17).

For both Andrei and Slava, the move into skinhead happened not as the result of a significant turning point, but rather as a progression from everyday provincial city gang life. For example, although Slava recounted in 2002 that he had become acquainted with a group of skinheads in Moscow, their communication soon dissipated and his existing peer groups and friendships appeared more important in his skinhead trajectory. These were closed, hierarchical groups routinely engaged in the physical resolution of disputes and economic extortion of subordinate members (Pilkington, 2007), in which core practices of independence, risk-taking, seeking 'action' and authority were established. Andrei explained in 2006 (aged 20) that the group was divided into sections, each with a leader: 'So I had four people with me – under me, that is. So if there were any problems, I, only I, would be rung. And it was my job to inform these four, gather them together. Nobody was phoned except me – all contact went through me. And it was the same with all the others ... It was all very serious.'

At the same time, adopting the subcultural code of 'skinheads' allowed individuals to stand out from the semi-criminal 'normal lads of our times' referred to by Valera above as the default cultural strategy in the city. Thus for Andrei and Slava, movement into skinhead had been part also of a 'progressive' (Pilkington, 2004) youth cultural trajectory out of earlier territorially based groups where they had shared their earlier teenage years.

Being skinhead: ideas, attachments, meanings

The symbolic significance of skinhead style – beyond the meanings attached to it by individuals involved in the movement – has been central to academic discussions (Clarke, 1993; Hebdige, 1982; Nayak, 1999). However, although style was not irrelevant to our respondents, it was considered to be of superficial significance only (Pilkington, 2010b), and we therefore focus on the meanings they themselves attached to 'being' skinhead.

Andrei was the most ideologically engaged respondent, investing skinhead with most political meaning. For him skinhead was about 'how you yourself understand the world around you', about being 'self-sufficient' and taking responsibility for change (2006, aged 20). He viewed ideology as meaningful only when firmly tied to action and characterized skinheads as a 'movement of action. They don't only think and talk – they act. They do everything they can to achieve their aim, to make sure our country, our people, are respected in the way they deserve to be ... I don't just sit around discussing with you – I take concrete steps.' It followed that for Andrei skinhead violence enacted a social or political ideal, and he spent considerable effort justifying it philosophically; he discussed it mainly in abstract terms, as something being done to the body of 'the other'. Primarily, however, skinhead provided a means of endowing a transcendent meaning to one's own life; this was typically articulated in discussions about what you would be prepared to die for:

> I live to change the world and for the sake of the continuation of our race [rod]. What does any person live for if not to ensure that his blood will be there in the future? Ian Stuart [Donaldson, frontman of Screwdriver] wrote that if a person doesn't know what they are prepared to die for, then what does he have to live for? (2006)

By contrast, for Slava and Valera the source of transcendent value embedded in skinhead was not an idea or political aim, but the bonds between people engendered in its performance. In discussing 'things I'd be prepared to die for' in 2006 when he was 21, Slava stated 'For the lads right here, for example'.

Following the split within the group in 2006, however, these bonds of loyalty increasingly shifted to other sites, especially work camaraderie. Through close work-based friendships, Slava shared the physical hardships of the job and enjoyed various adventures (evading 'the bosses', sneaking alcohol and other substances past the security). He also experienced a wider work team (brigada) camaraderie focused on its drinking traditions, and, in particular, the ritual of the 'table' (stolik) at which the group met every Friday to mark the end of the working week. For Slava these rituals had an added significance since they sealed the labour heritage from his dead father, whom he had followed into work at the power station and from whom he said he had inherited his strong work ethic (Omel'chenko, 2010a).

For Valera, the bonds forged through fighting within the skinhead movement were pivotal to the meaning he attached to it. These bonds brought not only a sense of solidarity, but also self-worth and authority. Unlike at home where he felt 'I was nobody ... Nobody fucking needed me, nobody paid me any attention', during an action and on the street he felt 'useful' and that he had authority and power: 'the young skinheads fucking idolized me – 'If Valera says so, then that's right.' I would tell them to follow me and 35 lads would set off in two rows, all behind me, wherever I led them (aged 19, 2006). He reminisced also about the loyalty and respect he himself felt for men like Andrei, claiming that 'for him I'd rip anybody's head off, I wouldn't give a fuck how old or how big they were. I wouldn't give a fuck. And if they rip my head off, fuck them. That's how it is. Fuck it. Andrei's the real deal.'

These articulations of what it meant to participate in skinhead suggest a quite different and more concrete relationship to its violence than

Andrei expressed, for example. Valera's life stories conveyed an image of him oscillating between being the victim of tough, physical discipline meted out by men (fathers, brothers, prison guards and other prisoners), of psychological hurt that he associated with women (especially his mother and former girlfriend but also a female teacher who expelled him from school) and of his *own* violent and 'out of control' behaviour. The latter almost resulted in his return to prison (his remaining sentence had been suspended) when his mother reported him to the police following a bout of drunken, violent behaviour on his birthday. In stark contrast to Andrei, therefore, for Valera, violence was not a means to a political end but an everyday experience to which skinhead – or rather the deep bonds of loyalty and respect that came with it – gave meaning.

Like Andrei, Lera saw the movement as committed to changing the world, arguing that 'the whole movement is based on ideas' with its main purpose to 'liberate Russia, cleanse it, ensure the future ... to make sure it was bright (*svetloe*, a Russian term evoking traditional Bolshevik slogans about Soviet society moving towards a 'bright future', but also indicating 'light coloured', giving an undertone to its use in this context). However, her prioritization of ideology and leadership over friendship bonds must be read in the context of the denial, by both young men and young women in the group, of the very possibility of 'real' friendship among women (Omel'chenko, 2010a, p. 69). Lera set up her own 'brigade' consisting entirely of young male skinheads. However, despite having apparently participated in the most serious act of violence reported to the researchers, Lera struggled to be taken seriously and her position in the group remained marginal. When a lad with whom she had had a romantic attachment left her and the movement to join the anti-fascists, her position as leader of the brigade was undermined, and her subsequent attempts to gain a position of authority within the Vorkuta skins met with resistance.

Nonetheless, she continued to place skinhead over gender solidarity. Explaining why there were no girls in her own skin brigade, she said that there was 'nowhere to recruit girls from now' and that she found it 'simpler with boys. A lot of girls see it as a way to show off ... to hang out with lads is great of course. Not everybody believes, not everybody is so serious about it. For the lads it is more serious' (2006, aged 18). She went on to joke about how girls might, in the middle of a fight, worry that they had 'broken a nail' or 'ripped their tights'. Thus, in considering the meanings attached to participation in the skinhead movement, it is important to take into account the highly restricted space for solidarity available to girls attached to the group and how this affects their wider cultural strategies.

Moving on: journeys out of skinhead

Continued engagement with respondents after the research, through social network sites, SMS communication, return visits to Vorkuta and face-to-face meetings in other cities where researchers and respondents intersected, provides some sense of how individuals have moved on from active engagement with the skinhead movement. Although none of them had 'switched sides' to join anti-fascist movements – a not uncommon trajectory according to Kimmel (2007, p. 215) – all had moved on from active, violent engagement in the movement and some had also renounced any ideological commitment to it.

Despite moving away from Vorkuta, Andrei maintained internal commitment to skinhead values, claiming that 'there is no such thing as a former skinhead': 'If you call yourself a "former" [skinhead] then you simply never really believed in it. But it's not a matter of belief, but of using your brains. So, you simply never grasped it fully' (2006, aged 20). Since our research ended, he has only sporadically participated in political action, most recently in a wave of protest in Russia over electoral fraud following the parliamentary elections in December 2011. Instead, he has developed his skinhead-related interests in pagan music, sport and in particular 'Fighting without rules' (*boi bez pravil* – in English referred to as 'ultimate fighting', 'extreme fighting', or 'kaged kombat'), in which he had begun to compete himself (Garifzianova, 2010, p. 82). Like Andrei, Lera too claimed that 'If it's in here [points to heart], you can't walk away' (2006). However, she also recognized that forms of activism change, with violent street practices being replaced by a greater concern with financial, organizational and promotional support for the movement.

For Slava, a dispute with Andrei in 2006 over how the group should use its basement gym (only for training or more sociable purposes) was a key turning point. It led to a definitive split between him and Andrei, a quarrel that recurred violently through to 2009, and also undermined the trust and loyalty that were essential to his sense of skinhead. He therefore moved on, describing this as a 'liberation' permitting him to 'progress' in his cultural interests (in practice to extend drink and drugs repertoires and hang out increasingly at club venues). By 2009, Slava was re-narrating his skinhead experience as a 'just cause' turned into violence by youthful alcohol abuse. He had removed all the skinhead paraphernalia that had previously decorated his room at home and conceded that, probably, 'our thinking was wrong'.

As already noted, Slava was particularly interested in the research process and reflected extensively on his own youth cultural trajectory. Employing an English loan word from information technology, he described his move out of skinhead as a process of 'upgrading' (*abgreid*) indicating a 'progressive' youth cultural strategy (see above) oriented towards constantly moving forward and acquiring new experiences. The research became part of his own mission to extend himself. In 2007, aged 22, he remarked that 'to be honest I don't understand myself and what I like most about myself is my lack of understanding of myself, that I am not friends with myself ... A lot of people are friends with themselves, but not me ... I adore self-bloody-criticism.' This echoes one of Kimmel's (2007, p. 217) respondents who talked about involvement in the skinhead movement as being a way of exploring his own identity, expressing and moving on from those elements of it that were 'destructive'.

Valera's trajectory was most subject to extreme experience and dramatic turning points, most significantly his time in prison during which, he said, 'I began to comprehend what I was doing' (2009, aged 22). Thus, although he had a swastika tattooed on his chest while in prison, it was less about loyalty to the movement and more a gesture of defiance towards the prison authorities (Pilkington, 2010b, p. 205): 'they beat us fucking all the time, constantly fucking broke us, in the cells, fuck it. Then I got the swastika done. Basically we had an inspection. We took off our fucking t-shirts, those who fucking could. And we laughed right at them' (2006, aged 19).

By 2009 Valera had thrown out all the attributes associated with skinhead and talked about having 'wasted 5 years' on it. He showed little nostalgia or sentiment, declaring, 'I want to forget about it! What went on before ... was terrible, ugly.' He expressed remorse for the actions in which he had participated and was saving money to get the swastika tattoo removed. Like Slava, Valera put down much of the change in his life to having 'stopped drinking': he had replaced alcohol with cannabis use in his leisure practices, and was even giving anti-alcohol talks at college. His example echoes Kimmel's (2007, p. 215) argument that many extreme-right activists are simply burned out by the constant drinking, fighting and anger.

Conclusion

This chapter has attempted a partial reconstruction of respondents' pre- and post-skinhead lives, based on their own accounts, in order to set skinhead activism in a wider context; firm conclusions about how this may have shaped their perceptions of the world or their wider youth cultural strategies are beyond its scope. The trajectories through skinhead of the four individuals introduced here, nonetheless, provide some corroboration of existing literature and suggest areas for future research.

The stories indicate the importance of family and peer contexts in shaping movement into and out of skinhead. Across the wider project too, respondents claimed tacit, if not open, parental support for their xenophobic views, confirming Nayak's (1999) suggestion that family histories of voting for far-right parties are important in forming racist views among young people. This to some extent supports the case that absent or abusive fathers are a significant factor in the backgrounds of violent racists (Kimmel, 2007, p. 210; Garland and Treadwell, 2011, p. 627). These factors have a structural dimension also; extreme deindustrialization as well as the harsh living and working environment of Vorkuta impact directly on families, which are often split by migration and premature death. This provides the conditions for early independent living and enhances peer influence on youth cultural strategies, even as young people may experience it as abandonment.

Peer social activities are not only important as 'gateways' into far-right movements (Kimmel, 2007, p. 210), however. The narratives here show the centrality of affective bonds formed within groups to becoming and remaining 'skinhead'. They indicate important continuities between past (semi-criminal) gang cultures and skinhead formations, in which skinhead ideology imbued pre-existing peer groupings with deeper meaning. These bonds provide protection and self-worth; breaking them can be a decisive moment in individuals' cultural trajectories, as they seek the existential comfort of solidarity elsewhere. Our research suggests the importance of tracing the interweaving of youth cultural with work and educational strategies, echoing existing arguments about the significance of experiences of bullying, and being bullied to trajectories into racist subcultures (Kimmel, 2007; Garland and Treadwell, 2011). In addition, it highlights the homosocial dimension of these bonds (see Omel'chenko, 2010b) and the constraints this places on young women's cultural strategies.

Respondent narratives confirm that in order to understand the continuing attraction of racist subcultures, we need to look beyond ideology and style. Even for those individuals who were ideologically engaged, 'around skinhead' interests in, for instance, pagan music, martial arts and other combat sports, as well as a range of drinking and recreational drug practices, were central to their everyday engagement with the movement and remained with them as they moved out of violent activism. The attraction of the ideological element of skinhead appears to be its capacity to provide transcendent meaning – purpose – to individual lives, whether articulated in terms of changing society or mutual support. Finally: if there is no single trajectory into, nor a single route out of, skinhead, perhaps the conclusion to draw from this is not that the movement has become fragmented but that research agendas have been left behind. Recounting these narratives as 'skinhead' stories misses the broader context, or as Slava puts it, that 'my whole life is here'.

Note

This research was part of a transnational European project on 'Society and Lifestyles' funded within the European Commission's Sixth Framework programme (STREP-CT-CIT5-029013). The article reflects only the authors' views and the Commission is not liable for any use that may be made of the information contained therein.

References

Becker, H. S. (1997). *Outsiders: Studies in the sociology of deviance*. New York: The Free Press.

Clarke, J. (1993). Style. In S. Hall and T. Jefferson (eds) *Resistance through Rituals: Youth Subcultures in post-war Britain* (pp. 175–91). London: Routledge.

Clarke, J., Hall, S., Jefferson, T. and Roberts, B. (1993). Subcultures, cultures and class: A theoretical overview', in S. Hall and T. Jefferson (eds) *Resistance through rituals: Youth subcultures in post-war Britain* (pp. 9–74). London: Routledge.

Cohen, P. (2005). Subcultural conflict and working class community. *Working Papers in Cultural Studies 2*. Birmingham: CCCS. Reprinted in K. Gelder (ed.) *The subcultures reader*, 2nd edn (pp. 86–93). London and New York: Routledge.

Connell, R.W. (1995). *Masculinities*. London: Sage.

Corrigan, P. (1993). Doing nothing: just bops' play? In S. Hall and T. Jefferson (eds) *Resistance through rituals: Youth Subcultures in post-war Britain* (pp. 103–5). London: Routledge.

Frith, S. (2004). Afterword. In A. Bennett and K. Kahn Harris (eds) *After subculture: Critical studies in contemporary youth culture* (pp. 173–7). Basingstoke: Palgrave Macmillan.

Garifzianova, A. (2010). "Upgrading": Cultural interests and strategies. In H. Pilkington, E. Omel'chenko and A. Garifzianova (eds) *Russia's skinheads: Exploring and rethinking subcultural lives* (pp. 75–96). London and New York: Routledge.

Garland, J. and Treadwell, J. (2011). Masculinity, marginalization and violence: A case study of the English defence league. *British Journal of Criminology, 51*(4), 621–34.

Hebdige, D. (1982). This is England! And they don't live here. In N. Knight (ed.) *Skinhead* (pp. 26–35). London: Omnibus Press.

Hodkinson, P. (2004). The Goth scene and (sub)cultural substance. In A. Bennett and K. Kahn Harris (eds) *After subculture: Critical studies in contemporary youth culture* (pp. 135–48). Basingstoke: Palgrave Macmillan.

Kimmel, M. (2007). Racism as adolescent male rite of passage: Ex-Nazis in Scandinavia. *Journal of Contemporary Ethnography, 36*(2), 202–18.

Nayak, A. (1999). "Pale Warriors": Skinhead Culture and the Embodiment of White Masculinities. In A. Brah, M.J. Hickman and M. Mac an Ghaill (eds) *Thinking identities: Ethnicity, racism and culture* (pp. 71–99). Basingstoke: Palgrave.

Nayak, A. (2005). White lives. In K. Murji and J. Solomos (eds) *Racialization: Studies in theory and practice* (pp.141–62). Oxford: Oxford University Press.

Nesterov, D. (2004). *Skiny: Rus' probuzhdaetsia.* Moscow: Ul'tra Kul'tura.

Omel'chenko, E. (2010a). "At home I was a nobody": The roots (and limits) of skinhead solidarity. In H. Pilkington, E. Omel'chenko and A. Garifzianova (eds) *Russia's skinheads: Exploring and rethinking subcultural lives* (pp. 49–74). London and New York: Routledge.

Omel'chenko, E. (2010b). In search of intimacy: Homosociality, masculinity and the body. In H. Pilkington, E. Omel'chenko and A. Garifzianova (eds) *Russia's skinheads: Exploring and rethinking subcultural lives* (pp. 166–86). London and New York: Routledge.

Pilkington, H., Omel'chenko, E., Flynn, M., Bliudina, U., Starkova, E. (2002). *Looking West? Cultural globalization and Russian youth cultures.* University Park, Pennsylvania: The Pennsylvania State University Press.

Pilkington, H. (1994). *Russia's youth and its culture.* London: Routledge.

Pilkington, H. (2004). Youth strategies for glocal living: Space, power and communication in everyday cultural practice. In A. Bennett and K. Kahn Harris (eds) *After subculture: Critical studies in contemporary youth culture* (pp. 119–34). Basingstoke: Palgrave.

Pilkington, H. (2007). Beyond "peer pressure": Rethinking drug use and "youth culture". *The International Journal of Drug Policy, 18*(3), 213–24.

Pilkington, H. (2010). No longer "on parade": Style and the performance of skinhead in the Russian far north. *Russian Review, 69*(2), 187–209.

5
From Local Gangs to Global Tribes: The Latin Kings and Queens Nation in Catalonia

Carles Feixa and Oriol Romaní

Prologue: an afternoon in Downing Street

In October 2011, the first author of this chapter was invited to participate in the international conference *Ending Gang Violence*, organized by the British Home Office in answer to the youth rioting the previous summer. The aim of that event, according to the letter of invitation, was 'to provoke discussion and debate with the objective of identifying best practice on tackling gang violence and examining what could be applied in England and Wales to strengthen and improve current approaches'. About 30 European and American experts participated at the conference, most of them police officers and intelligence agency members, although some academics, youth workers and civil society representatives of the neighbourhoods where the riots had taken place were also invited. Apart from Europol members and French police officers who had intervened after the *banlieues* riots in 2005, the main speakers were police officers from the United States who were experts in gangs, including Bill Braton, former chief of New York and Los Angeles Police Departments.

My participation came from the wish to know about the experience of mediating with Latino gangs that had taken place in Barcelona from 2006 – an experience which had some resonance through the British media and academic publications (Burke, 2006; Nilan and Feixa, 2006; Torres, 2006; Warden, 2006). In contrast with the strictly police-led approach defended mostly by the American experts, the academics and social workers who had the opportunity to participate in the event remembered the sociocultural roots of gang violence and the need to approach it from a more global preventative perspective. In one of the sessions I had the opportunity to explain how we had managed to work with some of the Latino gangs and how we managed to reduce significantly the conflicts between gangs, thanks to the cooperation of the Barcelona City Council and the Catalan Police force (the *Mossos d'Esquadra*), and thanks also to the involvement of some of the leaders of the main street youth organizations, which enhanced the visibility of gangs and the recognition of some of them as youth associations. In the afternoon of the last day, we were invited to visit 10 Downing Street, where the Home Secretary and the Prime Minister, David Cameron, received us. While I was talking to a British colleague, having a glass of wine served by Peruvian waiters, David Cameron came over and asked me what was the situation with the gangs in Spain. I answered briefly that we do have them, but they cannot still be compared to those in the United States, although some had an American origin: in order to intervene, we need to give a European response. In fact, our scientific and personal ties with the so-called Latin gangs had started a few years before, in 2004, following the death of a young boy in a secondary school in Barcelona.

Background: social context and methodology

On 28 October 2003, the Colombian adolescent Ronny Tapias was murdered as he was leaving his secondary school, in an attack by a group of youngsters in Barcelona. According to the investigation that followed, the murder was an act of revenge by members of a gang (the Ñetas) that supposedly mistook Ronny for a member of another gang (the Latin Kings) with whom they had fought at a disco a few days earlier. This case 'unveiled' the phenomenon of 'Latin street gangs' to the mass media and unleashed a wave of 'moral panic' that has continued ever since. A total of nine Ecuadorian and Dominican young persons were arrested within a month. Three of them were minors, who were tried and convicted (the alleged author of the crime was among them). The trial of the other six (aged over 18) was a major event followed with great expectation by the media. Gangs had a constant prominence during the trial, both as a reality and as a spectre. Behind the spectre of gangs there was an absent centre: the thousands of boys and girls of Latin American origin that had been arriving in Barcelona since the end of the 1990s (thanks in part to many family regrouping processes), exiled from their original places and social environments at one of the most critical times of their lives. These young people find frightened adults at their destination: busy mothers, absent fathers, insecure teachers and social assistants and scared neighbours. Behind this worrying presence another spectre can be found: the new forms of youthful sociability that cross geographical and time borders to reconstruct global identities – identities with a subcultural past, a nomadic present and a future to be constructed. This chapter outlines these developments, and presents the results of research about Latin American young people in Barcelona and their presence in the public life of the city.

After a few preliminary contacts in 2005 within the context of previous research (Feixa et al., 2006), we carried out fieldwork with this group during 2006–07, which consisted of interviews with their leaders and some Kings and Queens (grass-roots members), attended *Universales* and *Capítulos* (assemblies at different levels), leisure activities (football championships, the recording of a music album, concerts), and also more intimate events such as birthday parties, meals; but most importantly, we accompanied them during the process of their constitution as a legal association. Although the foundation myth of the Latin Kings and Queens dates back to the 1940s, The Almighty Latin King Nation (ALKN) did not emerge until the 1960s and 1970s as the union of all the Hispanic youth groups in Chicago, in order to fight against the discrimination that Latin people suffered. Today's characteristics were shaped during the establishment of the organization in New York during the 1980s, within the prison context, and in the 1990s in the streets, to fight for the improvement of living conditions of Latino communities; at this moment the feminine organization was founded in New York in 1991. The political awareness of the leader at that time, King Tone, promoted the transformation into a street organization, as opposed to street gangs (Brotherton and Barrios, 2004, pp. 122–48): the Kings and Queens of New York started to work for their community with other political movements such as the Black Panthers or the Young Lords (Ravecca, 2007, p. 35). The migration of the members spread the group's ideas and practices, from the United States into Ecuador, and from there into Spain and Italy, with the great migration wave at the beginning of the new century, adapting their meanings to the new territorial contexts.

The Latin Kings and Queens Nation is an organization with a pyramidal hierarchical structure that goes from the global, the nation as a rhetorical idea with transnational presence, to the local, as ideas are expressed by physical and concrete formulae that affect the members' daily lives. The *Nación* (Nation) is the biggest structure in the organization, which gathers all the tribes in the world, and at the same time identifies the organization at the local level. The tribe is the structure within the organization that corresponds to a country, although we can also find more than one tribe in the same country. Within a tribe there can be kingdoms or sectors, like the Kingdom of Madrid or the Kingdom of Catalonia in Spain. Finally, the chapters are the smaller-scale cells of the tribe and as a general rule they have influence on a more reduced area such as a district, a park or an underground station. In an assembly of the Almighty Latin Kings and Queens Nation Spain celebrated in 2006 in Barcelona, we gathered socio-demographic data from 118 members who answered a survey (out of the approximately 300 members of the group): 68.6 per cent were men (81) and 31.4 per cent women (37). The average age was 18.5 years, the men being a little older than the women with ages 18.81 and 17.83 per cent, respectively. About 70 per cent were Ecuadorian, and among the remaining 30 per cent most were Spanish (working-class background and migrant within Spain, with more women than men), followed by other Latin American nationalities. In general they left school early and unqualified and worked low-paid, precarious jobs often without a contract (Romaní et al., 2009, pp. 425–8). In short: these are transnational working-class young people.

Research object: a transnational nation

> Our long travel of discovery is over and our bark has drooped her weary sails in port (...) The temple of the sylvan goddess of the forest, indeed, has vanished and the King of the Wood no longer stands sentinel over the Golden Bough. (Frazer, [1890] 2006, p. 799)

In this chapter we propose a reflection on glocalization, using the neologism to refer to contemporary cultural phenomena composed of prominent elements that respond to both global and local dimensions. We consider the cultural imagery of youth gangs from our ethnographic fieldwork with members of the Latin Kings and Queens Nation in Catalonia, Spain. Catalonia is politically constituted as an autonomous region within the Spanish state in the northeast of the Iberian Peninsula; it has about seven million inhabitants, of which about four million live in Barcelona and its metropolitan area where we carried out the fieldwork. Approximately 15 per cent of the population are immigrants, among which Latin Americans feature prominently.

In his farewell to *The Golden Bough*, his book on mythology considered a classic of evolutionary anthropology, James Frazer returns to the myth of the forest king, guardian of the golden bough that protects the temple of Diana at Lake Nemi in the Lazio region, the origin of the

Latin confederacy that gave birth to the Roman Empire and to many of our myths and legends. The Golden Bough might well be the jungle of symbols of the Latin Kings and Queens Nation, a stateless and denied territory, but at the same time one that is rich in meanings, in which the darkness of the forest (an imagined community of subordination) is part of the royal *dorado* (an imagined community of empowerment), the colours of the flag of a nation without a state, a nation of youth, yet seeking its place in the world through symbolic work. Here we see the creation of a discourse of identity in which ethnic, generational and gender awareness produce new forms of political organization at the micro level, and new forms of public presence at the macro level. We will approach their reality through the oral stories of the protagonists, young migrants from Ecuador and other Latin American countries who have arrived in Spain since the beginning of 2000, and who staged a European 'third birth' of the Nation, after their previous births in the United States in the 1950s and in Ecuador in the 1990s. This is a story that revolves around the concept of nation, a homeland voluntarily understood as an imagined community – for young people who are stateless or from homelands in crisis. This concept draws on all the rhetoric of African American nations in the US melting pot (from the Nation of Islam to the Zulu Nation of Hip-hop), but fits within the post-national era, in which citizenship is constructed in the interstices of the nation state, in the migration of transnational actors and in the cyber-territories (Castells, 1996; Sassen, 2003).

Therefore, we start from a specific situation within this territory, which includes the relationships and interconnections of the Catalan tribes of the Latin Kings Nation with those in the rest of the world: their transnational connections, their different levels and their articulations. The first of these levels is precisely that the Nation, beyond its organizational characteristics, must be understood as a discourse that provides the rationale for specific practices, regarding both the organization, which is also the Nation, and each of the members, who feel identified with it by means of this discourse. The discourse offers a definition of who they are around a series of basic concepts such as the defence of the Latino culture, respect, brotherhood. It is a story that refers to the past, from the dichotomy of before and after being a Latin King or Queen, they are placed in the present in relation to the group to which they belong and to its values, and they are offered a future perspective based on the idea of progress. But this is not a univocal story: depending on the time or the context, it coexists with the story of the Nation as people, as a gang, as a tribe, as an organization, as a family and, last but not least, as a transnational community.

The nation as a people

Carles: What is a nation to you?

King M.:   A group of people who are governed by a single government, race, constitution, laws.

Carles: But this is a bit of a special kind of nation ...

King M.:   Well it is almost the same: we live here as a nation where we have a president, vice president, secretary, treasurer, a counsellor, a war chief, teachers, our policies, rules, we have a supreme court, judges ... Within our organization, we live as a nation within another nation, which is Spain.

According to the discourse of the Latin Kings and Queens, the Nation can be understood at three levels: (a) at the abstract level, as a sacred universe, which manifests its will and wisdom; (b) at the global level, as a global entity, an international organization that gives unity to the different ways of being Latin Kings in different sociocultural contexts; and (c) at the local level, as the people that make up a great family, who are each and every one of the brothers and sisters, and the way in which this takes place in everyday life. If we stick to the practices, people who form the Nation may have different situations in relation to these levels, and their experiences of it are also different. But if we focus on the discourse, what matters is a rhetoric that has been offering various levels, a definition and an identity that will allow them to respond to who they are (kings and queens), where they are located (in an 'organization') and what characterizes them (a 'purpose' around the idea of progress), although operating within such discourse becomes more complicated.

The Nation as 'sacred ground' is a metaphysical entity that is above the actions of its members: the will of the Nation would be independent from that of its individuals, who will sometimes accept assignments and responsibilities that are not totally understood, but are accepted because the Nation knows what it is demanding and why, and it may require some sacrifice or deprivation that ultimately will make sense taking into account the benefits to the Nation as a whole. The 'global level' would refer to the Nation as a transnational organization. While it is important for its members and their sense of belonging, and there is some internationalization in the Nation's nature, it also has limitations, as most members' experience of this connection is almost zero. They may be Latin in addition to the influences of the global culture, which affects, albeit differently, almost everyone with transcontinental connections through the new technologies (Internet, SMS), but in the same way as many other young people who are also migrants. In contrast, other connections exist between the leaders of the organization, which can be both mutual recognition and, at times, conflict, linked precisely to the process of expansion of the Latin Kings in very different contexts. Sometimes when a leader visits, it is when the base members of the Nation can experience more directly its transnational dimension, unlike what usually happens from day to day.

The nation as a gang

Carles: What is the difference between gang and nation?

King P.:   Gang is that everyone does what they want, while as a nation we are all united, all striving for the same reasons: if we suffer we all suffer if we have to laugh, we all laugh.

King T.:   The gang is almost a man, the leader. If he says, 'Go and steal', they will all steal. That's why we have our own Bible, our own laws. We have to abide by our laws, we are a Nation of organised people.

The political or cultural discourse of the Nation is not the first nor the most widespread, and it is often replaced and preceded by the discourse of the Nation as a street group, with criminal connotations (the gang) or identified with the informal sociability (the peer group). The discourse that the Kings and Queens have built to explain the Nation starts from denial, it is a discourse delivered from a subordinate position compared to that of the media who have identified them as a gang or criminal group, from prejudice and stigma, as has happened with other groups of young people. This was the imaginary we found when we began our research in Barcelona, in early 2005, and the one the brothers and sisters have to face and discuss at the beginning of each interview or press conference. However, beyond this negative view prevalent in the host society, the discourse of the 'peer group' coincides at the local, decentralized level: the collective (Delpino, 2007).

At the 'local' level, the persistence of the Nation's ideological discourse is experienced in the daily life, especially as a group of friends gathered around the 'chapter'. Boys and girls from the same neighbourhood are recruited through shared activities (school, public spaces, parks), and on several occasions there is a previous network of friends, in parks and sports grounds, acknowledged as Latino who eventually find membership in the Nation. This provides them with a strong identity, which they find useful in their relationships with their peers. Interaction with the other chapters tends to be monthly, so the daily life of the Nation takes place within a group of friends that make each of the chapters have few friends in common symbolic elements that allow them to clearly define the limits of their identity. One belongs to the Nation, then the chapter; coexistence and building support networks and mutual understanding will provide them with a discourse of identity that gives them meaning.

The nation as a tribe

King M.: Each tribe has its officers, its senior managers. STAE is a tribe, which is divided into several chapters. We are guided by the sacred tribe, within the empire. Chapters cover the tribes. All of that makes up an empire. For example ours is the Holy Tribe Spanish Empire, hence it is divided into chapters. Holy because it cannot be sacred yet. It is sacred when you have a leader, who has already achieved his independence. The process we are leading is to enable us to be recognised as a sacred tribe.

Our contact with the Latin Kings of Catalunya began in mid-2005; they presented themselves in the Youth House under the name Holy Tribe Atahualpa Ecuador (STAE). This was a second-level term, adopted for three reasons: first, because it was used as a 'second label' to avoid the term Latin Kings, then still stigmatized, which avoided doors closing from the very beginning: it worked in the Youth House where they had requested to meet, although a quick search for the name on the Internet soon confirmed the suspicions of what was behind that name. The second reason was that it corresponded to the second level of structuring of the powerful transnational Nation, representing the 'national' which produced the 'second birth' of the Latin Kings in Ecuador in the 1990s, after the first subdivision of the Nation into tribes, in the United States of the 1970s and 80s. The third reason was a politically correct alternative in the form of STAS (the Holy Tribe Atahualpa Spain), founded by King Wolverine in Madrid in 2001, which broke with the mother country and with its criminal drift. In the case of STAE, the tribe is preceded by the adjective Holy (as we have explained that evokes the mystic, symbolic dimension, of people in communion) and the double locative evokes both a remote source (Atahualpa, the last Inca who resisted the Spanish invader) and the origin (Ecuador, place of origin of 80 per cent of Latin Kings and Queens of Catalonia). The concept of 'tribe' has been labelled an 'obscure notion' by Godelier (1978), who denounces the use and abuse of the concept by anthropologists, often legitimating colonial or neocolonial political strategies (divide and conquer). Taking the example of the well-known Inca Empire, tribes were not always an evolutionary stage prior to the state, but they could be enhanced by the state structure, being a form of internal organization that could justify the subordination and hierarchy which corresponds to the process experienced by some factions within the Nation of Latin Kings and Queens.

The nation as an organization

King F.:   To introduce our culture, in it, right? Because we see that the culture here is different from our culture, then we have to try and say, hey, bring the two cultures closer and embrace the culture here a little, you know? Forget a little bit our ideals in our country, forget a little our culture, and adapt to what's here, you know? And adapt to the laws that are here, and the big differences between the countries, between Latin America and this country.

In the specific case of Barcelona, the positive definition of the Nation has also gone through the legal establishment of the 'Cultural Organization of Latin Kings and Queens of Catalonia', which clearly differentiates it from a gang, and represents the most symbolic and substantial change, as is their approach to various public institutions and services of Catalan society. At the same time it poses the challenge of giving content to its objectives in a stable manner over time and in a consistent way with their actions. We could say that becoming an association, which was not an easy process of negotiation with public institutions, was an element of 'acculturation' of the Catalan Latin Kings and, as such, perhaps it had more an operational value than the value of a full acceptance; not in the sense of setting a politically correct screen to hide obscure activities, but rather to acknowledge the limitations that underlie translating and adapting the whole scope of their phenomenon into the institutionally recognized models in the host country. Obviously, beyond what we have just outlined, the Latin Kings and Queens have other elements that define their Nation as an organized group fighting against social exclusion of Latinos, racism and xenophobia, while aiming to contribute to the progress of all its members so that they can have a prosperous future; statements that we might define as the 'official script' of the Born.

In our book *Jovenes Latinos en Barcelona* [Young Latinos in Barcelona] (Feixa et al., 2006), written when our study with the Latin Kings and Queens had not yet begun, we proposed the term 'organization' as an umbrella to encompass various forms of belonging to youth street groups (from the gang rule, to the Nation and the partnership). Some authors have criticized us for assuming a level of organization of the groups that did not correspond with the realities investigated by them (e.g., in Madrid), in which 'Latin gangs' appear as disjointed and marginalized groups, with little structure, which correspond to interpretations closer to social psychology and public policy: they see gangs as a way of compensating for self-esteem issues (Aparicio, 2008, p. 382). These authors are sceptical about the Catalan experience, because they presuppose that the real gang members are not the ones that participated in the organization. Since they have not contacted organized groups or leaders, they find it inconceivable that such realities could exist beyond speech or myth. Besides, the existence of a legally recognized entity does not necessarily replace other older and more profound organizations: the Nation as a form of (symbolic) kinship and as a field of (effective) power.

The nation as a family

King B.: I like the way people now realise that we are not the typical people that the press have always portrayed ... so now people realise that we are open to society and relate to everyone ... we are working people who want to be friends with everyone ... we are not racist like many people are here in Spain ... we want to live a quiet life without harming anyone ... we are with the Nation and we are with the family, which is one of the things that we want ... many say that if we are in the Nation it is because we are in conflict with our family, our family does not understand ... and this is a big lie, because I love my family and my family loves me ... But I like the Nation and I have time for all this ... for my family for the Nation, for work. I even have time to get my driving license. I have time for everything ... I do not lose because of the Nation, on the contrary, it has always given me ... has made me find the best friends in life ... and all that.

The group definition attempts to give a contrary view to the hegemonic one, and therefore must begin with the denial and then provide positive elements like the family or brotherhood. The family, as they define it, would be associated with a network of solidarity and mutual aid, and in this sense, the Nation, understood as a family, is primarily an organization that provides support and security, the main functions that characterize its raison d'être. In this regard, the functions performed by the Nation among young migrant workers would be similar to certain lifestyles that have characterized many European working-class districts in the twentieth century, such as neighbourhood networks and different types of partnerships that were articulated as forms of organization of a certain social class. Here we only want to make one point in reference to the relationship between the cultural imagination of the Nation and the rest of society, using the example of music produced by UGA Records, a group of young Latinos, most of whom belong to the Latin Kings. Using the musical language of hip-hop and rap allows these young people to bring to the forefront a media awareness of emigration and experiences related to it; although on the other hand, many songs make references to the identity of kings and queens, and tell stories that, although only some of them have seen them, they end up becoming almost a legend to the younger consumer. We know that 'Latino culture and race' are central in shaping the Nation, but when they speak of 'our culture' they refer to very heterogeneous elements from different backgrounds within the broad scope of 'Latino'. The immigrant community will always be fragmented, but its members have in common the experience of their integration into a new cultural reality, in this case, the insertion strategy also involves the construction and recognition of Latino culture as a valid model in a new social space. Thus, the creation of Latin music not only refers to the creation of a specific universe of 'Latinos', but speaks to the sociocultural context of the host society.

Catalan Kings *versus* Global Kings

Queen M.:   The integration of Latino youth in Spain has been and will be an uphill struggle as long as discrimination by the Spanish society and media go on, and there is lack of collaboration of many young people who are isolated and closed to change with the help and collaboration of all in general. Us Latino youth want and need our culture valued and help to integrate into society, with trust and not be labelled as part of a gang or criminal group.

Since the beginning of our investigation we have found that our analysis is more aligned with authors who have analysed gangs as social and political organizations (Conquergood, 1994; Brotherton and Barrios, 2004; Hagedorn, 2007), in contrast with other authors that also consider the criminal character of these groups (Klein, 1995; Klein et al., 2001). For instance, Brotherton and Barrios (2004) propose the concept of street organizations as the most appropriate for these groups, which they consider as resistance movements that oppose their counter-narratives and cultural practices to the hegemonic culture, while they make the experiences of belonging to the community possible and, ultimately, empowering. Although the reasons for choosing this concept were diverse, the main one was that it adapted much better than the other perspectives to the characteristics of the organizations that we were encountering, where cultural and social aspects prevailed far beyond criminal ones (Feixa et al., 2006). Other authors who have worked with the same organization in other regions have also identified these sociopolitical aspects: young people struggle against the invisibility of their subordinate status through processes of social and aesthetic reinvention (Queirolo and Torre, 2005; Cannarella et al., 2007). But in the long term this dichotomy was less clear and unambiguous: the sociopolitical and the criminal model were not so much alternative models as moments in a *continuum*: for this reason we proposed the notion of 'gangs-in-process' (Feixa et al., 2008).

Despite the usefulness of this theoretical perspective for the study of the Nation in Catalonia we found a paradox, as the character of resistance claimed by the organization was not easily identified in some key features of their discourse. From the perspective of the host society, this could be considered as conservative: different rules for men and for women, with a clear subordination of the latter, the fight against abortion, rejection of homosexuality, defence of hierarchy in decision-making, defence of more traditional family roles, defence of the 'Latin race'. In many cases, the narratives associated with joining the LK&Q could be identified with the 'stories of conversion' in which some followers of new religions take the path from 'darkness' into 'light', without appearing very combative towards the society in which they live. It seemed difficult, given the heterogeneity of their sources, that they could articulate a coherent political discourse which would be interpreted as a strategy for social inclusion, adaptation and recognition in the host society, defending values that they think are socially acceptable. But to avoid falling into simplistic assessments, we believe it is useful to consider the criticism from other perspectives that challenge the way Western political movements have tried to impose their agendas without considering the existing specifications, and the inequalities experienced by race, gender, social class, ability or subordinate colonial and neocolonial populations elsewhere (Bhavnani, 2001). In our case, it would be useful to highlight the different contexts where the basic literature of the organization has taken place, namely, the United States and Ecuador.

As regards the United States, Latin Kings arise from a population (Chicago and New York) with many social problems, from the immigration status of the group, to the subordinate position of the Latino population in the United States and their difficult relations with other groups. In this context, talking about the 'Latin race' has connotations related to the importance of the struggles of black people and the history of material and symbolic segregation of 'minorities'. Speaking of 'defence of the race', as members of the Nation often do has a very different meaning in the urban context of the United States than in the Spanish context, which brings us back directly to the language of Franco's dictatorship. The other major source of literature, lessons and prayers, is to be found in Quito, Guayaquil and other cities of Ecuador, where many members of the LK&Q come from. Individualism and hedonism are mentioned as two basic elements and would be complementary to existing forms of social control through the market: emotions that can be purchased, instead of the true enjoyment of life (Comas and Romaní, 2004).

Thus, consistent with the proposals that we have used as reference for research, also when considering the nature of the organization, we have to compare the discourse with the practices. So while we find that the first is embedded with elements that are conservative in our context, a close look at the practices, the ways in which their presence is confronted with the host society, we can see potential elements of resistance that a rigorous analysis cannot ignore. We refer to their claims of invisibility of the immigrant population, particularly the Latin, with both the discourse as embodied practice and cultural production – primarily music – to community-based approaches, and group involvement compared to the current hegemonic individualism in Catalan society. The management methods through solidarity and responsibility are opposed to the hedonism prevalent in other youth cultures, building a sphere of power and practice of 'social presence' in order to become a subject in a context of exclusion.

Postscript: the Barcelona Gang Model and beyond

While the Cultural Organization of Latin Kings and Queens of Catalonia was introduced in the register of associations in August 2006, the Sacred Tribe America Spain was declared an unlawful association by the Provincial Court of Madrid in March 2008, even if the sentence was ruled void by the Supreme Court and the trial took place again in 2010 (Feixa et al., 2011). To date (April 2012), the Latino gangs have consolidated their presence in Catalonia. The number of members, according to the Catalan Police, has remained stable (around 5000), although the number of groups has increased and diversified. The two most popular (Latin Kings and Ñetas) remain the most numerous, although smaller ones (Black Panthers, Vatos Locos, Trinitarios, Dominican Don't Play, Mara Salvatrucha, etc.) rival with them. The two entities created in 2006 (Cultural Organization of Latin Kings and Queens of Catalonia) and 2007 (Ñetas Socio-Cultural, Sports and Musical Association) continue to exist legally, but their activities are not so massive, novel or continuous. The Catalan Police themselves recognize that the process reduced significantly the conflict between gangs, although episodic fights and connections of some of its members with illicit activities did not disappear completely. The lack of support from government (which decided to put an end to our investigation after the media boom) implied that leadership was not consolidated and the autonomy of the organizations was questioned; some voices wanted to reclaim traditional views, both from within the groups (minority factions against legalization were created) and from outside (there were police unions and associations of educators who wanted the return of the tough anti-gang policy).

The so-called 'Barcelona model' of working with youth gangs was very successful nationally and internationally. The creation of entities offering an alternative to violence was exported to neighbouring regions (such as Valencia, the Balearic Islands, Murcia and Navarra), which formed or are in the process of constituting entities similar to those recognized by the Catalan Government. In other countries, such as Italy and Ecuador, initiatives were taken by people who had participated in or knew of the Barcelona Process. The British Home Office took it as an example of good practice, where we participated with about thirty policemen and researchers in the expert group 'Ending youth violence', described in our introduction.

Elsewhere, as in the community of Madrid, policing measures have prevailed, deportation and banning justified by some killings and explosions of xenophobia. The most significant example was the trial for illicit association against a group of Latin Kings held in the Madrid Provincial Court. After a conviction in 2007, the Supreme Court reversed the process in March 2009 for failure to prove beyond all reasonable doubt that the primary objective of the group was to commit crimes, 'such evidence by itself would not justify the qualification of illicit association without a failure in constitutional guarantee of the presumption of innocence' because 'there is not the slightest justification that authorises the transfer of offences from a strictly individual sphere to that of an organization' (Judgement 378/2009, p. 20.) The Court required the process to be repeated, keeping only the accusation of illicit association because allegations of coercion and threats were all acquitted in the first trial. The retrial was held in October 2010 and the verdict was guilty, but only of illicit association (i.e., they did nothing wrong but were organized to do so), reducing the penalties (see Feixa et al., 2011, for a full discussion).

The current financial crisis is hitting youth gangs hard, due to three risk factors: they're young, they're migrants and they're gang members. They and their families are being particularly affected by unemployment and find it difficult to access housing, which increases their social vulnerability. Furthermore, their presence in public space makes them easy scapegoats of the crisis and a focus for xenophobic reactions. As for the respondents that appear in the text, they have followed divergent paths: some remain committed to cultural organizations and live and work in Catalonia, others formed splinter groups and were deported to their country of origin, others are unemployed, others had children and left the group and some others ended up in jail. For all of them – as for us – the process was a research experience and an experience for life.

References

Aparicio, R. (2008). Psicología evolutiva, psicología social y bandas latinas en Madrid. In J. García Roca and J. Lacomba (eds). *La inmigración en la sociedad española. Una radiografía multidisciplinar* (pp. 379–402). Barcelona: Bellaterra.

Bhavnani, K.K. (ed.). (2001). *Feminism and race.* Oxford and New York: Oxford University Press.

Brotherton, D. and Barrios, L. (2004). *The Almighty Latin King and Queen Nation. Street politics and the transformation of a New York City gang.* New York: Columbia University Press.

Burke, J. (6 October 2006). Row erupts in Spain over treatment of Latin Kings. *The Guardian.* Retrieved from http://www.guardian.co.uk/world/2006/oct/05/spain.gilestremlett.

Cannarella, M., Lagomarsino, F. and Queirolo Palmas, L. (eds). (2007). *Hermanitos. Vita e politica di strada tra i giovani latinos in Italia.* Verona: Ombre Corte.

Castells, M. (1996). *La era de la información.* Madrid: Alianza.

Comas, D. and Romaní, O. (2004). El control social. Reflexiones en torno a controles sociales y control social. In VV.AA. (ed.). *Consumo y control de drogas: reflexiones desde la ética* (pp. 119–35). Madrid: Fundación Ciencias de la Salud – FAD.

Conquergood, D. (1994). How street gangs problematize patriotism. In H.W. Simons and M. Billing (eds). *After postmodernism. Reconstructing ideology critique* (pp. 200–21). Sage: London.

Delpino, M.A. (2007). *La inserción social de los adolescentes latinoamericanos en España: algunas claves.* Madrid: Ministerio de Trabajo y Asuntos Sociales.

Feixa, C., Canelles, N., Porzio, L., Recio, C. and Giliberti, L. (2008). Latin Kings in Barcelona. In F. van Gemert, D. Peterson and I.-L. Lien (eds), *Street gangs, migration and ethnicity* (pp. 63–78). Devon (UK): Willan Publishing.

Feixa, C., Porzio, L. and Recio, C. (eds). (2006). *Jóvenes 'latinos' en Barcelona: espacio público y cultura urbana.* Barcelona: Anthropos.

Feixa, C., Scandroglio, B., López, J. and Ferrándiz, F. (2011). ¿Organización cultural o asociación ilícita? Latin kings entre Madrid y Barcelona. *Papers. Revista de Sociología, 89.*

Frazer, J.G. ([1890] 2006). *La rama dorada: magia y religión.* México: FCE. [*The Golden Bough.* New York: Macmillan].

Godelier, M. (1978). *Perspectives in Marxist anthropology.* Cambridge: Cambridge University Press.

Hagedorn, J. M. (ed.). (2007). *Gangs in the global city: Alternatives to traditional criminology.* Urbana: University of Illinois Press.

Klein, M. W. (1995). *The American Street gang: Its nature, prevalence and control.* Oxford University Press: New York.

Klein, W. M., Kerner, H.-J., Maxon, C. L. and Weitekamp, E. (2001). *The Eurogang paradox: Street gangs and youth groups in the US and Europe.* London: Kluwer Academic Publishers.

Nilan, P. and Feixa, C. (2006). *Global youth? Hybrid identities and plural worlds.* London and New York: Routledge.

Queirolo, L. and Torre, A. (eds). (2005). *Il fantasma delle bande.* Genova: Fratelli Frilli Editori.

Ravecca, A. (2007). Buscando la historia nelle metropoli e nelle carceri americane. In M. Cannarella, F. Lagomarsino and L. Queirolo (eds). *Hermanitos: Vita e politica di strada tra i giovani latinos in Italia* (pp. 34–44). Verona: Ombre Corte.

Romaní, O., Porzio, L., Rodriguez, A., Canelles, N., Giliberti, L. and Maza G. (2009). De nacions, reialeses i marginacions. L'organtizació dels 'reyes y reinas latinos' de Catalunya, un estudi de cas. In VV.AA. (ed.). *Recerca i immigració* (pp. 419–38). Barcelona: Secretaria per a la Immigració.

Sassen, S. (2003). *Los espectros de la globalización.* México: FCE. [*The spectres of globalization*].

Torres, G. (27 September 2006). Latin kings: del mito a la realidad. *BBC World.* Retrieved from http://news.bbc.co.uk/hi/spanish/misc/newsid_5384000/5384426.stm.

Warden, R. (15 October 2006). Hard cases show soft side. *Times Higher Education.* Retrieved from http://www.timeshighereducation.co.uk/story.asp?storyCode=205826&sectioncode=26.

6
Dissenting Citizenship: South Asian Muslim Youth in the United States after 9/11

Sunaina Maira

Introduction: youthscapes and exceptionalisms

Youth are the locus of deep anxieties about local, national and global politics, for as a liminal category associated with the transition from childhood to adulthood, they are assumed to embody the future and the possibility of change or continuity. The notion that youth is an inherently unstable or shifting ontology means that they are also the objects of overt nationalizing, disciplinary and repressive practices that are revealed when youth are their objects. My research builds on the framework of 'youthscapes' that analyses the intersections between popular culture, national ideologies and global markets and migrations (Maira and Soep, 2005). Elisabeth Soep and I developed this conceptual, epistemological and methodological framework for studying youth to integrate an analysis of expressive cultural forms produced and engaged by youth with materialist and historicist approaches, while interrogating the production of the category 'youth' itself. Young people are often situated at the centre of debates about national identity and globalization – and often in charged, symbolic and overdetermined ways, given the construction of youth as a 'transitional' category in relation to the social order and civic personhood and one on which the tension between dissent and conformity is often pinned (Maira and Soep, 2005).

This chapter is based on an ethnography focused on South Asian Muslim immigrant youth in the United States and their notions of cultural citizenship in the post-9/11 moment. The larger study explores how national belonging and citizenship are experienced on a daily basis in the spheres of education, popular culture, family and labour for young immigrants from communities targeted in the War on Terror (Maira, 2009). If the category 'youth' has been viewed as a critical stage for the development of political and national identity, as the generation that embodies social protest, then immigrant or second-generation youth are perceived as doubly liminal subjects, with suspect national allegiances. For Muslim American youth this perception is even more acute; they are constructed in mainstream discourse as culturally or religiously alien, vulnerable to 'radicalization' by Islamist or anti-American movements, and as potential threats to the nation. Furthermore, the category of 'Muslim youth' often stands in for a certain politics that the imperial state opposes and must challenge in order to justify its global policing.

My research explores young people's everyday relationship to the state and their understandings of citizenship in encounters with institutions such as the school, workplace, media or immigration bureaucracy, at a time when the political views, religious practices and social networks of Muslim youth in the United States are under greater scrutiny than ever before. 'The effect of the state' is created through structural and everyday processes that produce the state and manifest its disciplinary power in everyday contexts – what Timothy Mitchell describes as 'small-scale polymorphous methods of order' (2006, p. 177). However, the experiences of grappling with the state, and the social and political identities developed in the spheres of work, cultural consumption, subcultural affiliation and cross-ethnic solidarity have been underexplored in work on Muslim American youth. Many studies have a rather narrow and Orientalist focus on issues of Islam, gender, cultural clash and intergenerational conflict and exist in uneasy relationship with the state's desire to map, classify and track Muslim American youth. My research challenges the dominant fiction about Muslim immigrant youth and the desire to 'know' them as a distinct, and potentially threatening, 'other', by tracking also the dominant investments in particular constructions of Muslim youth.

Islamophobia and racial profiling of Middle Eastern communities in the United States long preceded the events of 11 September 2001. However, in the wake of the 9/11 attacks, questions of citizenship, racialization, religion and national belonging took on urgent meanings for South Asian Muslims living in the United States and Muslim and Arab Americans more generally – as well as those mistakenly profiled in the post-9/11 backlash, particularly (turbaned, male) Sikh Americans. The national allegiances of Muslim, Arab and South Asian Americans have come under intense scrutiny for signs of betrayal to the project of 'freedom' and 'democracy', regulating what is deemed proper or 'good' (moderate) Muslim politics and unacceptable or 'extremist' (radical) political subjecthood. It is important to note that the current 'state of emergency' affecting Muslims and Arabs in the United States, which entails the suspension of civil rights and the targeting of certain groups by sovereign violence, has also affected other immigrant and minority communities. In fact, it is constitutive of an imperial governmentality which rests on the exclusion of certain groups from citizenship at various historical moments (Agamben, 2005; Ganguly, 2001). The 'state of exception' is permanent for a warfare state which, as a rule, exercises repressive, preventive and military force. This everyday state of exception is particularly acute for young people from communities that are labelled as culturally antithetical to Western modernity, for youth, as a category, is also seen as potentially deviant and threatening to the social order. This dual exceptionalism makes the predicament of Muslim, South Asian and Arab American youth in the post-9/11 era an important one for youth studies to theorize.

Cultural citizenship and empire

This project examines everyday experiences of inclusion or exclusion, or cultural citizenship, in a particular moment of US empire (Ong, 1996; Flores and Benmayor, 1997). The notion of cultural citizenship highlights how the trope of national belonging, so powerful in modernity, is based not just on the political and economic dimensions of citizenship but also defined in the cultural realm of belonging. Cultural definitions of citizenship and 'American' national identity mediate the rights afforded to citizens and immigrants via cultural constructs of immigrant aliens or terrorists ('jihadists'). Muslim youth, particularly young males, are associated with the spectre of radical Islam and fundamentalist militancy and as an ever-present threat. Muslim women and girls are viewed in these Orientalist imaginaries as objects of rescue who must be liberated by Western democracy or feminism. At the same time, cultural citizenship is still intertwined with legal distinctions between citizens and non-citizens that have powerful material consequences for young people, as much as anyone else.

Citizenship, I argue, is not just embedded in but constitutive of the workings of empire and the management of its subjects, as well as their resistance. Linking immigrant youth to US empire shifts the frame of analysis from worn dichotomies of assimilation/ethnicization, and a nation-based focus on immigration, to an analysis of the domestic *and* global faces of the imperial state's policies of constructing citizen-subjects. Empire works on two fronts, the domestic and the foreign, so the experiences of Muslim American youth must be situated in relation to both US foreign policy and the 'policing of domestic racial tensions' and disciplining of subordinated populations through gender and class hierarchies at home (Pease, 1993, p. 31). However, the link between the two fronts of imperial power is obscured, given that the history and nature of US imperialism have generally been repressed, erased or obfuscated (Kaplan, 1993).

US imperialism is marked by invisibility, secrecy and flexibility in its operation of power – including covert and proxy interventions – and by nebulous, non-territorial forms of domination that do not resemble traditional forms of 'colonialism' (Kaplan, 2005). While the United States was founded as a settler-colonial state, it has a long history of 'imperialism without colonies' (Magdoff, 2003). The rhetoric of democracy and freedom has been used to cloak the US imperial project in a discourse of 'benevolent imperialism' – a project for global political, economic and military hegemony legitimized by a universalizing language of human rights and multicultural inclusion. Given the ambiguity in the dominant or everyday discourse about the nature of US empire, it is not surprising that this term is one that many people do not explicitly invoke in daily conversation, including immigrant youth. The unique challenge as well as contribution of youth studies has always been the analysis of young people's politics as they emerge in the quotidian and through a language that expresses political subjectivity, without necessarily resembling what is recognized as 'properly' political.

Youth who are immigrant, Muslim and South Asian are caught in the national security state's conflation of internal and external enemies and wrestle with questions of national belonging that are laced by the politics of citizenship, race, religion and generation (Stoler, 2006, p. 12). Here, I will focus specifically on the practice of dissenting citizenship in order to illuminate some of the complexities and contradictions of political dissent for youth targeted in the War on Terror.

South Asian Muslim youth in Wellford

The ethnography on which this chapter is based was conducted between 2001 and 2003 and explored the experiences of Muslim immigrant youth from India, Pakistan and Bangladesh (see Maira, 2009). The South Asian immigrant youth in this study were students at a public high school in a small, predominantly white town in the northeast, which I call 'Wellford'. They had mostly migrated to the United States within the preceding seven to ten years and were predominantly working to lower middle class, with minimal to moderate fluency in English. Their parents generally worked in low-income, service-sector jobs, and they themselves worked after school in fast food restaurants, gas stations, retail stores, and as security guards. Their immigrant and class locations were a major reason why they were not involved in political organizing, but this was also a moment in which there was a heightened fear among Muslim American youth about public political engagement, or even discussions of geopolitics. This study is based on interviews with South Asian Muslim immigrant students, second-generation South Asian youth and other Muslim immigrant students, parents, teachers, staff, youth programme organizers, community and religious leaders and immigrant and civil rights activists, and on fieldwork in the school, homes, workplaces, and at social, cultural and political events. While doing this ethnography, I was also volunteering in the high school through a programme that offered tutoring and academic and cultural workshops for immigrant South Asian students.

These youth would not conventionally be defined as 'activists' and did not belong to any organized political or community groups. Thus the research questions what it means to express dissenting views *outside* of formal political movements and at a moment of political repression, surveillance and profiling based on national origin, religion and political speech. What does it mean to be 'political' when the notion of politics itself is fragile and is used to surveil and discipline subjects? How do young people engage with 'local' and 'global' politics if they are imagined as an intrinsic, and violent, threat to the national and even global order?

I begin with a brief vignette from my fieldwork that touches on some key themes of nationalism, warfare and racial violence that marked the politics of Muslim American youth in this moment.

Adil: 'freaked out ... But not afraid'

Of all the South Asian immigrant boys in the high school I met that year, Adil was perhaps the most outgoing and gregarious. It seemed to me that this was not just because he had lived in the United States longer than the others and so was more fluent in English and comfortable in the city, but also because of his self-assured personality. Adil, whose family had migrated to Wellford from Gujarat in India, said that on 11 September 2001, his mother called him on his cell phone at 2:30 p.m., the minute that classes ended. She told him, 'I want you to come home RIGHT now, don't go anywhere, don't stay at school, come right home and stay inside!' Adil remembered how worried his mother was about him, especially because she knew that Adil did not like 'sitting at home'.

One Friday night in fall 2001 when he was downtown, he had an encounter that disturbed him much more. It was late at night, and he was driving with his friend Walid, his cousin, and some Pakistani and Indian friends through a neighbourhood known for its clubs and bars. 'Six white guys' in an Explorer accosted Adil and his friends and one young man got out of the car and threatened him. Adil said he 'knew there'd be cops' around the corner and so he immediately reported the incident to the police, who later came to his house to follow up on the complaint.

I asked him, 'Did you feel afraid or freaked out after the incident?'

'A little freaked out,' Adil replied. 'But I wasn't afraid. When Walid and I are together, we are not afraid.'

I asked him what the other students in the school thought about the events of 11 September. Adil seemed to think that the tragedy had traumatized white students much more than black Americans. 'I think the black people are not so into it,' Adil responded. 'It's the white people who are really into this thing, because more white people got killed in those buildings.' But Adil was cautious to qualify his statements about the war in Afghanistan, for when I asked him if he thought that blacks supported the war as much as white Americans, he replied, 'It depends. Because black people have different feelings. Like you and I have different feelings about things.'

When I pressed Adil on what he thought about the invasion of Afghanistan, he responded equally thoughtfully, 'You have to look at it in two ways, it's not right that ordinary people over there, like you and me, just doing their work, get killed. They don't have anything to do with the attacks in New York but they're getting killed. And also the people in New York who got killed, that wasn't right either.'

Adil and I were chatting as he walked out of the school to his car, a gleaming golden Toyota parked on a nearby street. 'Do you like my car?' Adil was clearly excited about it, saying that it was a used car bought by his sister. He laughingly said he worked every day to 'stay out of trouble', remarking, 'Like today, I wasn't meant to be going into work, but my friends are going to Foxwood Casino, so I decided to sign up for more hours [at work].' Adil slipped a CD into the car's audio; he had to go straight to work after school, so he got into the car and sped down the street, dance music pounding.

Dissenting citizenship

My conversation with Adil revealed how these young people's experiences of public space had been (re)shaped by Islamophobia and the construction of young Muslim, or 'Muslim-looking' men, in particular, as the 'enemy'. But it also suggested how some youth felt perhaps compelled consciously to resist the feeling of fear, and to insist on some semblance of normalcy in their everyday life and leisure activities. Adil was also explicitly critical of the US war on Afghanistan and the killing of innocent civilians, at a moment when the US invasion was seen as a 'just war' in retribution for the 9/11 tragedy, but also critical of the attacks on the Twin Towers. Adil's life was shaped by concerns about work, pleasure in his car and in music and a sense of responsibility that kept him 'out of trouble' on the streets or in casinos – spaces of youth culture not typically associated with Muslim American youth in the reified narrative that has positioned them primarily in relation to national security and religion.

While the youth in this study did not use a formal political vocabulary of state and empire, they offered critiques of racism, Islamophobia, war and foreign policy after 9/11 and grappled with an ethics of belonging. Criticism of the state's rationale for the collective punishment of Muslims and the US War on Terror was pervasive among these youth. For example, Ayesha, from India, observed, 'Just because one Muslim did it in New York, you can't involve everybody in there, you know what I'm sayin.' A week after 9/11, Ayesha chose to write the words 'INDIA + MUSLIM' on her backpack. For her, this was a conscious gesture of defiance for she knew well the possibility of repercussions, including physical assault, for those publicly identified as Muslim. Zeenat, a newly arrived Indian immigrant, thought that the bombing of Afghanistan in response to the attacks of 9/11 was 'wrong' because the United States was targeting innocent civilians. She observed, 'After September 11, they [Americans] hate the Muslims ... I think they want the government to hate the Muslims, like, all Muslims are same.' Zeenat seemed concerned that both civil society and the state were Islamophobic and constructing Muslims as a homogenized category of collective guilt.

Several youth denounced both the terrorist attacks of 9/11 and militarized state aggression as a means of retribution, as did Adil, emphasizing the importance of political justice and respect for international human rights. Jamila, a young Bangladeshi woman, was one of several students who spoke of the need for the US government to provide 'proof' of who was really culpable in the 9/11 attacks, and who condemned the killing of 'innocent people who had nothing to do with it' in the US invasion of Afghanistan. She held the state accountable for offering evidence to justify its War on Terror and invasion of Afghanistan, legitimized by the presence of al-Quaeda in Afghanistan and by a racialized imperative to save Afghan women from the Taliban. All of these youth challenged the state's rhetoric about the 'liberation' of Afghanistan and the 'collateral' killings of civilians, linking it to nationalisms and state-sponsored terror. Their persistent, if not strengthened, identification as Muslim after 9/11 seemed to be partly a defiant response to Islamophobia, scapegoating and collective punishment. In other cases, youth also asserted regional, national and pan-South Asian identities, as I explore in the larger project.

As the state acquired sweeping powers of surveillance and detention with the Patriot Act, there were numerous reports of FBI and police investigation of 'un-patriotic' statements or activity that were variously frightening and absurd. In the face of such repression, many of these South Asian Muslim immigrant youth seemed to be engaged in a form of dissenting citizenship, that is, an engagement with the nation state based on a critique of its power and rhetoric, but still situated within the framework of the nation state and citizen and immigrant rights. The dissent of these Muslim immigrant youth was driven by two factors: they had been forced to deal with state and civil society discrimination soon after arriving in the United States, and they were from a region that was experiencing a US military invasion (in Afghanistan). So their political critique should not be idealized and in fact, over time, deep fissures emerged between Muslim Americans who supported the US War on Terror and the project of 'regime change' and 'democraticization', as well as racial and religious profiling in the name of national security, and those who challenged these policies as imperial violence and racial/religious discrimination by the state.

Interestingly, for these Muslim immigrant students, the high school was one of the few, if only, public spaces where they felt comfortable discussing politics, mainly because of the support of progressive teachers and staff in what was known to be a liberal school. Schools are considered a primary site of teaching informal and formal citizenship lessons to youth, constructing beliefs and skills that are considered necessary for the national citizenry and workforce (Buckingham, 2000, p. 11; Ong, 2006, p. 139). The public school inculcated ideals of multicultural, civic engagement and liberal democratic notions of racial justice and civil rights in the classroom as well as in numerous after-school programmes and activities. For example, after an anti-Muslim incident in the high school involving Adil and Walid, the school organized an assembly featuring two Arab American speakers who discussed the War on Terror and challenged the attack on civil liberties. Adil, Walid, and an Indian Muslim, Shireen, delivered eloquent speeches condemning racism to an auditorium filled with their peers. Adil spoke of his experience of being threatened in the city and Shireen said, 'We have to respect each other if we want to change society. You have to stand up for your rights.' Even though these immigrant youth did not have the time to participate in organized activism, they seemed to have become spokespersons in the public sphere and engaged with rights talk.

However, the notion of dissenting citizenship is not meant to suggest that dissent by South Asian Muslim immigrant youth, or South Asian or Muslim Americans more generally, was overt or consistent, let alone that it is guaranteed. Not all the students were as bold as Ayesha in challenging the profiling of Muslims and publicly claiming a Muslim identity. In the aftermath of 9/11, especially in the first one or two years, South Asians, Arabs and Muslims across the United States were increasingly hesitant to speak publicly about political issues. As Corey Robin (2004) points out, repression historically works on two levels to silence dissent: on a state level and on the level of civil society, where individuals internalize repression and censor themselves. Furthermore, regimes of racial violence, incarceration and deportation that have long targeted other groups in the United States, such as African Americans, Asian Americans and Latino(a)s, not to mention the brutal subjugation of Native Americans, represent 'political technologies of the body' whose disciplining effects are not restricted to those bodies actually targeted but also to those of others who internalize these disciplinary regimes (Hansen and Steputat, 2005, p. 12).

Furthermore, dissenting citizenship is still a form of cultural citizenship and engages with the role and responsibility of the nation state and the question of rights, so it encapsulates the contradictions of challenging the state while petitioning or seeking inclusion within it. Dissenting citizenship is marked by the ambivalence expressed by these youth toward the United States, which is simultaneously a place invested with their parents' desire for economic advancement and their own hopes for belonging, and also the site of alienation, discrimination, fear, frustration and outrage. Most of these young immigrants desired US citizenship to enable them to work, travel and gain the protection afforded by citizen rights, however contingent or partial (especially after 9/11). As migrants with transnational ties, these youth and their families strategically used the framework of immigrant and citizen rights, trying to advance from one category of protection and entitlement to the next. A few young immigrants had expectations that the United States would live up to its ideals of freedom and equal rights, but most seemed to emphasize simply that US actions should be held to an international standard of justice that should apply to all nation states, including India and Pakistan. On the first anniversary of 11 September, the International Student Center organized another student assembly, and Samira (Shireen's younger sister) and another young Indian woman, Mumtaz, made public speeches. Mumtaz spoke of her sadness at the events of 9/11 and commented, 'It's not right to go after Pakistan and Afghanistan and all [the] Muslims who had nothing to do with it.' Samira mentioned that a reporter from the local media was videotaping the event and had for permission to quote the students' speeches. Samira seemed pleased by this request but also slightly hesitant, given the targeting of Muslim and Arab Americans for political dissent and political speech after 9/11. Public political critique thus came with an unease or anxiety about what this kind of performance meant at a moment of FBI interrogation, detentions and deportations that had even targeted youth.

Dissenting citizenship was inextricably intertwined with the politics of race, gender and class for these immigrant youth. In a high school where African American students were the largest minority group, some Muslim youth were drawn to cross-ethnic affiliations with other youth of colour based on a shared experience of alienation from a dominant nationalism and exclusion from cultural citizenship, as alluded to by Adil.

It is apparent that 9/11 seemed to have drawn some of these immigrant youth into an understanding of citizenship based on racialized fissures in claims to national identity, and solidarity with other youth of colour. Some of these Muslim immigrants were drawn to identify with other groups who provided a model of dissenting citizenship and a larger critique of the exclusion inherent to citizenship and the nation's history of slavery and settler-colonialism.

However, these 'polycultural' and cross-ethnic affiliations among youth did not exist in the absence of inter-racial tensions between South Asians and other minoritized communities, including anti-black racism (Prashad, 2000). Moments of tension and suspicion between groups coexist with multicultural attempts at 'inclusion' of those same groups, as evident after 9/11. Furthermore, as Wendy Brown (2006, p. 6) observes, the War on Terror is legitimized by supposedly apolitical regimes of tolerance and intolerance in everyday life that produce essentialized notions of 'cultural difference' and 'civilizational conflict', distinguishing between 'free' and 'unfree' peoples and cultures. Multiculturalism can be a manifestation of imperial nationalism, in other words.

Dissenting citizenship is, thus, not without tensions that animate its expression. I found that these young immigrants implicitly understood the limits of citizenship, in its economic, cultural and political senses, and of 'rights' afforded by the nation state. Muslim immigrants from India, in particular, had to consider the failures of both home and host states – India and the United States – to guarantee protection and equal rights to Muslim subjects. The anti-Muslim massacres in Gujarat in spring 2002 as well as other attacks by right-wing Hindu movements in India, and the military standoff between India and Pakistan that preceded it, reinforced for Indian Muslim youth their ambiguous location between religious and national identification; their national allegiances are questioned in India by diasporic Hindu nationalist movements as part of a larger discourse about 'Islamic terrorism' and a 'fifth column' that echoes that in the United States (Kurien, 2003).

Furthermore, it must be noted that dissent is waged by youth not only against the War on Terror but also in response to the neoliberal capitalist regime which is articulated with the global war for democracy and freedom. The notion of 'freedom', 'as a specific kind of "choice"' and 'symbol of [American] nationalism', key to the War on Terror's rationale of defending the American 'way of life', is marketed through American popular culture that circulates globally (Grewal, 2005, p. 206). The immigrant youth in this study understood themselves as consumers of not just commodities or media but also of the promise of a 'way of life' that compelled their parents to migrate from South Asia. The notion of 'choosing' freedom and democracy, presumably over other ways of life and in opposition to those who 'hate' America, is a central tenet of late imperial culture. However, these working-class youth are ambiguously positioned in relation to the US neoliberal ideology of productivity and consumption (Ong, 1996, p. 739). The mythologized promise of the American Dream was often shattered soon after their arrival. Soman, a young Indian immigrant, worked in his family's Bengali restaurant after school where he often waited on more affluent South Asians. He said, 'Here, you live in a golden cage, but it's still a cage ... My life is so limited. I go to school, come to work, study, go to sleep.' Soman's comment about being imprisoned by the 'golden cage' of the American Dream is profound because it captures the glittering appeal of American capitalism *and* the confining imprisonment, not just of the lifestyle it engenders, but also of belief in this illusion. Dissenting citizenship is layered with critiques of imperial warfare, racial violence and neoliberal notions of autonomy and productivity.

Dissenting feelings

An incident involving a Pakistani immigrant student, Samir, helped me think about the ambiguity of political dissent expressed by South Asian Muslim youth after 9/11 and where one locates 'politics' in a climate of repression and surveillance. My conversation with Samir took place in the International Student Center, where immigrant students often hung out and used the computer terminals, since most did not have computers at home. This is an excerpt from my field notes in September 2002:

> I'm in the International Center one morning when Samir comes in and sits down at one of the terminals. I ask him if he has a webpage and though Samir is generally a bit quiet, he calls me over excitedly and pulls it up. It has links to 'Lollywood' [Pakistani] films, Bollywood film music, and also to 'funny pictures'. I ask him if I can see the pictures, and when he clicks on the link, pages and pages of images of [George] W. [Bush] appear, a row of him wiggling his hips, a row of him looking like a chimpanzee, a row looking like Superman.
>
> 'This is great,' I say, laughing, 'So you think the same thing about Dubya [W]?'
>
> Samir doesn't seem to understand the reference, and he also doesn't respond.
>
> 'So you don't like George Bush?'
>
> 'No,' he says, 'I just saw these and I thought they were funny.'
>
> Then he scrolls down and there's a digitally produced photograph of a bearded Bush looking like Osama bin Laden with a white turban coiled around his head, and a picture of the Statue of Liberty draped in a hijab. I ask Samir what he thinks of them and why he chose to put them up, and he simply replies that someone sent them to him. Yet these are the only 'funny' images he has up, and also the only images related to America or to politics. They are clearly, grotesquely, about 9/11 and about George W. Bush.

I spent a long time wondering about Samir's funny pictures and his responses to me: was this a vernacular mode of dissenting citizenship? Despite his verbal denial, was Samir placing these images on his website as a way of expressing a coded critique of Bush? The images, obviously, did not collectively produce a consistent critique; the veiled Statue of Liberty reified notions of gender and Islam and evoked anxieties about the transformation of cherished symbols of 'American freedom' by Islam. In contrast, the image of Bush grinning in a bin-Laden-esque turban played visually with the question of who the 'real' terrorist might be. This image, which circulated on postcards and on the Internet after 9/11, digitally mashed together signifiers of the President and 'the terrorist' to question Bush's own civilizational discourse of a clash between 'Western' modernity/democracy and Islamic fundamentalism/ anti-modernity, suggesting the two were not as sharply dichotomous as the 'clash of civilizations' framework suggests. On a deeper level, the image could also challenge the presumed binary between the rational violence and 'just wars' waged by the United States and the irrational violence and militant fanaticism associated with the 9/11 attacks, fusing the two symbols of the clash between 'good' and 'evil'. And the caricatures of Bush as chimp and Superman clearly mocked the President's heroic crusade as leader of the free world.

Were the 'funny pictures' Samir's way of grappling with the anti-Islamic caricatures pervading American popular culture by responding with caricatures of his own choice, resituated on a webpage that was swathed in green and decorated with the Pakistani flag? Or was it that Samir thought these images were, simply, 'funny'? Either way, the choice of these pictures did not seem accidental but suggestive of an attempt to play with the images of Islam, terrorism, and US power circulating in public culture at a time when overt political critique was extremely risky, and had resulted in FBI surveillance, including electronic surveillance, and even detention and deportation for Muslim Americans. The seemingly contradictory juxtaposition of these images may not express an explicit or consistent political critique, but they hint at some unease with the dominant discourse about Islam and 'terrorism' and, clearly, a dissenting humour.

This encounter was one of the moments in the study that gave me the most pause, for it forced me to think about how young people engage with the political, and the subtle ways in which they may express a range of responses to questions of power, the state and resistance, at a moment when overt resistance comes with a high price. These moments of ambiguous dissent, potentially expressed from multiple locations and against various forces, are important to consider when thinking about the political subjectivity of youth, especially those targeted for political speech. Potentially they illustrate techniques of resistance of repressed groups that infiltrate the 'public transcript' of political discourse in ways that are 'intended to be cryptic and opaque' to escape retaliation: Samir's images are perhaps a form of 'hinted blasphemy' that exists on a continuum of challenges to dominant interpretations of 'terrorism' or 'fundamentalism' (Scott, 1990, p. 137, p. 152). The subtle play with the political and the permissible and the refusal to verbalize political critique shows the many ways dissent can be coded, especially for youth and those considered enemy subjects at a time of war.

Samir's funny pictures also suggest the affective dimensions of dissent as a feeling, as something that is not simply caught in the binary of resistance and complicity but that is expressed in subtle and complex ways. Thinking about dissenting feelings does not mean giving up on the tangibility of dissent and collective mobilization, and the pressing need for resistance in the face of state-sponsored violence. On the contrary, understanding dissenting feelings allows us to acknowledge the range of expressions of resistance, especially among those who are coerced into silence by repressive state measures or who are outside traditional organized movements, while not falling prey to a romanticization of heroic protest or passive victimhood based on familiar tropes.

Conclusion: de-exceptionalizing youth and empire

Questions of cultural citizenship for these immigrant youth are deeply shaped by the politics of global warfare and imperial power, and by the cultural imaginaries of media and technology. It is crucial not to idealize the possibilities for political expression available to youth through the consumption of media, while exploring how popular culture offers 'symbolic resources' to young people in engaging with politics outside of official institutions and formal citizenship (Willis, 1990, pp. 131–149). Youth studies can help us understand that the production of the notion of 'youth', not just as a collection of bodies defined by age but as an ideological apparatus, is very much a part of processes of the state and empire. Understanding youthscapes as a site that produce empire, just as empire is a site that produces youthscapes, would help us challenge the exceptionalisms that bedevil thinking about youth as well as late imperial culture.

References

Agamben, G. (2005). *State of exception*, translated by Kevin Attell. Chicago and London: University of Chicago Press.
Brown, W. (2006). *Regulating aversion: Tolerance in the age of identity and empire*. Princeton: Princeton University Press.

Buckingham, D. (2000). *The making of citizens: Young people, news, and politics.* London and New York: Routledge.

Flores, W. V. and Benmayor, R. (eds). (1997). *Latino cultural citizenship: Claiming identity, space, and rights.* Boston: Beacon Press.

Ganguly, K. (2001). *States of exception: Everyday life and postcolonial identity.* Minneapolis: University of Minnesota Press.

Grewal, I. (2005). *Transnational America: Feminisms, diasporas, neoliberalisms.* Durham, NC: Duke University Press.

Hansen, T. B. and Steputat, F. (2005). Introduction. In T. B. Hansen and F. Steputat (eds). *Sovereign bodies: Citizens, migrants, and states in the postcolonial world* (pp. 1–36). Princeton: Princeton University Press.

Kaplan, A. (1993). Left alone with America: The absence of empire in the study of American culture. In A. Kaplan and D. Pease (eds). *Cultures of United States imperialism* (pp. 3–21). Durham: Duke University Press.

———. (2005). Where is Guantánamo? In M. Dudziak and L. Volpp (eds). *Legal borderlands: Law and the construction of American borders,* special issue of *American Quarterly 57*(3), 831–58.

Kurien, P. (2003). To be or not to be South Asian: Contemporary Indian American politics. *Journal of Asian American Studies 6*(3), 261–88.

Magdoff, H. (2003). *Imperialism without colonies.* New York: Monthly Review Press.

Maira, S. (2009). *Missing: Youth, citizenship, and empire after 9/11.* Durham, NC: Duke University Press.

Maira, S. and Soep, E. (eds) (2005). Introduction. *Youthscapes: The Popular, the National, the Global* (pp. 15–35). Philadelphia: Temple University Press.

Mitchell, T. (2006). Society, economy, and the state effect. In A. Sharma and A. Gupta (eds). *The anthropology of the state: A reader* (pp. 169–186). Malden, Mass.: Blackwell.

Ong, A. (1996). Cultural citizenship as subject-making: Immigrants negotiate racial and cultural boundaries in the United States. *Current Anthropology 37*(5), 737–62.

Robin, C. (2004). *Fear: The history of a political idea.* New York: Oxford University Press.

Pease, D. (1993). New perspectives on US culture and imperialism. In A. Kaplan and D. Pease (eds). *Cultures of United States imperialism* (pp. 22–37). Durham: Duke University Press,.

Prashad, V. (2000). *The karma of brown folk.* Minneapolis: University of Minnesota.

Scott, J. C. (1990). *Domination and the arts of resistance: Hidden transcripts.* New Haven: Yale University Press.

Stoler, A. L. (2006). Intimidations of empire: Predicaments of the tactile and unseen. In A. L. Stoler (ed.). *Haunted by empire: Geographies of intimacy in North American history* (pp. 1–22). Durham and London: Duke University Press.

Willis, P. (1990). *Common culture.* Buckingham: Open University Press.

Part III
Media and Consumption

7
Looking East: Young Koreans Consuming Japanese Media in the Intra-Asian Youthscape

Kyong Yoon

Introduction: youth in intra-national cultural flows

The rapid process of globalization has led to an increase in transnational cultural practices among young people who are 'using global resources to deal with local conditions' (Wise, 2008, p. 63). In particular, alternative popular cultural resources made available through transnational digital technologies allow young people to negotiate the symbolic and geographic boundaries of the nation state. In this regard, youth cultural studies need to acknowledge the emerging 'youthscape' (Maira and Soep, 2004), in which imagined places and people are integrated into young people's lives. The evolving global youthscape, however, does not necessarily promise young people enhanced freedom and mobility; instead, it often involves particular power struggles in which young people's lives are constrained by the intersection of global, national and local forces.

A critical examination of the emerging youthscape should consider the tensions between forces that are motivated by global capitalism and forces that resiliently remain within the boundaries of the nation state, silencing local subjectivities. In so doing, we can move beyond the fallacy of simply equating the local with the national (Fung, 2007, p. 266); this scenario has been evident in East Asia, which has experienced a state-led and often militant modernization since World War II (Moon, 2005). The robust sense of the national in which state-led national and hegemonic ideologies predominate over local cultures has recently been challenged by the emergence of 'post-national subjectivities' that question the myth of a homogeneous national culture (Cho Han, 2000). In particular, young people have been introduced to new media platforms through which local cultures can be reimagined beyond the boundaries of the nation state (Yoon, 2010).

The trans-Asian media flows and forms of fandom described by the media and critics as 'Waves' (e.g., 'the Japanese Wave' and 'the Korean Wave') that have appeared since the early 2000s seem to present an aspect of translocal cultures emerging *from below* that move beyond the hegemonic national culture (Chua, 2004; Iwabuchi, 2002; Otmazgin, 2008; Zheng, 2011). These translocal forms of youth cultural practice in the East Asian context, however, have been largely overlooked in previous studies of 'global youth culture' (e.g., Pilkington and Johnson, 2003), which have focused on the non-Western localization of Western youth cultural forms. The case of young East Asians who have increasingly appropriated media content and styles from other East Asian countries may provide an insight into the non-Western localization of non-Western youth cultures.

With this context in mind, this chapter discusses how young people's cultural practices, carried out via new media technologies, are reconstructing an intra-regional youthscape. Drawing upon data collected in a series of in-depth interviews conducted in 2004 and 2007 with 32 young South Korean (Korean, hereafter) fans of Japanese media, the chapter explores the cultural implications of the emerging intra-Asian youthscape as a technologically mediated playground where post-national subjectivities and consumer identities are formed. Given that Korean fans of Japanese media have been identified in previous studies as relatively young and well-educated (Chua, 2004; Kim, 2003; Lee, 2006), the field studies for this chapter focused on middle-class university students who considered themselves as fans of Japanese media (especially TV series and/or pop music) and were members of at least one fan club associated with Japanese popular culture. In both studies (2004 and 2007), respondents who had been enthusiastic about Japanese media for 3–10 years were asked to provide their 'life histories' as fans of Japanese media culture. The recollections and current narratives of these young people show how the intra-Asian youthscape has developed in a particular local context.

Together, offline ... and counter-hegemonic? – *Donghohoe*-based fandom pre-2004

Young East Asians' engagement with intra-Asian flows of media content is a relatively recent phenomenon in such countries as China, Hong Kong, Japan and Korea, since trans-Asian imports of media and popular culture were constrained by the boundaries of the nation states throughout the twentieth century. Indeed, national media and popular cultures were the dominant resources for youth cultural styles in East Asian countries, while Western media and popular cultures were introduced and filtered by national governments. The dominance of the national media and the supplementary role of Western media in East Asia implied that media content from other Asian countries was scarce and unpopular among Asian media consumers. While this was partly a function of cultural barriers such as language differences, it was more significantly to do with the broader geopolitical contexts of the region.

Korea had been colonized by Japan between 1919 and 1945 and was then 'liberated', or more precisely 'occupied', by the US Army between 1945 and 1948. As a belatedly established nation state in 1948, Korea sought to achieve two key national goals (among others): removing the legacy and trauma of colonization and catching up with the West. First, in the process of encountering colonial traumas, Koreans detested the former colonizer, and this was often expressed as an aspect of 'national sentiments' (*gukmin jeongseo*) (Han, 2001); ultimately, imports and sales of literally all Japanese media commodities were banned in Korea for several decades. The lifting of the ban progressed slowly, beginning in 1998 with the initial 'opening up' (*gaebang*) phase of the Korean market to Japanese media content, but the substantial introduction of Japanese media to Korea was not made until 2004, when imported Japanese cable television series and satellite broadcasting were allowed (Park, 2007). Second, in the process of catching up with the West and modernizing the nation, American media and culture had powerful and long-lasting effects on the Korean media industry and its audience (Kim and Won, 2008). Korea's efforts to achieve its postcolonial goals as a new nation state were evident in frequent media panics about the 'Japanization' of culture (Lee, 2002), primarily referring to the influx of popular Japanese cultural styles, while the 'Americanization' of culture was deemed to be an unavoidable consequence of modernization. In fact, Americanization was more readily tolerated by the mainstream media and the government (Kim and Won, 2008).

It can be argued that by 'looking West' and 'ignoring East', Korea's process of militant modernization in the second half of the twentieth century resulted in a form of 'self-Orientalism', through which Asia was negatively conceptualized as 'non-Western'. In contrast, the West was regarded as an imagined destination of modernity. Throughout the twentieth century, Japanese media content in Korea was so suppressed that its consumers were primarily young people with relatively diluted 'national sentiments' towards Japan (Chua, 2004; Kim, 2003; Lee, 2006). Many respondents in my research recalled the marginalized position of fans of Japanese media before the early 2000s. They remembered the prevailing negative perceptions of Japanese media and popular culture among their friends, families and the public in the early period of their involvement in the consumption of Japanese media. Most respondents felt stigmatized at school for their fandom. For instance, *Sona*, a 19-year-old female interviewed in 2004, recalled some of her classmates from the early 2000s saying to her, 'You love *jjokbali* (a very contemptuous Korean slang term to refer to Japanese as "short-sized people") SO MUCH ... Why don't you go live in Japan?'

It seems significant that females were more likely to experience such stigmatization. Some female respondents recalled that they had often been described contemptuously by their peers as *illbba* (i.e., fanatics obsessed with Japanese popular culture). This slang term combines *il*, which denotes Japan, with an abbreviation of *bbasuni*, which refers to a female popular culture fanatic. *Nami*, a 22-year-old female, noted; 'I hated being called *ilbba*. *Ilbba* is even more insulting than *bbasuni*.' Associating the penchant for Japanese popular culture with 'fanatic' female fans may demonstrate how 'national sentiments' towards Japanese culture were constructed through the patriarchal and gendered social order, which contributed to reinforcing the hegemony of the nation state during the period of rapid and militant modernization (Moon, 2005).

The degradation of Japanese popular culture in Korea seemed to stem from a prevailing binary opposition between the 'other above' (the West) and the 'other below' (the non-West) (Monteiro and Jayasankar, 2000). In this framework, the hegemonic nationalizing forces undermined Japanese culture as the taste of 'the other below' and therefore as something to avoid. Many respondents realized that consuming Japanese media meant that they could not ignore ongoing historical and political tensions between Japan and Korea. For instance, an 18-year-old woman said in my 2004 interview, 'I could not dislike *L'Arc* [a Japanese pop band], although I do not like the historical memory related to Japan. At the same time, I cannot simply come to like Japan's history only because I love the band.' In other words, the respondents sought to maintain an imagined distance between postcolonial memories of Korea's relationship with Japan and their own cultural tastes.

It was extremely difficult to access Japanese media content in Korea until the early 2000s due to government regulations. Korean fans of Japanese media had to form amateur underground fan clubs known as *donghohoe* (literally meaning 'the gathering of people with a similar taste'). According to research participants' recollections, *donghohoe* activities in the late 1990s and the early 2000s were characterized by particular patterns of consumer behaviour, such as collective consumption and an appreciation for authentic materials. First, media consumption tended to be accompanied by some form of collaboration with other fans in *donghohoes* online and at offline events. By organizing events, such as viewing music videos together and going on shopping trips to Japan, Korean fans purchased, exchanged, shared and copied Japanese media materials. The collective and collaborative nature of consumption was also evident in the exchange of meanings attached to Japanese commodities at events or online forums. As Fiske (1992) asserts, subcultural fan activities may give rise to 'enunciative productivity', which involves the creation and communication of meanings between fans in relation to certain cultural objects or topics. In the culture of *donghohoes*, the sharing of materials, information and meanings appeared to provide fans with a sense of belonging as sharers of forbidden cultural tastes.

Second, as a number of respondents recalled, the notion of authenticity was highly regarded in the culture of *donghohoes* during the pre-2004 period. As it was very difficult for young Koreans to purchase authentic materials made in Japan, the possession of Japanese materials was highly valued among Korean fans in the *donghohoe*. As *Yujin* (female, 22 years) noted, shopping trips to Japan were occasionally made for purchasing authentic materials:

> It was quite difficult to get Japanese stuff here in Korea at that time [i.e., the early 2000s] and I didn't want to have pirated stuff. So, at times I had to ask my friends who were the members of my *donghohoe* and were going to Japan for shopping to buy pop music CDs, books, and magazines. *Donghohoe* people would go together to Japan in order to buy those things.

Although the appreciation of authentic Japanese material did not fade away after 2004, research participants in 2004 and 2007 noted that possessing authentic materials had seemed more important before the opening up of the country in 2004. Most of the respondents who became interested in Japanese media in the late 1990s or early 2000s recalled how much they had longed for authentic materials during the pre-2004 period. For instance, *Jinsoo* (male, 19 years) noted that he had little interest in licensed materials that were translated and reproduced by Korean distributors:

> My friends and I (who are enthusiastic about Japanese pop music) would not buy Japanese pop music CDs licensed in Korea even if

they were legally released in Korea. That's because we have been much more interested in the original materials made in Japan. Licensed ones would feel strange.

Interestingly, some respondents remained cautious about Korea's growing accessibility to Japanese media commodities and those reproduced in Korea since 2004. Legitimately licensed materials were deemed 'inauthentic' merely on the basis that they were not made *in* Japan.

Collaborative and authenticity-seeking consumption seemed pervasive among Korean fans of Japanese media in the pre-2004 period. This pattern might have been influenced not only by the limited availability of media resources due to the official ban on Japanese items, but also by the limited capacity of the Internet at this time. Indeed, many respondents remembered that the early version of the text-based Internet system, called *PC Tongshin* in Korea, contributed to the formation of intra-Asian media fans' subcultural consumption patterns. The technological constraints of *PC Tongshin* in the late 1990s, which included long downloading times and limitations in file size, meant that the activities of *donghohoes* were largely carried out offline rather than in online fan networks (Lee, 2006). Consequently, Japanese pop music, television dramas and animations were often circulated in the form of hard copies – CDs and VCDs – as in other Asian countries (Hu, 2005).

Until the early 2000s, therefore, intra-Asian cultural practices constituted a particular cultural economy of fandom that was different from the official economy associated with the mainstream media industry. Some political connotations were linked to the fan economy of *donghohoes*, regardless of the intentions of individual members. Since cultural tastes for Japanese media and popular culture in Korea had been viewed negatively by the general public and media for a long time, developing and expressing one's interests in Japanese media unintentionally implied a challenge to, or a critique of, the hegemonic national discourse, at least until the early 2000s. The cultural objects that the *donghohoes* appropriated were categorized as illegitimate by the pre-2004 cultural regime; accordingly, the cultural practices of *donghohoes* – many of which were merely gatherings of people who liked Japanese media – might have been considered to some extent as subversive.

Technology-based tribal consumers and global commodities: the emergence of *Ildjok*

The explosive emergence and popularity of numerous UGC (user-generated content) sites, as well as the Korean government's deregulation of Japanese media content in 2004, offered Korean consumers greater access to Japanese media. As a consequence of heavy investment in the IT industry since the 1990s (Yoon, 2010), Korea has consistently ranked first in penetration of high-speed broadband Internet among OECD member countries since the 2000s (97.5% as of 2010) (OECD, 2012). The new cultural and technological environment allowed young Koreans in the mid-2000s to access Japanese TV series via Korean cable TV channels and through fan-based voluntary labour, such as promptly uploading the latest episodes and producing subtitles (Kang, Kang and Kim, 2012). The older media platform of television gradually became obsolete, as *Hyuna* (female, 22 years) stated in 2007: 'Kids like me always watch Japanese TV series on the Internet. Whenever new episodes are uploaded on file-sharing sites, I get them and watch them. I hardly watch them on TV. Watching Japanese TV series on TV is kind of strange!'

As cultural tastes for Japanese media content were gradually accepted by the Korean media and public during the neoliberal regime, the social stigma attached to fandom of Japanese media slowly decreased (e.g., Jeon, 2007). Research participants, especially in 2007, reported that they had become relatively comfortable about consuming Japanese media. In addition, the respondents indicated that they became less committed to the collective practices of the *donghohoes* with the advent of the new cultural and media environment that allowed individualized access to and consumption of Japanese media content; thus, *donghohoes'* roles and organizational structure changed. The term *ildjok* (meaning 'Japanese drama tribes') most vividly reflects these changing consumption patterns; it has been widely used since the mid-2000s to identify Korean fans of Japanese TV drama series, both by fans themselves and by critics (e.g., Jeon, 2007). The term seems to be resonant with Maffesoli's (1996) conceptualization of postmodern consumers as 'neo-tribes' who form highly flexible micro-subcultures. The *ildjok* as a form of *neo-tribe* or *post-subculture* (Bennett, 1999; Bennett and Kahn-Harris, 2004) represents a tendency towards fluid and technology-based micro groupings that differ from the *donghohoes*, which were organized by a few leaders and defined by bonding of the members via regular on-/offline events. While *donghohoes* have not completely disappeared during the post-2004 cultural regime and the term is still used by fans, their influence has been significantly weakened. Whether or not fan clubs continue appropriating the term *donghohoe*, fan activities have become increasingly flexible, fragmented, anonymous and technologically mediated.

Thus, most of the respondents in 2007 identified themselves as members of the *ildjok*, and commonly showed some post-subcultural traits in their fan activities. First, *ildjok* members tend to pursue individualized patterns of cultural consumption, while refusing to follow *donghohoe* rules that depend upon hierarchies between fans who have accumulated 'authentic' Japanese materials and those who have not. Participants in the 2007 study (and sometimes in the 2004 study) frequently described *donghohoes* to which they used to belong as old-fashioned and authoritarian. For instance, *Sangmi*, a 23-year-old female who had been a member of a few *donghohoes*, noted:

> I left a popular online *donghohoe*, because its managers sucked (...) They thought they had power to control the club and that they owned it. They had lots of rules and regulations ... But, they've got to know the *donghohoe* was not theirs.

It was especially apparent in the 2007 research that the fans' commitment to *donghohoes* had been gradually undermined as the pleasures attached to the content of Japanese media had become accessible to individual fans without club memberships. The *donghohoe's* gatekeeping role was perceived as unnecessary since fans of Japanese media were engaging in individual activities to pursue their cultural tastes. In particular, the formalities and rules of *donghohoes*, such as obligatory online logging in and posting on a regular basis, were severely criticized by some of the respondents who sought more egalitarian forms of sharing cultural knowledge and resources.

Second, *ildjok* members do not attach themselves exclusively to a single cultural style or form; instead, they move freely from one style to another. They are likely to join several different online or offline communities simultaneously without establishing any long-term commitments. In addition, distinctions between different cultural tastes are somewhat more ambiguous. For instance, some respondents in the 2007 study did not perceive Japanese, American and Korean cultural forms to be in conflict with each other, although they identified themselves as fans of Japanese media in one way or another. Especially in 2007, respondents were critical of 'obsessive' or *otaku* fans who were seen as committed exclusively to Japanese popular culture and media without attempting to appreciate any other forms, such as American and Korean TV dramas. The *ildjok* members who responded in my 2007 study tried to distinguish themselves from such fans: for instance, *Sora* (female, 23 years) claimed that 'those *otaku*-type kids' were 'obsessed only with Japanese stuff. They are kind of creepy. (...) They sometimes look like ghosts. They even speak Korean with Japanese accents.' In contrast to those seemingly obsessive fans, the *idjok* members in my study generally described themselves as consumers who were flexible and 'right'. Some declared that they were thoroughly enjoying Japanese and American television series at the same time. Their interest in a variety of cultural styles was indicative of the fact that they did not attribute 'national sentiments' to any particular style. At times, the *ildjok* emphasized not only differences but also similarities between Japanese, Korean and Western cultural content in terms of genre and format, as *Nami* (female, 22 years) said: 'I like love stories. It doesn't matter whether they are Japanese or American.' In fact, some respondents proudly claimed that they had initiated the recent boom (since the mid-2000s) in American television series viewing among young Koreans, known as the *mid boom* (i.e., the boom in American television dramas):[1]

> In a way, *midjok* (i.e., American television drama tribes) actually evolved from *ildjok* (i.e., Japanese television drama tribes). Kids watching Japanese television dramas via the Internet became interested in American dramas and began to download and upload American television series as they had done for Japanese television dramas. *Ildjok* was looking for something new, thinking, 'Why don't we try American TV dramas?' (*Mira*: female, 23 years)

As this suggests, it is not unusual for Japanese television drama fans to enjoy American drama at the same time, without any apparent contradiction. The technological skills used for downloading and sharing intra-Asian cultural content is easily transferable to American cultural content.

Third, the *ildjok* has renegotiated the notion of authenticity as it relates to Japanese media, now that a wider range of Korean consumers can access these media. It was observed by most respondents in 2007 and some participants in 2004 that feelings about authenticity, which had been acquired primarily by possessing Japanese-made materials, were increasingly replaced with an emphasis on certain attitudes towards, or cultural literacies relating to, Japanese media. As described below, respondents pointed out that 'being a fan' meant more than accumulating materials:

> Japanese things are massively available these days, so I don't have as strong a desire to possess them as I had before. While often downloading the files [of Japanese music or television dramas], I don't keep them or burn them to CDs, except for a few of them that

I REALLY like or consider REALLY high-quality stuff. (*Boryung*, female: 20 years)

For *ildjok* members, the possession of, or access to, cultural commodities made in Japan is no longer a sufficient criterion for being a fan. According to the respondents, appreciation of quality is most important. Some respondents criticized 'fake fans' who were not culturally literate and who did not truly appreciate Japanese media and popular culture. *Taesan*, a 22-year-old male, observed, 'Having lots of J-Pop MP 3 files or CDs does not necessarily mean they are true fans. I think what matters more is to know how to appreciate the music.' In other words, a qualified fan is no longer defined as a person possessing 'hard' evidence (the accumulation of content or commodities), but as a person exhibiting 'legitimate' cultural knowledge and literacy. In this regard, most research participants attempted to distinguish themselves from those who had recently become fans, especially since the mid-2000s. For example, *Arang* (female, 22 years) tried to distinguish herself from novice fans who seemed to enjoy the greater availability of Japanese content by saying, 'I'm kind of annoyed by kids who suddenly pretend to be TRUE fans even though they just got to know Japanese stuff and buy things obsessively.' The respondents' accounts affirm the claim by Hills (2002) that fandom is often about knowing the 'right' or 'appropriate' things.

Fourth, the *ildjok* operates in a participatory cultural atmosphere where egalitarian exchanges of intra-Asian cultural resources occur anonymously and voluntarily. Fan-subtitled videos ('fansubs') are good examples of the *ildjok*'s Internet-based, voluntary and egalitarian cultural translations 'from below'. Fansubbers have recently been recognized as crucial players in the post-subcultural consumption of global media content in Korea (Kang et al., 2012). Respondents in my studies argued that fansubs offered prompt and rich translations of Japanese cultural content that were more reliable than official translations offered by importing television stations. *Boryung* (female, 20 years), who identified herself as a decent Japanese speaker, pointed out that fansubs were often products of voluntary and collaborative labour that reflected the perspectives and ideas of multiple users:

I think fans can translate these things much better than professional translators can, and fans' translations catch the subtle nuances of dialogue. (...) Fan-made subtitles go around lots of people, and I feel they get better and better. Those pirated subtitles are often much better than the official translations on TV. (...) I tried several times to translate and fansub. That was fun but also little bit demanding if I had to complete a whole episode or two. These days I would rather revise and re-post subtitles posted by others only if I notice that they need to be revised for a better translation.

In comparison to the early fansubs of *donghohoes* that were provided and maintained by only a few 'managers' (*sisab* or *unyongja*), the fansub culture of the *ildjok* appears to be led by a larger number of individual contributors. However, not all respondents in 2004 and 2007 vigorously contributed to UGC. While a few respondents like *Boryung* had actual experience of creating and circulating UGC, others were more interested in *using* content. It appears that in this emerging intra-Asian youthscape, a particular form of cultural literacy – Japanese language skills – often required for fansubbing encourages certain fans to be more producer-like than others. The two groups of the *ildjok,* whom I refer to as *producerly* and *semiotic consumers* based on Fiske's (1992) categorization of fan productivity, are relatively fragmented in comparison to the earlier *donghohoe*-based fans, in that the *ildjok*'s participation and consumption are not necessarily collective but rather loosely collaborative and anonymous. In my research, the majority of fans appeared to be semiotic consumers whose participation was largely symbolic. However, it should be noted that those semiotic consumers were sometimes, if not often, involved in material economies as well as symbolic ones. For instance, the *ildjok*'s enthusiastic pursuit of certain Japanese TV series, films and popular fiction on UGC sites occasionally prompted the import of those items into the official market for a wider audience. While more *ildjok* members seemingly remained semiotic recipients of UGC, the boundaries between semiotic and producerly consumers were not firm but rather obscure. It appears that user agency on UGC sites tends to be increasingly hybridized (van Dijck, 2009), and participants are involved in both material and symbolic economies of fandom.

While the consumption of Japanese media during the pre-2004 period implied possible challenges to the hegemony of the national culture (Kim, 2003), today's neo-tribal and semiotic consumers seem relatively ambiguous in terms of their political positions. Since the nationalizing forces that used to prohibit imports of Japanese media into Korea are no longer conspicuous, consumption by the *ildjok* does not necessarily signify any counter-hegemonic meanings. For some respondents, Japanese media were perceived as global commodities without any anti-national cultural connotations. It should be noted that some respondents in the

2004 and 2007 studies attempted to neutralize the political nuances associated with Japanese media by devaluing them as simple commodities: as *Sungmin* (male, 21 years) noted, 'I wouldn't really call Japanese popular songs and animations *culture* [my emphasis] ... I like those things anyway. But I don't identify myself with them.' Among Korean fans, Japanese media content has gradually been conceptualized as a global commodity without the stigma linked to colonialism; further, it connects the national and the West, since these commodities are also massively popular worldwide.

Conclusion: cultural politics and subjectivities in the hybrid intra-Asian youthscape

This chapter has traced the complex and changing nature of the intra-Asian cultural flows that are apparent in young Koreans' engagement with Japanese media. In the emerging intra-Asian youthscape, where translocal imagination is facilitated by the changing media landscape and by changing national regulations, young East Asians encounter and appropriate cultural forms that are neither national nor Western. This new youthscape has evolved since the 1990s through subcultural negotiations of the regulatory nation state and collective struggles for new resources that move beyond rigid and defensive national boundaries. During the pre-2004 period, when Japanese content was largely forbidden in the Korean market and the Internet-based UGC system was not yet established, *donghohoe*-based fans' subcultural consumption represented an implicit challenge to the hegemonic national culture. While early fans of Japanese media enjoyed a collective sense of belonging, and often organized their activities in relatively hierarchical and exclusive ways, since the mid-2000s young Korean fans have gradually become more fluid and fragmented in their consumption patterns. *Ildjok* members with different cultural tastes, who have emerged in the post-2004 cultural regime, enjoy surfing and shopping in the current globalized and technologically mediated media environment. For the neo-tribal *ildjok*, the intra-Asian youthscape is perceived as a hybrid, virtual and flexible cultural arena in which the global is imagined and experienced through the lenses of individuals, without being dominated by collective national voices or mediated by subcultural gatekeeping. The neo-tribe seems less interested in the origin of the media content; and the process of globalization 'makes it impossible to single out the absolute symbolic center that belongs to a particular country or region' (Iwabuchi, 2010, p. 92).

The hybridity of this intra-regional media culture, which seemingly questions the dominant national cultural regime, presents some questions for further exploration. First, we can ask whether the intra-Asian youthscape can be considered as a 'virtual public sphere' for deliberative conversations between local subjects. As recent studies argue, UGC sites and social networking sites do not necessarily provide platforms for expressions of collective knowledge and opinions; instead, they represent the interests of narcissistic individuals who are insulated in their 'filter bubbles' (Pariser, 2011). In the case of Korean fans of Japanese media, heavy reliance on the Internet as an almost exclusive channel for media consumption, along with increasingly fragmented ways of acquiring Japanese materials, may adversely affect the potential for deliberative social engagement. Bearing in mind sceptical views of virtual political engagement as merely a form of 'point-and-click politics' (van Dijck, 2012), it needs to be further investigated how the *ildjok* can be engaged with political agendas in ways that might prove empowering.

Second, it is uncertain what kind of subjectivity is emerging in the seemingly liberal and hybrid intra-Asian youthscape. The highly individualized, technologically mediated pursuit of a supermarket of styles may risk replacing the previous myth of homogeneous national subjectivity with another problematic myth: a neoliberal subjectivity that commodifies and homogenizes almost every cultural item in the name of global capitalism. Given that young Korean consumers' UGC activities have increasingly been sponsored and commercialized by the IT and entertainment industry (Jin, 2010), it could be argued that fans of Japanese media are merely being mobilized as 'free' labour power (Terranova, 2000) for the emerging intra-Asian media market.

These issues clearly require further debate; yet it seems important to stress the dynamic relationships here between structure and agency. This chapter has shown that youth culture is increasingly articulated with diverse forms of globalization, different local and national conditions and the emerging economic and technological forces associated with neoliberal capitalism. Yet the empirical data has also shown how young people make their own meanings of the global by appropriating intra-regional media commodities, reworking the historical memories of the region in the pursuit of their own cultural tastes and practices.

Note

1. Although American television dramas have remained steadily popular in Korea for the past few decades, largely due to terrestrial television

programming, some portion of which was covered by America television dramas, it was not until the mid-2000s that an extensive range of American television series began to be enthusiastically received by Korean viewers – especially via illegal online downloading.

References

Bennett, A. (1999). Subcultures or neo-tribes? Rethinking the relationship between youth, style and musical taste. *Sociology, 33*(3), 599–617.

Bennett, A., and Kahn-Harris, K. (eds). (2004). *After subculture: Critical studies in contemporary youth culture.* London: Palgrave.

Cho Han, H. (2000). "You are entrapped in an imaginary well": A feminist critique of modernity and Korean culture. *Inter-Asia Cultural Studies, 1*(1), 49–69.

Chua, B. H. (2004). Conceptualizing an East Asian popular culture. *Inter-Asian Cultural Studies, 5*(2), 200–221.

Fiske, J. (1992). The cultural economy of fandom. In L. A. Lewis (ed.). (1992), *The adoring audience: Fan culture and popular media* (pp. 30–49). London: Routledge.

Fung, A. (2007). Intra-Asian cultural flow: Cultural homologies in Hong Kong and Japanese television soap operas. *Journal of Broadcasting & Electronic Media, 51*(2), 265–286.

Han, S-H. (2001). Consuming the modern: Globalization, things Japanese and the politics of cultural identity in Korea. In H. Befu (ed.), *Globalizing Japan: Ethnography of the Japanese presence in America, Asia and Europe* (pp.194–208). London: Routledge.

Hills, M. (2002). *Fan cultures.* London: Routledge.

Hu, K. (2005). The power of circulation: Digital technologies and the online Chinese fans of Japanese TV drama. *Inter-Asia Cultural Studies, 6*(2), 171–186.

Iwabuchi, K. (2002). *Recentering globalization.* Durham: Duke University Press.

Iwabuchi, K. (2010). Undoing inter-national fandom in the age of brand nationalism. *Mechademia, 5*(1), 87–96.

Jeon, J. (2007, March 21). *Midjok, ildjok, bidjok* ... Which *jok* do you belong to? *Munhwa Ilbo,* p. 28.

Jin, D. Y. (2010). *Korea's online gaming empire.* Cambridge, Massachusetts: MIT Press.

Kang, J. S., Kang, Y. G. and Kim, M. C. (2012). Internet fansubbing culture: An in-depth interview study with foreign film and TV show fansubbers. *Korean Journal of Broadcasting Studies, 26*(1), 7–42.

Kim, D. and Won, Y. (eds). (2008). *Americanization: The Americanization of Korea since the liberation.* Seoul: Purun Yeoksa.

Kim, H-M. (2003). The inflow of Japanese pop culture and the historical construction of fandoms in South Korea. *Korean Journal of Cultural Anthropology, 13*(1), 149–186.

Lee, D-H. (2002). Media discourses on the other: Japanese history textbook controversies in Korea. *Proceedings of the Media Ecology Association, 3.* Retrieved from http://www.media-ecology.org/publications/MEA_proceedings/v3/Lee03.pdf

Lee, D-H. (2006). Transitional media consumption and cultural identity: Young Korean women's cultural appropriation of Japanese TV dramas. *Asian Journal of Women's Studies, 12*(2), 64–87.

Maffesoli, M. (1996). *The time of the tribes: The decline of individualism in mass society*. London: Sage.

Maira, S. and Soep, E. (eds). (2004). *Youthscape: The popular, the national, the global*. Philadelphia: The University of Pennsylvania Press.

Monteiro, A. and Jayasankar, K. P. (2000). Between the normal and imaginary: The spectator-self, the other and satellite television in India. In I. Hagen and J. Wasko (eds), *Consuming audiences? Production and reception in media research* (pp. 301–321). NJ: Hampton Press.

Moon, S. (2005). *Militarized modernity and gendered citizenship in South Korea*. London: Duke University Press.

OECD (2012, July 18). OECD broadband portal, Retrieved from http://www.oecd. org/sti/broadbandandtelecom/oecdbroadbandportal.htm

Otmazgin, N. K. (2008). Contesting soft power: Japanese popular culture in East and Southeast Asia. *International Relations of the Asia-Pacific, 8*(1), 73–101.

Park. J. (2007). A study on broadcast professionals' and researchers' perceptions of lifting the ban on Japanese broadcast programs. *Korean Journal of Cultural Policy, 19*, 245–265.

Pariser, E. (2011). *The filter bubble: What the Internet is hiding from you*. New York: Penguin Press.

Pilkington, H. and Johnson, R. (2003). Peripheral youth: Relations of identity and power in global/local context. *European Journal of Cultural Studies, 6*(3), 259–283.

Terranova, T. (2000). Free labor: Producing culture for the digital economy. *Social Text, 18*(2), 33–58.

van Dijck, J.(2009). Users like you? Theorizing agency in user-generated content. *Media, Culture & Society, 31*(1), 41–58.

van Dijck, J.(2012). Facebook as a tool for producing sociality and connectivity. *Television and New Media, 13*(2), 160–176.

Wise, J. M. (2008). *Cultural globalization: A user's guide*. New York: Wiley Blackwell.

Yoon, K. (2010). The representation of mobile youth in the post-colonial techno-nation of Korea, S. Hemelryk, T. D. Anderson, and D. Spry (eds), *Youth, society and mobile media in Asia* (pp. 108–119). New York: Routledge.

Zheng, K. (2011). Karaoke bar hostesses and Japan–Korea wave in postsocialist China: Fashion, cosmopolitanism and globalization. *City & Society, 23*(1), 42–65.

8
Learning to Act Your Age: 'Age Imaginaries' and Media Consumption in an English Secondary School

Patrick Alexander

Introduction

In this chapter I explore the relationship between 'age imaginaries' and media consumption in an English secondary school I have called Lakefield School. I argue that the concept of age imaginaries is valuable for understanding how both students and teachers negotiate multiple notions of age while in school. In the ethnographic examples presented here, age is imagined within the realms of youth, growing up and adulthood; but these categories emerge concurrently, rather than being necessarily mutually exclusive. This has significant implications for research into 'youth cultures' because it undermines the fixity that this term and other age-based markers of identity often imply. I also argue that media consumption is an important means for negotiating these multiple, concurrent imaginings of age. I begin by explaining the concept of 'age imaginaries' and then situate this concept, and my arguments about the role of media consumption in imagining age at school, within a broader ethnographic context. In the second part of this chapter I consider ethnographic vignettes from Year 11 (age 15–16) Media Studies lessons at Lakefield School. I conclude by arguing for the value of age imaginaries in understanding 'youth' culture and media consumption. The ethnographic vignettes presented here are particularly revealing in terms of what they show about how 'youth' culture and media consumption are negotiated in creative and surprising ways within the context of secondary education – a space normally imagined in the literature on youth culture as the restrictive institutional opposite to more romantic, supposedly 'free' locations for media consumption, such as the street, the club or the bedroom. Finally, I argue for the power of age imaginaries as a means for placing adults firmly within the landscape of 'youth' culture, both as arbitrators and as co-constructors of 'youth' through media consumption. First, however, I start with a story.

On a sunny May afternoon, Mr O'Reilly, a teacher at Lakefield School, is running a Year 7 tutor group session on the theme of 'rights and responsibilities'. (Students in Year 7, which is generally the first year of secondary school in England, are aged 11–12; in this case tutor groups were used to deliver the Personal Social and Health Education (PSHE) curriculum.) Mr O'Reilly approaches his theme by talking about the rights of children. As the lesson begins I sit in the bottom left-hand corner of the horseshoe of tables and chairs in Mr O'Reilly's classroom, next to Steven, who is as usual excitable and distracted. Mr O'Reilly quietens the class in order to introduce the theme of the lesson while Steven, finishing a giggling, spluttering conversation about something on his mobile phone, turns back around to listen. Mr O'Reilly starts by talking about how certain rights, like the right to education, come with responsibilities (e.g., acting responsibly when at school), and how certain rights and responsibilities increase with age (voting, marriage, driving, and so on). He briefly describes the universal rights that the UN Convention on the Rights of the Child (UNCRC) is supposed legally to protect, then screens a DVD. In the half-darkness of the room, and against the faint sound of a netball game being played outside, the video focuses on the differences between children in Africa and in Britain, contrasting scenes of African children hauling water, playing dusty games of football or attending lessons in sparse, overcrowded classrooms, with scenes of life at school in Britain. Afterwards, class discussion continues, with Mr O'Reilly pointing out that while the idea of not going to school might seem 'brilliant', going to school is a lot better than having to do the kind of heavy labour that the children in the video were expected to undertake (across the room Sarah comments, 'God, I'd much rather be in school than do that work [shown in the video] – even maths!'). Segueing into the plenary of the lesson, Mr O'Reilly argues that going to school is in this sense a privilege, not a chore:

So next time you're moaning to your mum about getting up in the morning to come to school, or you've got homework to do, or whatever, you have to remember that in other places there are children who would love to go to school, they would love that opportunity ... So you've got it quite good, really.

Meanwhile, amidst the slow crescendo of books being slipped into bags as the lesson draws to a close, Steven twists around again to show his phone to Jake, a boy with spiky gelled hair two seats away. Both turn red and guffaw with stifled laughter. When Steven glances at me, sizing up my response, I ask him what is so funny. He checks that Mr O'Reilly isn't looking before showing me his phone under the table. A lurid, pixellated image of the cartoon character Betty Boop, naked, dances back and forth jerkily on the screen. He looks back at me, hissing laughter through his teeth, as the bell goes to mark the end of the lesson.

This story highlights the ways in which students and teachers are engaged in the moment-by-moment negotiation of age as an aspect of social identity at Lakefield, and the vital role that media consumption and digital technology can play in this process. Here we see age imagined in relation to a universal, essentialized vision of childhood and children's rights, which in turn is set against media representations of cross-cultural differences in the lived experiences of children. We also see age imagined in the way that the delivery of the curriculum encourages the students to act responsibly – to engage in the process of 'growing up' and to be 'mature' about their rights as children. We see the role of media consumption in forging these imaginings, first through the watching of a DVD about childhood and then, more interesting still, through Steven's fleeting but, nevertheless, important forays into imagined 'adult' spheres online through his mobile phone.

This account thus raises a number of broader questions that I address in this chapter. How do students and teachers manage to maintain this precarious balance between different and sometimes divergent imaginings of age; and, if they do this on a daily basis or even moment by moment, why do they continue to place so much value in age-based categories as seemingly rigid markers of identity? What is meant by 'age' in the first place, and how does the concept of 'age imaginaries' make sense of the above story and the ethnographic descriptions that follow?

The concept of 'age imaginaries'

'Age' is a sphere of social inquiry claimed by diverse and sometimes disparate traditions within the social sciences (Pilcher, 1995). In ethnographic studies of schooling, age represents a fundamentally important aspect of social life at school, yet commonly remains a 'backdrop' for thinking about other issues such as class, gender or ethnicity. The quiet ubiquity of age as a 'backdrop' in social science research in this sense means that it is particularly difficult to pin down as a discrete field of study. Indeed, it is perhaps better to see 'age' currently existing at the crossroads of multiple fields of study, rather than as a field of study in its own right. 'Age' itself, then, is a word that does not immediately lend itself to dextrous analytic use, because it potentially encompasses so many different aspects of human experience.

Nonetheless, the idea of 'age imaginaries' can capture the complexity of 'age' as a social phenomenon; it deals with the common everyday practices that combine to provide us not only with a sense of individual age-based identity, but also with a sense of belonging and/or positioning within broader, normative age-related categories of social organization. Just as Anderson (1983) argues for the notion of the 'imagined community' as a means for understanding how ideas about national identity are developed, negotiated and sustained (see also Yoon in this publication), I argue that the notion of 'age imaginaries' is useful for describing the complex ways in which we make sense of ourselves and our relationships with others in relation to imagined, and imaginatively constructed, ideas of age-related identity (James and Prout, 1997; James et al., 1998; Prout, 2005). Individuals must negotiate understandings of age as an aspect of identity in relation to their own lived experiences; but they must also do so in relation to an imagined set of broader social categories – of generation, of consumer demographics, of legal ages, of age sets, of school year groups, of 'childhood', 'youth', 'adulthood' and so on – through which age-based notions of belonging and difference are nurtured, reinforced and negotiated relationally (Alanen, 2001).

Following Castoriadis' conception of the social imaginary (1987 [1975]), there is a constant interplay between taxonomies of known age imaginaries – the recognized, dominant order of institutional practices and discourses through which age is made sensible in the school – and moments of improvisation and alterity when age is imagined between staff and students in ways that move beyond these taxonomies. Making sense of these novel imaginings of age and articulating them within the context of the school requires them to be reconciled with the existing taxonomies through which age is normally negotiated; with the result that taxonomies of known age imaginaries exist concurrently with the novel, improvised and sometimes contradictory age imaginaries that emerge from the relational exchanges between staff and students. Thinking about age imaginaries in this way allows us consider how, in the context of Lakefield, staff and students are able at once to negotiate and make sense of diverse and sometimes contested ideas of age in their interactions with one another, simultaneously shaping their own notions of age-based identity while also engaging with an imagined sense of how things 'ought to be' in terms of their interactions with others (Strauss, 2006; Taylor, 2002). The idea that multiple and seemingly paradoxical imaginings of age are negotiated concurrently and relationally by staff and students is therefore at the centre of the concept of age imaginaries.

Conceptualizing age and media consumption in secondary schools

In studies of 'youth' in English school settings, media consumption has often served as a marker of social identity for students (Ball, 1980; Hebdige, 1979; McRobbie, 1991; Willis, 1977). Whether in the form of pop music, magazines, television programming or other media, this consumption has been associated, mainly in an unproblematic way, with teenage life – with 'youth' as an experience bounded and discretely linked to chronological 'youth' or adolescence during the teenage years. A number of recent studies have highlighted the social importance of patterns of consumption (and gender) on identity in school settings, again, with age emerging as a background theme (Livingstone, 2009; Nairn and Griffin, 2007; Phoenix and Frosh, 2001). Importantly, however, these studies reflect a general move within sociological studies of youth towards a more complex conceptualization of both the nature of 'youth' and the patterns of consumption (Griffin, 2001). It is arguable, for example, that there is today no clearly defined line that distinguishes 'adult' spheres of consumption from those of 'young' people – not least in the context of converging, deregulated digital media (Miles, 2000). It is important therefore that adults are also incorporated into an understanding of how age is configured and negotiated through consumption in the day-to-day of life at school. A more complex interpretation of 'youth', and an interest in consumption as an aspect of young people's lives, can be seen in a number of recent ethnographic studies of schools (Buckingham, 2000; Dover, 2007; Hollands, 1995; Phoenix and Frosh, 2001; Rampton, 2006).

To add to these examples, let us now return to Lakefield School and consider a number of ethnographic narratives that illuminate something of the complex relationship between media consumption and age imaginaries. The next part of this chapter explores how both students and teachers imagine age in the context of Year 11 (age 15–16) Media Studies lessons: in their media consumption, in articulating ideas about age and media consumption and ultimately in their interactions with one another. Gender and class emerge as important aspects of these configurations of age imaginaries, as I explain in my concluding remarks.

Sampling Age: imagining belonging and difference in Year 11 Media Studies

Year 11 Media Studies was made up primarily of some of the 'less able' and 'more disruptive' members of the year. This particular group of students had been relegated to the peripheries of the curriculum because of their inability to conform to the broader academic and behavioural expectations of the school, and to the rigours of the examination system. Media Studies was seen as a 'soft' option reserved for students who were not deemed capable or well-behaved enough to undertake other formally examined subjects. Arguably, this positioning of Media Studies at Lakefield reflects the marginality of Media Studies within the GCSE curriculum in Britain more generally speaking. Although Buckingham draws our attention to the impact that studies of youth subcultures and consumption have had on the development (and significance) of Media Studies as a field of study within secondary education (2003), teachers of Media Studies still struggle to overcome its negative stereotyping, either as a subject without substance or as a vehicle for teaching technological skills, rather than as a means of developing a more rigorous and critical form of media literacy. This 'generally inhospitable climate', as Buckingham describes it (2003, p. x), certainly hindered rather than helped Media Studies teachers and students in these particular lessons.

Imagining age in opposition to the Media Studies curriculum: 'tapes and records'

The Media Studies syllabus being followed by Year 11 was regarded by both the students and their teacher, Mrs Garrison, as outdated and behind current trends in media consumption. In an introductory Media Studies lesson, for example, the class openly mocked the textbook for being 'well old-fashioned' because it talked about popular music consumption in relation to 'tapes and records' – units of music consumption with which these students were personally almost wholly unfamiliar. In the same lesson students voiced other opinions about the relationship between different media and ideas of age. Mrs Garrison had brought in a selection of newspapers for the class to look at and compare in terms of supposed audience and readership. When asked who they thought read newspapers, Richard pointed to the broadsheets and said, 'You think of an old granddad, don't ya, sitting on the toilet or something. When you see it's about politics and things you just switch off, don't ya.' The others in the class agreed that they thought newspapers were for 'old' people and that they would never read them – even *The Sun*, which they preferred because of its sports and celebrity sections. To this Mrs Garrison agreed that she didn't read the papers either. The discussion then moved on to other forms of media. When asked to describe who they thought the audiences were for radio, again they agreed that radio was for 'old' people – even though they also agreed that they all listened to the radio from time to time (particularly to BBC Radio 1 and BBC 1 Extra, the latter an RnB and hip-hop station).

Imagining age-based difference though media consumption

In the Media Studies curriculum itself, then, these students were presented with an 'old-fashioned' vision of the media that was at times in stark contrast to their imaginings of their own media practices. From the outset, this appeared to provide grounds for distinguishing themselves, as young people, from an imagined sense of adult media consumption that involved technologies and texts of another, bygone, era – such as newspapers, radio, tapes and records. Building on this image, they also distinguished between their media consumption habits and those of adults in other spheres as well. In the introductory lesson mentioned above, the students were asked to compile their own 'media profile', detailing their own patterns of media consumption. As we talked about the content of some of the newspapers – the haircut of one of the singers in the girl group *Girls Aloud,* the popular TV talent show *X Factor*, the Madeleine McCann abduction case – Robert explained the kinds of things that he liked to watch on television. These he described as TV shows that were for 'young people – children ... well, people my age', rather than 'old people'. The TV programmes listed included the satirical American cartoon *Family Guy* and music TV channels such as *TMF*, as well as programmes such as the comedy *Only Fools and Horses*. Despite Mrs Garrison's claim that she also watched these kinds of programmes, and my own similar claims, Robert was adamant that these were media for 'young people', not adults. The latter example, *Only Fools and Horses,* is particularly interesting in this case, given that it was produced mainly between 1981 and 1991, before Robert was born and when Mrs Garrison, on the other hand, was a teenager. Other students chimed in with their own suggestions, such as *MTV Base,* the soap operas *EastEnders, Emmerdale* and *Coronation Street* and the American sitcom *Friends*. Again, Mrs Garrison claimed that she was also a fan of these programmes and channels. While they could see that she might be a fan of *EastEnders* or *Friends* – after all, they said, they had watched these shows with their parents – they were much less convinced when it came to the idea of Mrs Garrison watching MTV Base or something similar.

Meanwhile, on the other side of the classroom, some of the girls had become preoccupied with other things – in particular, with an online social networking site called *Hi5*. This was not a generally popular social networking site online among young people in the United Kingdom at the time of my research, compared with more prominent sites such as *Bebo, Myspace* or *Facebook*, or chat facilities such as *MSN Messenger*. However, it was popular with Lakefield students because, unlike all those others, the IT Support staff had not yet blocked access to it in school. Students therefore used *Hi5* as a platform for chatting and meeting people online: these sometimes included friends in other lessons around the school, but because the site was not restricted either by location or by age, students could also chat with young people and adults from all over the world. While the boys were flipping through the newspapers and talking about the things that 'young people – children ... people my age' watched on television, Janie, Zara and Layla were developing their online *Hi5* profiles and searching the site for other people. Layla put her hand on the screen in embarrassment when I walked past her, laughing and saying, 'Oh God, don't look!', quickly followed by similar protestations from the other girls. She had uploaded a picture of herself striking a model-like pose and, although she was 15, had listed her age as 16. Later, however, the girls relaxed and started to talk about the politics of 'unfriending' someone online (removing someone from one's list of networked online friends). When I asked them who used the site, they agreed that it was probably mostly young people because '*Hi5* is for young people' [Layla] (i.e., *designed* for young people). They did not seem particularly concerned or convinced by the idea that adults might also be using it to interact in a virtual, age-fluid space. This was particularly ironic given that they had also been discussing 'pretending to be other people' in online chat facilities: Janie, for example, had said 'yeah, last night I was Dave and I was 44!' when talking about 'messing around' in a chatroom. However, confirming their idea that *Hi5* was an unknown social world among adults, Mrs Garrison came over to have a look at the site, asking what it was and saying that she had never seen it before.

In this one Media Studies lesson, then, there were various interesting and nuanced examples of students expressing ideas about their own media consumption, or engaging in media consumption practices that were positioned in opposition to an imagined sense of how adults – such as Mrs Garrison, myself and the writers of the Media Studies text-book – might consume media. There was in particular a sense that media focusing on trends in popular culture, such as music video channels, and particular social networking sites, such as *Hi5*, were beyond the pale of adult experience, while newspapers and radio were emblematic of the stuffy, boring, technologically retrograde adult sphere. At the same time, however, the informal discussions and activities suggested a more complex picture. There were obvious points of overlap and intersection in the television viewing preferences of Mrs Garrison and the 15- and 16 year-old boys that she was teaching (and myself), even if the students were reluctant to acknowledge this fact. There were also examples of the girls attempting to appear more 'grown up' or adult through media consumption (even to the extent of Layla literally changing her recorded chronological age). While disengaged from the formal Media Studies curriculum, which they saw as boring, outdated and representative of 'old people', students were engaged in complex and interesting sets of practices that revealed something nuanced about how they used media and technology to imagine age in multiple different ways.

Mobile phones and music: Puff Daddy (or is that The Police?) and Bluetooth

Despite the seeming contradictions between what students and their teacher *imagined* to be the relationship between media consumption and age, and their more messy *lived experiences* of this relationship in school, there were numerous other occasions where students in particular used media consumption practices to carve out imaginings of age in opposition to the adults around them. This is apparent in the following three examples of simultaneous boundary building and border-crossing.

On a languid and somewhat directionless Thursday afternoon, a student called Janie, sitting in the back row of a near-empty classroom, got out her new phone and started comparing it with the phones of other students in the class. She was impressed when I told her that my phone was the same model as hers (and therefore somewhat up-to-date, apparently unlike my clothes), and we began to discuss its different features. At the time she was listening to music on her phone through one surreptitious earphone cupped in her hand. When, after a while, I asked her what she was listening to, she gave me a withering look and scoffed 'errrr, nothing *you'd* know!' before turning back to thumb her phone. After a bit of persistent questioning she agreed to let me hear what she was listening to, this time by playing her phone on its external speaker. Janie said she was listening to Jay-Z, a popular American hip-hop artist. When I told her that I was a fan, she looked sceptical but was won over when I could name a few popular Jay-Z songs. The song that she was playing sampled another song entitled *Every Time You Go Away*, by Paul Young, a popular 1980s British pop singer (whose version in turn was a cover of the original by American singers Hall & Oates, released in 1980). Upon hearing this sample, Mrs Garrison looked up and rolled her eyes, moaning 'God, I know I'm old when they start sampling songs I used to listen to when I was a teenager!'

Two weeks later, in another Media Studies lesson based in a narrow, dingy computer room, the class were supposed to be researching the structure of film plots. Most, however, had become distracted by other things online and were huddled around computers looking at different sites about graffiti. In one corner, Shane was watching an online episode of *Waterloo Road,* the popular school-based TV drama, on BBC iPlayer (the on-demand section of the BBC website). Janie, at the other end of the room, was staring intently at her new phone again. She decided to enable the Bluetooth function on her mobile in order to see which other phones in the vicinity were also active. When the search was finished a number of different phones emerged on Janie's screen, including Mrs Garrison's. Slightly embarrassed, but also quite innocent of Bluetooth technology, Mrs Garrison took her phone out of her handbag to see how Janie was connecting her phone to her teacher's. Recognizing Mrs Garrison's ignorance of this function, Janie exclaimed 'Oh my days, old people are so rubbish with phones! I bet you don't even know how to turn it on!' She wanted to show Mrs Garrison how Bluetooth worked, and so asked her to name a song she would like Janie to send her. Janie busied herself organizing her MP3 files into a playlist and, in her usual flamboyant way, decided to play sections of each song (loudly) to see which one Mrs Garrison might like, discussing each with Mrs Garrison and myself. The first track was by the hip-hop artist Timbaland, which had received a lot of radio play at the time (particularly on BBC Radio 1, which Mrs Garrison had told me she sometimes listened to on the way into work in the mornings), and was in the top 10 in the charts. Since Mrs Garrison said that she liked it, Janie said she would send her the file from her phone. Mrs Garrison was at first unsure about giving Janie access to her phone because she thought that this would allow Janie to pass on her mobile number to other students; but with assurances that this was not how Bluetooth worked, Mrs Garrison allowed the file-sharing to take place.

Janie continued to play songs loudly on her phone, now discussing them with me as she went through different play lists. Putting on *Missing You,* from the American hip-hop artist Sean Combs (or Puff Daddy), which had returned to the charts in 2007 after he performed it at a Princess Diana memorial concert earlier that year, Janie said that it had been played at her cousin's funeral recently. I replied by telling her that the song had been first released when I was in the sixth form, in 1998, and that it reminded me of being in school. Mrs Garrison then interrupted to query the year of the song's release, because she also associated it with being at school but was some 10 years my senior. Then she realized her mistake: the song that we were now listening to in 2007 *had* been released in 1998, but it was built around a sample from a song released in 1983 by the band The Police, entitled *Every Breath You Take.* Again, Mrs Garrison rolled her eyes and made a comment about how she felt old because the songs being sampled 'nowadays' were songs from her own youth. At this point the bell rang, and the class slowly dispersed to move across the school for English.

Sampling age

The vignettes above provide nuanced and rich material for thinking about the relationship between age imaginaries and media consumption. To begin with, music consumption becomes a topic of conversation and a vehicle for articulating and acting out ideas about age through the medium of mobile phones. In the course of both lessons described above, Janie reinforces an imagined sense of age-based difference between herself and Mrs Garrison by emphasizing the latter's lack of knowledge and competency in the arenas of popular media and digital technology (specifically, in terms of Bluetooth file-sharing). Her exclamations about Mrs Garrison's lack of knowledge of phones as an 'old person' implicitly position Janie as a young person who, seemingly by virtue of belonging to this category, has a greater degree of 'savvy' when it comes to digital technology. This is emphasized by the fact that traditional teacher–student roles are reversed in this lesson: Mrs Garrison learns about new aspects of media from her students, rather than the other way around. As we have seen above, it seems that students in this class learn little about the media from the formal Media Studies curriculum in terms of literacy, but are able to show a complex level of competency in the media-based activities in which they are engaged when they are supposed to be studying. In this instance, this issue is cast into stark relief by the fact that the teaching and learning taking place relates neither to the curriculum nor to a conventional understanding of a teacher's authoritative subject knowledge. An imagined sense of traditional adult authority – the idea that adults, by virtue of their age, 'ought to be' inherently more experienced or knowledgeable – is in this way also undermined by the exchanges that take place around media consumption in these lessons.

For her part, Mrs Garrison also does some work to establish a sense of age-based difference and distance in time between herself and Janie, particularly through her discussions and comments about the samples being used in the songs to which Janie is listening. Mrs Garrison feels 'dated' by the conversation that we have about Puff Daddy sampling The Police because this serves as a reminder and confirmation that she is now 'old' relative to her students. Whereas the Police song in question evokes Mrs Garrison's own school days, in its newer, sampled form, it reinforces the fact that those days are gone and that therefore she is 'old' now compared to the teenagers that she teaches.

Listening to the Puff Daddy track has multiple resonances for Janie and Mrs Garrison relative to their different imaginings of age as a marker of difference between them. And yet, in their shared tastes in popular music, both also implicitly undermine the imagined generational barriers that they conjure between one another. The idea of sampling in particular seems to serve here as a metaphor for the ways in which imaginings of age are spliced and intermixed through the process of consuming particular forms of media. Both the Jay-Z track (which Mrs Garrison doesn't know) and the Puff Daddy one (which she knows as well as the original Police song that it samples) serve as links between Janie's media consumption practices in the present and Mrs Garrison's own teenage media consumption practices. This literal mixing of 'older' sampled songs with new material imbues these particular media texts with significances as songs that serve as reference points to an imagined sense of youth, even when consumed simultaneously by people of different chronological ages, imagining different 'youths'. And as in the case of the Puff Daddy track, they can also serve as points of shared media consumption located in the present.

Conclusions

In this chapter I have drawn on a range of ethnographic vignettes to explore how age imaginaries are negotiated in the classroom both in the content and in the delivery of the curriculum, and in contexts where the curriculum itself becomes peripheral to the activities taking place in the classroom. Frequently these peripheral spaces in the classroom are sites for 'illicit' media consumption that also serves in helping students and teachers to imagine age. While particular imaginings of age are presented and reinforced in the content and delivery of the curriculum, then, students and teachers are also actively engaged in negotiating their own age imaginaries through the lived experience of taking part in lessons, often via media consumption. This involves both engaging in and diverging from dominant discourses of age.

In these Media Studies lessons, students and staff were attempting to use media consumption practices to reinforce notions of age-based difference – although in the process of doing so they also pointed to similarities across generations. The examples of media consumption presented here represent an important vehicle for negotiating age imaginaries at Lakefield, both in terms of reinforcing established categories of age and in imagining age beyond these categories. While at times more traditional, popular ideas (or ideals) of age-based difference may be reinforced through media consumption practices (e.g., between 'media-savvy', *avant garde* young people on one hand, and 'out-of-date', technophobic adults on the other) there are also frequent moments where media culture and new digital technologies serve as common cultural reference points that trouble traditional age-based categories of identity. Here this is crystalized in the description of 'sampling' above. The complex nature of age as an aspect of identity means that these different understandings of the relationship between age and media consumption – as markers of imagined difference and as moments of generational border-crossing – are not necessarily mutually exclusive. Instead, potentially contradictory imaginings of age in relation to media consumption emerge simultaneously. In the vignettes presented here it is in the emergence of these concurrences, and in the ongoing, relational negotiation of age, in part through media consumption, that the complexity of age as an aspect of self-making can be perceived.

References

Alanen, L. (2001). Explorations in generational analysis. In B. Mayall and L. Alanen (eds). *Conceptualizing child–adult relations*. London: Routledge Falmer.
Anderson, B. (1983). *Imagined communities: Reflections on the origin and spread of nationalism*. London: Verso.
Ball, S. (1980) *Beachside comprehensive: A case-study of secondary schooling*. Cambridge: Cambridge University Press.

Buckingham, D. (2000). *After the death of childhood: Growing up in the age of electronic media.* Cambridge: Polity Press.

Buckingham, D. (2003). *Media education: Literacy, learning and contemporary culture.* London: Wiley.

Castoriadis, C. (1987 [1975]). *The imaginary institution of society.* Cambridge, MA: MIT Press.

Dover, C. (2007). Everyday Talk: Investigating Media Consumption and Identity Amongst School Children. *Particip@tions, 4,1,* Retrieved from http://www.participations.org/Volume%204/Issue%201/4_01_dover.htm

Griffin, C. (2001). Imagining new narratives of youth: Youth research, the 'new Europe' and global youth culture. *Childhood, 8*(2), 147–166.

Hebdige, D. (1979). *Subculture: The meaning of style.* London: Routledge.

Hollands, R. (1995). *Friday night, Saturday night,* Newcastle: Newcastle University Press.

James, A., Jenks, C. and Prout, A. (eds) (1998). *Theorizing childhood.* Cambridge: Polity Press.

James, A. and Prout, A. (eds) (1997). *Constructing and reconstructing childhood: Contemporary issues in the sociological study of childhood.* London: Falmer.

Livingstone, S. (2009). *Children and the Internet: Great expectations, challenging realities.* Oxford: Polity Press.

McRobbie, A. (1991). *Feminism and youth culture: From 'Jackie' to 'Just Seventeen'.* Basingstoke: Macmillan.

Miles, S. (2000). *Youth lifestyles in a changing world.* Buckingham: Open University Press.

Nairn, A. and Griffin, C. (2007). "Busted are cool but Barbie's a minger": The role of advertising and brands in the everyday lives of junior school children. In K. Ekstrom and B. Tufte (eds). *Children, media and consumption: On the front edge.* Goteborg University: Nordicom Press.

Pilcher, J. (1995). *Age & generation in modern Britain.* Oxford: Oxford University Press.

Prout, A. (2005). *The future of childhood: Towards the interdisciplinary study of children.* London: RoutledgeFalmer.

Phoenix, A. and Frosh, S. (2001). Positioned by 'hegemonic' masculinities: A study of London Boy's narratives of identity. *Australian Psychologist, 35,* 27–35.

Rampton, B. (2006). *Language in late modernity: Interaction in an urban school.* Cambridge: Cambridge University Press.

Strauss, C. (2006). The imaginary. *Anthropological Theory, 6*(3), 322–344.

Taylor, C. (2002). Modern social imaginaries. *Public Culture, 14*(1), 91–124.

Willis, P. E. (1977) *Learning to labour: How working class kids get working class jobs.* Farnborough: Saxon House.

9
Charver Kids and Pram-face Girls: Working-Class Youth, Representation and Embodied Performance

Mary Jane Kehily and Anoop Nayak

Introduction

> Chavs are for the most part, extremely stupid. However, some of them render a form of low cunning, which can be misinterpreted as intelligence. However this is false. A Chav has no desire to better themself through honest means nor learn anything outside of car modification ...

> Commonly thought to be of inferior intellect, the Chavette surprises us with its cunning plan to avoid taking up a professional career and provide itself with free accommodation supplied by tax payers by spawning multi coloured mini chavs at a early stage in life, usually mid teens.
>
> > http://www.urbandictionary.com/define.
> > php?term=chav accessed 19 March 2013

The invocation of the 'chav' in these examples from the Urban Dictionary conjures up well-worn responses to a substratum of working-class youth, laden with disgust and condemnation. As shorthand for the unrespectable poor, *Little Britain*'s pram-pushing character Vicky Pollard serves as a recognizable representation of the modern-day 'chav'. With her scrunched-back hair, day-glo tracksuit, hooped ear rings and predilection for smoking, drinking and swearing, Vicky Pollard's chav identity is written on the body. Transnational depictions of 'trailer park trash' in the United States, 'bogans' in Australia, 'neds' in Scotland, 'pikies', 'scallies', 'hoodies' and 'chavs' in England are all ways in which those who are young, poor and white are brought into being in the contemporary global era. While a number of authors have critically discussed these representations, producing rich insight into the reworking of social class delineations in late-modernity (e.g., Adams and Raisborough, 2011; Hayward and Yar, 2006; Jones, 2011; Lawler, 2005; Tyler, 2008), surprisingly few have sought to engage with the voices of dispossessed youth themselves. Little is known about how young people speak back to these representations, transfigure or dissent from them.

This chapter is concerned with the intra-group differences that characterize working-class youth and the ways they are brought into being through performance and media representation. We consider how relations of affect are produced through popular media representations as well as the way in which these felt intensities are lived. We ask what work the representational does, and how it impacts upon the lives of young people themselves. Through an analysis of two popularly maligned youth groups, teenage mothers and socially excluded young men, we consider how they negotiate signs of social class disgust and signifiers of shame. Our research shows young people's awareness of the deeply pejorative nature of these representations and their attempts to displace them by reimagining themselves instead as competent carers and active citizens. We also explore the potential for digital culture to extend the canvas for comment and construction at a general level (see Soep, this volume).

Our analysis of these young people, referred to colloquially as 'charver kids' and 'pram-face girls', demonstrates how academic readings can benefit from connecting the 'encoded' messages of social class representations with their 'decoded', felt and affective understandings (Hall, 1980). By moving beyond textual analysis and engaging with the wider 'circuit of culture' (Johnson, 1986), we adopt a more performative approach in which the 'work of representation' can be seen as a type of 'doing', and images and stereotypes are in a continual process of struggle and re-articulation. While we would agree that being labelled a 'chav/charver' or 'pram-face girl' is pejorative, the testimonies of charver kids and teenage mums suggest that some forms of negotiation, resistance and re-appropriation are possible and that by listening to these experiences and 'working with emotions' a more intimate and intricate understanding of working-class life can be evinced. In this, we concur with the urban ethnographer Les Back (2007), who has urged sociologists to 'listen with the eye' in an effort to avoid reproducing distant, disembodied and sanitized readings of everyday working-class life.

'Listening with the eyes' to working-class youth

Scholars of youth culture have long been concerned with questions of representation. Landmark texts in the youth studies canon by Hebdige (1979), Hall and Jefferson (1976) and Cohen (1972) critically explore how young people come to present themselves through subcultural affiliation, whilst simultaneously exploring the constitutive role of mediated representations. A rich history of research on youth culture and subcultures has illustrated how young people construct identities in dialogue with the way they have been represented by others. While early studies focused on labelling and patterns of deviance (Becker, 1963; Cohen, 1972), later work drew attention to the creativity of young people and their ability to mobilize forms of self-expression and symbolic resistance (Cohen, 1972; Hebdige, 1979; Willis, 1990).

Our account here is based on studies by the authors in two different areas of the United Kingdom, which attempted to interweave representational analysis with qualitative empirical fieldwork. Mary Jane's study is part of a five-year project, *The Making of Modern Motherhood,* exploring the identity changes involved in the transition to motherhood among a diverse sample of first-time mothers in the southeast of England (Thomson et al., 2011). Recognizing the social and demographic changes affecting women's lives, our central research questions asked if motherhood was becoming a site of new social divisions between women (see Kehily and Thomson, 2011a). Aspects of the study were concerned with how far media representations, expert advice and practices of consumption feature in the project of pregnancy and new motherhood. An initial questionnaire provided background data on participants' regularly used and preferred media forms and the research team carried out a content analysis of pregnancy magazines commonly available and read by women in the study. Digital photography was used to record how women were preparing for the birth of their first child. Diverse media images (advertisements, magazine and newspaper features and promotional material) were used as prompt material in interviews, generally introduced towards the end. Our key aim was to invite women to explore the boundaries of the common culture of mothering, identifying points of identification and difference by speaking to feelings generated by the images (Kehily and Thomson, 2011b). This chapter draws from a data set of 62 interviews with first-time mothers, focusing particularly on a subset of interviews with 10 mothers aged 15–19 years.

Anoop's account focuses upon 'charver kids' in the Nailton district of Newcastle in northeast England. The city contains over 292,000 residents, of whom 70,000 reside in the Nailton area. The urban area surrounding Newcastle city centre is made up of a band of old inner-city locales formerly designed to service armament workers at William Armstrong's plant, once producing guns, arms and battleships. Having employed 700,000 workers at its peak, today the area is predominantly post-industrial containing some business parks, local services and varying types of employment in public healthcare, as well as relatively high levels of unemployment. Many of the neighbourhoods in Nailton are regarded as socially deprived compared with wealthier suburbs lying to the east of the city. The urban ethnography is derived from living in the area for two years, and includes interviews and multi-site participant observations with young people through daily encounters in schools, neighbourhoods, pubs and clubs, in the city centre and other local spaces (see Nayak, 2003; 2006). The chapter also draws on an Internet forum established following the screening of a regional TV documentary about 'chavs/charvers' in which Anoop appeared. The forum invited responses from young people whose working-class lifestyles are more commonly pilloried and mocked in and by the media: it therefore sheds some light on how young people come to position themselves in and against these tropes and the intensities of feeling they carry.

The 'bringing into being' of chav and pram face

As a class-cultural formation created by processes of industrialization, the status of the working class in the post-industrial age appears as a fragile chimera of the past. The decline of a manufacturing base in the West and diminished need for manual labour creates a stratum of young people as a working-class-without-work. The multiple losses encountered in the domino-effect collapse of livelihood, identity and intergenerational inheritance suggest that this group remains least touched by the gold dust of 'new times' and promises of freedom and mobility heralded by youth commentators of the global media age (Harris, 2004, McRobbie, 1994). Unemployed youth, referred to in government policy terms as NEETs (not in employment, education or training), and teenage mothers are identifiable social categories capturing aspects of youth experience that are often overlooked in celebratory accounts of leisure and style, yet are prominent in studies of social exclusion and policy initiatives. In contrast to the expressive subcultures of earlier studies, these groups appear 'ordinary' and unspectacular, not part of a subculture (post- or otherwise) and not easily interpellated as neoliberal subjects able to craft a unique biographical narrative of self. Yet patterned and repeated popular media representations turn the ordinary into something other than ordinary, 'bringing into being' chav and pram face as recognizable categories of class derision in late modernity.

More recently the term chav has stretched to include the 'bling' and excess of the newly moneyed: social class transgressors such as footballer's wives and girlfriends (WAGS), reality TV stars, glamour models, working-class lottery winners, white rap artists and a host of figures celebrated and parodied in reality TV programmes such as *Marbella Belles, Geordie Shore, The Only Way Is Essex* and *Big Fat Gypsy Weddings*. However, the more mundane, commonly held meaning (prominent in our research participants' accounts) refers to what has been termed the 'new underclass' (Hayward and Yar, 2006) in which the chav is stereotyped as young, relatively uneducated, wearing tracksuits and baseball caps, listening to hi-energy trance or drum 'n' bass and engaged in street crime. The abjection attributed to charver kids is compounded where they are seen as 'scruffy whites' (Rhodes, 2011), 'feral youth' forming part of a 'white trash' underclass markedly different from these newly minted chavs, emblematic of a reconfigured nouveau riche. In schools where uniforms were compulsory, students identified charver kids by their allegedly unkempt appearance, referring to them as 'soap dodgers' with nits, fleas and bad body odour.

Though its precise etymology remains uncertain, the term charver holds negative race/class undertones. Local English etymology suggests that it is a hybrid combination of the supposedly working-class names, Sharon and Trevor (i.e., Shar/vor), and the term has also been said to derive from the word 'chavi', a term for a small child popularly used by Travellers and those of Romany ancestry. 'Chav' accoutrements such as sovereign rings and large hooped gold ear rings are also associated with Travellers, adding to the 'not-quite-white' status of charver kids. At a transnational level, comparisons can be made between representations of Britain's Travelling population and America's rural 'trailer park trash', both of whom occupy a precarious 'off white' status in their respective national body politic. Even a 'celebrity chav' such as Cheryl Cole, the popular singer who hails from Newcastle, has been constructed as 'dirty white', with emphasis placed on her strong regional accent, occasional violent outbursts (she was once arrested for punching a nightclub toilet attendant) and black boyfriends such as footballer Ashley Cole and American dancer Tre Holloway. Charvers are represented as society's new urban primitives, dwelling in 'sink estates' beyond the restorative powers of gentrification and urban regeneration.

Most studies of the chav investigate how classed subjectivities are represented in popular media (Adams and Raisborough, 2011; Hayward and Yar, 2006; Lawler, 2005; Tyler, 2008). However, commentators such as Owen Jones (2011) are critical of both popular media and academics for focusing upon 'spectacular' examples of working-class experience, whether in TV drama, reality TV, talk shows or news stories. These illustrations iteratively 'bring into being' a version of working-class life that can obscure the lives of 'ordinary' working-class youth. Semiotic readings and textual analysis alone risk 'scaling up' and making extraordinary the socially impoverished, escalating fears about difference by drawing upon the excessive representations paraded on media websites, social documentaries and tabloid newspapers. For sociologists only too aware of the historical silencing of working-class voices, this is innately problematic, as Tyler observes in the conclusion to her insightful media analysis:

> The figure of the chav is mobilised in ways that justify the continued division of society into those who can speak, act, and feel and those who are 'spoken for'. (Tyler, 2008, p. 32)

'Speaking for' working-class youth can elicit a complex and at times contradictory representational bind. Substituting the 'bad', denigrated and comic images that appear in popular culture for 'good', deconstructive and socially aware academic interpretations, does not get around the complex question of who speaks for whom and on what terms – an issue our own interviews and ethnography with young people cannot fully escape either. Yet the silencing of working-class voices is a tendency that empirical research can go at least some way to arresting.

In addressing these issues in our own research, we suggest that charver kids and pram-face girls are relational constructions emerging within the context of social change and the growing gap between rich and poor in Western late modernity. The figure of the chav and the teen mum exist in the representational sphere as 'abject others', a repository for fears and anxieties concerning the corrosion of white respectability and social class mobility. As figures of abjection, charver kids and pram-face girls serve to maintain the boundaries of the 'normative', holding in place otherwise fragile configurations of class, ethnicity and gender, while engendering a myriad of popular representations from which it becomes possible to speak the unspeakable.

Teenage motherhood is a particularly feminized route to poverty, with the additional prospect of lack of respectability and 'underclass' status.

While it remains a largely 'working-class affair' (Walkerdine et al., 2001) in the contemporary era, it is an arena in which socio-economic differences between women are defined and compounded by distinct cultures of childrearing (Byrne, 2006; Clarke, 2004; Tyler, 2008). Walkerdine et al. (2001) argue that, despite the apparent 'remaking' of modern girlhood, it is vital to acknowledge how social class continues to shape girls' experiences of education, academic attainment and their subsequent life trajectories. Their analysis shows how the regulation of femininity is related to sexuality and works differently upon the bodies of working-class and middle-class girls. For middle-class girls the emphasis is upon educational success, and the possibility of early motherhood is more likely to end in termination. By contrast, academic success for working-class girls involves identity rupture and a transformation of self. Working-class girls bear the emotional cost of becoming bourgeois subjects in forms of pain, loss and fragmentation. From the perspective of working-class young women, early pregnancy may be an attempt to resolve some of the contradictions in the transition to adult womanhood. Becoming a mother bypasses the educational process while affording young women a particular role and status in the local community. Walkerdine et al. suggest that in these ways working-class and middle-class girls become 'each other's Other' (2001, p. 209), cautionary examples of what you could become by transgressing the regulatory framework of class and gender.

A central finding of the Motherhood study (Thomson et al., 2011) lies in the significance of age as the 'master category' in shaping the maternal experience. This is reflected in representations of pregnancy and new motherhood as the apex of feminine achievement and a celebration of romantic coupledom. The idealization of pregnancy as presented in magazines, for example, addresses an imagined readership of 25–35-year olds in long-term heterosexual relationships and with established careers. For this age group pregnancy forms part of an individual choice biography and is a feat of synchronicity, bringing together the right man with financial and emotional security. Teenage mothers rarely feature in these publications. Their pregnancies appear aberrant in the context of planned and delayed motherhood. Furthermore, the work/career orientation of such magazine features excludes young mothers who have not yet established themselves in the world of work.

These forms of popular culture celebrate the increased visibility of pregnancy and the confidence of mature motherhood. The pregnant body emerges as an 'on show' display encoding versions of 'pregnant beauty' (Tyler, 2001) and respectability. Pregnancy magazines emphasize the individual satisfactions of pregnancy in straplines such as 'it's all about me, me, me', 'bumptastic' and 'it's the time of your life'. New mothers are encouraged to pamper, indulge and embrace an expanded project of self, principally realized through new practices of consumption. Such practices also take on an age-based character. While older mothers are depicted as hosting pink champagne baby showers spilling over with designer accessories, a recurrent theme in younger women's accounts is a shift in consumer identity from 'teen' to new mother-with-responsibilities, a moment to re-evaluate spending priorities, cutting back on 'going out' and fashion wear to focus on the baby rather than themselves.

By using visual prompt material in our interviews with first-time mothers, we aimed to encourage women to look beyond the immediacy of their personal experience. Many of the images highlighted the idea of pregnancy as a time of increased visibility, when women are on show. Fashion features on maternity wear profiled the gloriousness of the pregnant tummy. Celebrity pregnancies profiled how to do it or not do it. For example, a feature entitled *Pregnant and Fabulous* showed celebrity mothers in designer garments such as an 'off-the-shoulder black dress showing plenty of cleavage', a maroon and gold sari and a red ball gown, highlighting statements such as 'you feel more feminine when you're pregnant, sexier'. By contrast, however, another image showed glamour model and reality TV star Jordan/Katie Price wearing a cropped, see-through top and size 6 jeans, her heavily pregnant tummy fully exposed between the microgarments. While most of our respondents enjoyed the pregnant-and-stunning look modelled so beguilingly by the celebs, they distanced themselves from Price's style, describing her as 'improper', 'tarty' and 'ridiculous'. Such responses, commenting on her borderline respectability as a celebrity and a mother-to-be and invoking notions of propriety and respectability, indicate how the mothers-to-be in our study felt a need to position themselves in relation to these broader discourses about femininity (Skeggs, 2004) – discourses that find renewed focus in pregnancy. Women made significant investments in the embodied display of pregnancy, feeling strongly that 'how you wear your bump' mattered. Images of pregnant celebrities appear to encode a particular feminine aesthetic, a notion of 'pregnant beauty' (Tyler, 2001) that can be both inspirational and regulatory in its appeal to women to measure themselves against their celebrity counterparts and to compare celebrities with each other.

By contrast, the image of Vicky Pollard with her multiple babies in buggies produced immediate peals of laughter and derision. Epitomizing a chav identity, the Pollard character has become associated with excessive working-class femininity as a ubiquitous signifier for the unrespectable poor whose profligate ways define 'bad mothering'. Women in the study commonly did not comment on social class directly, although responses to Katie Price and Vicky Pollard provided glimpses into class-inflected perspectives and practices. Thus, a 42-year-old respondent commented that many young women in her rural county town looked 'just like' Vicky Pollard, pushing prams, smoking and shouting at their kids, implying that the reality is not so far removed from the media portrayal. Many younger respondents, however, found Vicky Pollard 'funny' but unrelated to reality, being quite unlike them or anyone they knew. Such contrasting views suggest that the fault lines of gender and class, while structurally significant at so many levels, can also shape-shift at the local level, creating scope for multiple acts of recognition and misrecognition, as we consider below.

Stigmatized bodies, representation and dissimulation

Can young people 'speak back' to these mediated forms? And how are these projections assimilated, rejected and negotiated by young people themselves? In this section we argue that more ambivalent readings of chav and pram face emerge in young people's own responses. Ethnographies of people and place (Nayak, 2003; 2006) and biographies of young lives (Shildrick and MacDonald, 1997) can offer counter-representations of 'chav' and unemployed youth more generally. The young people in both our studies show agency and appear articulate and knowledgeable about how they and others are represented.

For young women in Mary Jane's study, having their first child between 15 and 19 years meant they were acutely aware of how their pregnancy was viewed by others. In a broader social context where delayed pregnancy is becoming the norm, teenage mothers-to-be can be made to look and feel aberrant. For them the pregnant tummy was a potential source of shame, a point of judgement and something they had learned to be defensive about:

> Some people look at you funny because you're young and you've got a bump ... two ladies were sitting on the bus the other day talking about how young people were getting pregnant and how it was a disgrace and all this lot. And I wanted to say something but I couldn't because I didn't want to be rude ... [At the parenting classes] some girls cover their bump and some girls don't. I usually do but

sometimes my tops do rise and I think that's what they were shocked about 'cos some of my tummy was hanging out. (Zoe, age 17)

Aware of the shock prompted by being young and pregnant, but without saying anything herself, Zoe's swollen belly 'talks back' to the women on the bus. Displaying the tummy can act as a gesture of defiance, a 'what you gonna do about it?' flash of resistance designed to unsettle adults around them. The 'tummy flash' was most in evidence in moments of conflict with staff in the young parents' support centre where they attended classes. In this context exposing the pregnant tummy was a fiery, non-verbal response that challenged adult authority without risk of admonishment. However, as a young mother-to-be, Zoe has embodied resources associated with youthfulness, such as enhanced health, energy, elasticity and renewal that give her a certain physical capital in enabling her to cope with the demands of motherhood. Zoe is attuned to these differences and offers a counterpoint to contemporary 'age-appropriate' discourses of first-time motherhood:

What's the difference between having a baby now and having a baby when you're older? There's still the [absence of] knowledge, you can't change the fact that you're gonna have a baby for the first time. No matter how old you are it's the same set of issues, you know, sleepless nights, breastfeeding, changing the baby and you're not gonna know any different because you're 17 or you're 30. Older people don't think like that. They judge you because you're young and having a baby ... I love being pregnant. I absolutely love it. I'd go through it again and again.

In claiming new motherhood as a universal experience, Zoe demonstrates her command of the knowledge necessary for her new role. Keen to assert that youth should not be a barrier to motherhood, she has enjoyed the embodied experience of pregnancy and is prepared for the transition to parenthood. Zoe's assertion of her readiness to parent has a poignant, double-edged quality. In a context where material resources to support a child are considered significant, Zoe's claim on motherhood can be seen as a fragile defence as well as a statement of desire.

In keeping with Zoe's reconstruction of motherhood, the 'charver kids' in Anoop's study could reposition and oppose popular representations of the 'charver'.

Jez: The thing that really annoys me is how certain newspapers act like they invented the chav (and for the record it's cha-r-v) and glamorise their lifestyle. People like [journalist] Julie Burchill really haven't got a clue, these [charvs] aren't people making a fashion statement and challenging class systems.

Jez's response identifies how local understandings (charv) have become supplanted by national stereotypes (chav). In particular he challenges the celebratory reading provided by the journalist and commentator Julie Burchill (2010) of chavs as heroic transgressors of bourgeois etiquette. Burchill has even appropriated the label for herself, but for her this is a 'choice' identity she has the power to assume or relinquish. As Jez suggests, most young people lack a similar mobility to move through class signs while remaining relatively unaffected; these signs adhered to them, their neighbourhoods and lifestyles so that in turn they too risked being stuck in place.

Even so, subtle transformations of meaning and new claims to respectability were in evidence. In the open web forum Anoop established with the BBC, young people made a qualitative distinction between the representational and the performative aspects of what it means to be a charver:

Steven: I think what people don't realise is that wearing 'charver' clothes or listening to 'charver' music doesn't make you a charver. They may look like one but a real charver (because the term does get thrown around these days) is basically a thug that is up to no good (e.g., smashing glass bottles off peoples' heads for no reason). I have respect for people that like the music and dress like that but aren't actually charver as they are decent human beings.

Anth: I listen to rave and have a pair of trackies. Does this mean I'm a charver? In the eyes of society I would be, and just for those two simple facts, I would be a thief, a binge drinker and have loads of kids. It's all a stereotype. Of course there will be people who wear trackies and listen to rave who will be what I describe above but this is a minority.

Aaron: Being a charver is about sticking in with a fashion with all your friends, respecting all your friends – and getting alcohol obviously.

While Steven associates 'real' charvers with violence, he constructs other young people who listen to hardcore music and wear casual leisure gear as 'decent human beings', thus refiguring popular representations of working-class youth. Whilst not denying the reality of violence in urban life, he does not accept it as intrinsic to impoverished youth communities. Similarly, Anth and Aaron affiliate with the subcultural aspects of charver style, wearing tracksuits and listening to rave, but disconnect from the thuggery casually attributed to young men like themselves. Their contributions avoid reducing charvers to animalistic typologies, a familiar trope in media reportage, or elevating them to 'noble savages' who can challenge bourgeois privilege and entitlement, as Burchill claims. In other words, these young people were enmeshed in a complex recalibration of what it means to be a charver, subtly distinguishing 'what you look like' from 'who you are'. What it means to 'be' a charver is then performed and embodied, as is illustrated in this extract from a discussion with a group of 11–12-year-olds:

Anoop: Are the charvers lads or girls?
Sam: Both. They all wear Kappa [brand].
Nicola: The boys do 'charver' [peroxide bleach-blonde] their fringe, actually.
[...]
Sam: All the charvers have a skinhead all the way round, and they shave it with just the fringe left.

In northeast England the trainers, tracksuits and street-wise ensemble 'is also about being hard, being survivalists in a brutalized, gendered, conservative culture' (Campbell, 1993, p. 273). Some young people Anoop encountered interpreted the overall appearance – fake tan, heavy jewellery, bleached hair – as 'bad taste' and a wilful display of lower-class credentials. However, young people living in stigmatized areas characterized by long-term intergenerational unemployment could resituate such interpretations:

Nicola: Our street isn't posh cos there's loads of charvers 'round our street.
Anoop: Who are the charvers?
Michelle: Like, they're from Nailton, like Nicky, with dyed bleached hair, like you [laughs at Nicola] and they all wear Kappa and they've got hair really lacquered back and they talk [affects deep voice] 'like this mon'.
[....]
Michelle: They're all clueless, wearing these baggy pants.
Nicola: Don't say 'clueless'.

[...]
Michelle: They hang 'round the shops and cars.
Nicola: We don't.

Nicola's challenging of representations of charvers as 'clueless' and 'hanging round' reveals a struggle for working-class respectability occurring between and within class fractions themselves. As Skeggs (1997, p. 6) has shown in her discussion of respectability amongst white working-class women, such representations 'are not straightforwardly reproduced but are resisted and transfigured in their daily enactment'. Nicola is willing to embody a charver identity (note her use of the term 'we'), but, nevertheless, refuses to be seen as 'clueless', thieving and not respectable. By portraying charver kids in these ways, other working-class youth implied by contrast that they were respectable, a continual iteration that only serves to evince their own insecurities and the 'emotional politics of class' (ibid., p. 162).

Given the derogatory connotations of the term charvers, it is generally presumed that it is wholly rejected. Steph Lawler argues that 'though the term chav/a now circulates widely in Britain as a term of disgust and contempt, it is imposed on people rather than being claimed by them' (Lawler, 2005, p. 802). However, detailed ethnography with young people suggests they have a more complex and ambivalent relationship to the term, deploying and appropriating its markers at certain moments and within particular peer situations. Thus Nicola's remarks are important in revealing the complex manner in which such heavily laden class identities are negotiated, rebutted and reworked. Similarly, some young people who spoke disparagingly about charver style in one context admitted that they were 'a bit charver' in their tastes for rave music and certain elements of fashion, which could be 'toned down' or 'played up' according to time and place. For them, being a charver could be a more mobile and flexible affiliation, not always anchored by a weight of negative affect:

Lil: Us charvers treat our mates like family, and respect them ...
Kathy: I have been classed as a charver for years now. I am 19 and since I was about 12 I have been classed as one. I don't wear fake trainers and tracksuits, now but the best for me. I may be a charver but I go to college and have been going for 3 years now and plan to be a barrister. I go to the new monkey [a Hardcore music event taking place in a Sunderland nightclub] and used to go every week. All I can say is don't judge a book by its cover.

Spoiled identities

In the extracts above, Lil and Kathy do not shy away from the label 'charver', but actually reconfigure it as 'respectful'. Lil interpellates herself as one of 'us charvers'; Kathy recognizes she is 'classed as a charver' and may even 'be charver', but argues that this is not a fixed, essentialist label. Such accounts challenge semiotic readings of chav culture that speak 'for' working-class respondents rather than engage in the serious art of listening (Back, 2007). They show how young people are critical agents who reject some aspects of social class stereotyping even as they acknowledge the existence of class formations. The ethnographic engagement further indicates how young people may partially identify as chavs/charvers, re-signify terminology or resist national media encoding through locally grounded and culturally inflected decoding.

Tracey, a mother of two writing on the Internet forum, explains how a charver identity is part of a broader coming of age:

Tracey: I am a 37 year-old married mum of 2 teenage girls (14–15) who are both 'charvers' they are both doing well at school, have each got their own set of friends. The clothes are expensive but if they did not wear them they would not look popular as they say! [...] Come on give the 'charvers' a break what else have they got to do when they finish school – sit in their bedrooms and then get a big shock when they leave school and go into the big wide world without seeing any of it!!!!!

While Tracey seems happy to locate her daughters within the vilified repertoire of the charver, she is quick to declare they are 'both doing well at school'. She also sees 'street knowledge' as a valuable asset of working-class experience and is scathing of the closeted 'bedroom culture' (McRobbie, 1978) associated with middle-class femininity and an increasingly domesticated childhood. Like our teen mother Zoe, Lil, Kathy and (to some extent) Tracey also expose the limits of media representations and authorial voices which symbolically decode and 'read off' meaning in abstraction from working-class experience. They suggest it is inadequate to deconstruct meaning from representations without paying close attention to the deep 'structures of feeling' (Williams, 1977) and complex social class dialogues happening at the level of everyday experience. By contrast, the ethnographic and Web-based data discussed here demonstrate how some young people may embrace or re-signify the term charver within local circuits of production and reshape it within their everyday 'youthscapes'. Rather than being simply a term of rebuke owned by middle-class subjects, it is revealed as a more subtle, mobile, contingent and flexible point of identification and dissimulation, even as it has come to be amplified and given new meaning through the wider 'circuit of culture' (Johnson, 1986).

As we have shown, the 'spoiled identities' (Goffman, 1963) of charver kids and young mothers can be figured differently when seen alongside the counter-articulations and understandings derived from marginalized working-class communities themselves. Here, we gain sharper insight into the struggle for representation as an activity that is open to contestation and always in process. Despite the intensities of feeling that bring into being the charver kid and teenage mother as societal figures of abjection and abhorrence, seemingly fixed taxonomies of class disparagement can also be momentarily rendered into sliding signifiers as young people contest, resist and struggle to overturn representations that cast them as 'filth', 'scum', 'dirty whites' and even subhuman. Their readings may displace, though not entirely remove, their feelings of stigma and abjection, and whilst they are partial, incomplete and forever subject to the power of dominant media representations, they reveal the value of eliciting the perspectives of marginalized youth, and their efforts to reconfigure social norms and hollow out the markings of stigma.

Note

The Making Modern Mothers study was funded by the ESRC Social Identities programme (RES 148-25-0057). The project team comprised Rachel Thomson, Mary Jane Kehily, Lucy Hadfield and Sue Sharpe.

References

Adams, M. and Raisborough, J. (2011). The self-control ethos and the 'chav': Unpacking cultural representations of the white working class. *Culture & Psychology 17*(1), 81–97.

Back, L. (2007). *The art of listening.* London: Routledge.

Becker, H. (1963). *The outsiders.* New York: Free Press.

Burchill, J. (2010). Those who call Jordan a chav are just insecure and undersexed. *The Independent,* 25 November.

Byrne, B. (2006). *White lives.* London: Routledge.

Campbell, B. (1993). *Goliath: Britain's dangerous places.* London: Methuen.

Clarke. A. (2004). Maternity and materiality: Becoming a mother in consumer culture. In J. Taylor, L. Laynes and D. Wozniak (eds) *Consuming motherhood.* New Brunswick, NJ: Rutgers University Press.

Cohen, S. (1972). *Folk devils and moral panics*. London: Paladin.

Goffman, E. (1963). *Stigma: Notes on the management of spoiled identities*. New York: Simon and Schuster.

Hall, S. (1980). Encoding/decoding. In S. Hall et al. (eds). *Culture, media, language*. London: Hutchinson.

Hall, S. and T. Jefferson (eds) (1976). *Resistance through rituals: Youth subcultures in postwar Britain*. London: Hutchinson.

Harris, A. (2004). *Future girl*. New York: Routledge.

Hayward, K. and Yar, M. (2006). The 'chav' phenomenon: consumption, media and the construction of a new underclass. *Crime, Media, Culture* 2(1), 9–28.

Hebdige, D. (1979). *Subculture: The Meaning of Style*. London: Routledge.

Johnson, R. (1986). The story so far. In D. Punter (ed.). *An Introduction to British Cultural Studies*. Harlow: Longman.

Jones, O. (2011). *Chavs: The Demonization of the Working Class*. London: Verso.

Kehily, M.J. and Thomson, R. (2011a). Displaying motherhood: representations, visual methods and the materiality of maternal practice. In Dermott, E. and Seymour, J. (eds). *Displaying Families*. Basingstoke: Palgrave.

Kehily, M.J. and Thomson, R. (2011b). Figuring families: Generation, situation and narrative in contemporary mothering. *Sociological Research Online* 16(4).

Lawler, S. (2005). *Mothering the self: Mothers, daughters, subjects*. London: Routledge.

McRobbie, A. (1978). Working class girls and the culture of femininity. In Centre for Contemporary Cultural Studies, *Women take issue*. London: Hutchinson.

McRobbie, A. (1994). *Postmodernism and popular culture*. London: Routledge.

Nayak, A. (2003). *Race, place and globalisation*. Oxford: Berg.

Nayak, A. (2006). Displaced masculinities: Chavs, youth and class in the post industrial city. *Sociology*, 40(5), 813–83.

Rhodes, J. (2011). 'It's not just them, it's whites as well': Whiteness, class and BNP support, *Sociology*, 45(1): 102–117.

Shildrick, T. and Macdonald, R. (1997). Biographies of exclusion: Poor work and poor transitions, *International Journal of Lifelong Education*, 26(5): 589–604.

Skeggs, B. (1997). *Formations of class and gender: Becoming respectable*. London: Sage.

Skeggs, B. (2004). *Class, self, culture*. London: Routledge.

Thomson, R., Kehily, M.J., Hadfield, L. and Sharpe, S. (2011). *Making modern mothers*. Bristol: Policy.

Tyler, I. (2001). Skin-tight: Celebrity, pregnancy and subjectivity. In S. Ahmed and J. Stacey (ed.) *Thinking through the skin*. London: Routledge.

Tyler, I. (2008). Chav mum, chav scum: Class disgust in contemporary Britain. *Feminist Media Studies*, 8(4), 17–34.

Walkerdine V., Lucey, H. and Melody, J. (2001) *Growing up girl*. Basingstoke: Palgrave Macmillan.

Williams, R. (1977). *Marxism and literature*. Oxford: Oxford University Press.

Willis, P. (1990) *Common culture: Symbolic work at play in the cultures of the young*. Milton Keynes: Open University Press.

Part IV
Participation

10
Youth Media and Its Global Digital Afterlife

Elisabeth Soep

As a researcher working at the intersection of youth, learning and media culture, I probably should have anticipated the extent to which digital developments have redefined our fields of study, research relationships, conceptual frameworks and strategies of analysis. Yet evidence of these changes took me by surprise when I was working on a book about youth media and learning (Soep and Chávez, 2010). My ethnographic site was Youth Radio, an organization where I play a dual role, as both participant – Senior Producer in the youth-driven newsroom – and researcher. I'd been associated with Youth Radio for eight years or so. At the time, I was reworking a chapter called 'Converged Literacy', about the new learning demands and opportunities created when young people produce media reaching massive audiences. In the chapter, I discussed a radio story a teenaged Youth Radio reporter, Finnegan Hamill, had produced called *Emails from Kosovo*, which excerpted his correspondence with a girl living in Kosovo just as war was breaking out in that region. The story turned out to be huge. It ran as an eight-part series on National Public Radio, was quoted verbatim by the then president Bill Clinton and subsequently won the prestigious Alfred I. DuPont award for journalistic excellence. All this attention and impact turned Finnegan into a public figure. He'd been reporting the news, and then he *became* the news – making appearances on CNN, The Today Show, even People Magazine.

Using this as a shining example, I was applauding the sophisticated literacy practices collaborative media projects can foster in young producers. And then, double-checking the spelling of his name, I came across a blog post Finnegan himself had written years after the series ran. Called *My Year as Kosovo Boy*, it included some harsh reflections on his experience. Describing how the Today Show host Katie Couric

169

asked him what he had learned from working on the series, Finnegan confessed to his blog readers, 'I couldn't think of a damn thing.'

It was a humbling moment, to say the least. I'd been developing an argument about all that young people can learn by producing high-impact media content; and then, through an Internet search, I accidentally discovered some crucial data I hadn't known existed that collided with my own analysis. Who was the observer here, and who the observed, I had to ask as I read Finnegan's blog, since as a researcher and producer at Youth Radio, I was both analysing and implicated in his critique.

I don't want to overstate the case. Youth media research has a tendency to assign a kind of automatic 'authenticity' to expressions of youth voice (Fleetwood, 2005) – as if hearing directly from young people is all we need to do to understand the complex and sometimes fraught meanings attached to youth-produced texts. Finnegan was already in his twenties when he wrote the post, looking back on a teen production. And although he raised some important questions about the relationship between media production and learning, these contributed to but did not trump the varied interpretations others, including his editors and peers at the time, the story's audiences and I, could legitimately put forth. But his account, and the fact that it, like my own, would be permanently available anywhere and at anytime, to anyone who had access to an online search engine, profoundly unsettled the conventional research dynamic. No longer can researchers who study youth media production single-handedly demarcate the beginnings, middles and ends of the processes we examine. The making and remaking continue long after we leave our field sites, beyond the superimposed and arbitrary boundaries we erect to wall off our units of analysis. Nor can researchers assume that it will be our academic peers, for the most part, who hold us accountable – in documented, public, retrievable ways – for our arguments and conclusions. Youth media producers themselves, as research 'subjects', have always formed their own interpretations and accounts of the experiences we analyse. What's different now is that they're publishing their assessments alongside our own.

In this chapter, I examine the digital afterlife of youth-produced content: what happens in the comments sections and link-rich online conversations that transpire past the 'completion' of a given media project. This phase of participation reflects the ease with which content circulates now, as a result of new technological and economic structures that enable users to share media across platforms, via 'social networks that link people through the exchange of meaningful bytes' (Jenkins,

Ford and Green, 2013). The digital afterlife of youth-made media is governed by a different set of players, agendas, stakes, consequences and rules of engagement than those associated with the original production process, especially in the case of projects originating from community-based organizations. Youth media projects typically aim to promote youth development and literacy as well as a range of other positive outcomes (Buckingham, 2003; Goldfarb, 2002; Kirwan, Learmonth, Sayer and Williams, 2003). Attesting to the ambitions behind these efforts, it takes practically a full paragraph for JoEllen Fisherkeller (2011, p. 2) to articulate a definition: '[Y]outh media projects and programs provide young people with a variety of intellectual, aesthetic, social, and technical knowledge and skills they need to use, comprehend, and evaluate media, and – especially – to create and circulate media that are variously critical, appreciative, and proactive in nature, thus providing youth with transformation opportunities.' Projects such as these are attracting new attention, and not just because they might be trans-formative: increasingly, they are also asked to fill gaps left by schools, entry-level jobs and other training contexts – once relied on by youth and backed by governments – to build skills and professional pathways.

This cluster of prosocial goals and practices is not necessarily shared by participants who join the conversation post-production. Nor are these afterlife producers beholden to funders or non-profit norms, which often operate somewhere behind the products youth organizations release to the world, as evidence of both mission-driven achievements and grant-driven compliance.

Researchers know little about the imaginative work that takes place inside the new digital 'architectures' for co-creation (Karaganis and Jeremijenko, 2007; Sefton-Green, 2005) or about their implications for study methods. Ethnographers are always creating and negotiating boundaries. What information do we consider? What do we leave out of data collection and analysis? When do we start looking? When do we stop? These matters of site and time (the what and when questions) are less straightforward than ever for researchers who focus on digital media production. We investigate processes and products that by defini-tion spread and sprawl, via links, uploads and downloads and remixes, and that have the potential to be never-ending and ever-extending, as authors and users keep on making and engaging, long after the original work has been published. In a sense, even the absence of 'conversation' below a youth-produced media post is its own kind of statement, an empty comment field, often marked with a bleak 'comment (0)', publicly branding the product as failing to engage an audience.

In light of such developments in digital culture, I examine here the meanings and politics of researchers' protocols for 'bounding' our sites and times of study, advocating the anthropological framework of 'multi-sited ethnography' (Marcus, 1998) even within single sites. I argue also for a conception of youth culture that aims to reconcile two contradictory realities. On the one hand, key social achievements including agency and transnational identity, to name two, are best understood not as fixed states but emergent, irregular and contingent processes that shift over time. On the other hand, increasingly, young people's expressions of these processes through media are harnessed and algorithmically reorganized through digital channels youth and their mentors can neither predict nor control. This set of conditions calls for new literacy practices, which I'll return to at the chapter's end (indebted to Zuckerman, 2011).

The research site on which I focus here is Youth Radio–Youth Media International, a hybrid youth development organization and professional production company headquartered in Oakland, California, with bureaus and correspondents across the United States. The coverage is transnational, with stories developed by young people in Afghanistan, Iraq, Ireland, Israel, Palestine, India, Pakistan, South Africa, Ghana and other locations throughout the world. Founded in 1992 by Ellin O'Leary with San Francisco Bay Area high school students Deverol Ross, Chano Soccarras, Ayoka Medlock, Noah Nelson and Jacinda Abcarian, the organization serves primarily low-income youth and young people of colour, recruited for its free programmes from local under-resourced, re-segregating public schools. Students can move from introductory to advanced after-school converged media classes into paid internships as peer educators, facility administrators, reporters, producers and engineers (approximately 50 young people annually are on payroll at any given time). The organization's production company, Youth Media International, generates content for its own website; outlets including National Public Radio, The Huffington Post, National Geographic, PBS and the San Francisco Chronicle; as well as local commercial and public radio stations, niche blogs, YouTube, and the Internet's varied social media sites. Having won US broadcast journalism's most prestigious honours, including the George Foster Peabody and Edwards R. Murrow Awards as well as the DuPont for *Emails from Kosovo*, the organization is unusual. And yet Youth Radio's engagement with young people as media producers, and its work across formats (audio, video, photography, print) and platforms (online, broadcast, mobile), provide a rich context for analysing dynamics affecting both makers and researchers at a contradictory moment of promise and challenge (Soep, 2007).

I work at Youth Radio as a maker alongside young people, within a model I have characterized elsewhere as 'collegial pedagogy' (Chávez and Soep, 2005), and I also research our own work and related projects across the United States, with a focus on implications for learning, literacy and civics. This double perspective of researcher and producer is not always comfortable, and certainly there are things I can't (or don't want to) see because I am 'in' the work and not standing outside. But, indebted to traditions of community-based participatory research and participant action research (Morrell, 2004; Torre and Fine, 2006), it is my view that there are also special affordances that come with this unorthodox research position. Equally relevant here is a capacity to watch what happens to individual media projects long after an outside researcher would probably have moved on, and to participate with young people in navigating how that afterlife unfolds.

Youth media examined

Youth media researchers have bound their units of analysis and sites of study in various ways. There are surveys of the field that seek trends and patterns evident across practice and scholarship – for example, studies that identify the range of organizational goals espoused, media genres taught and populations served, or those pinpointing the tendency for researchers to advocate for youth media's benefits rather than explore deeply its contradictions and limitations (Buckingham, Burn and Willett, 2005). There are regularly released reports by the Pew Research Center, the Kaiser Family Foundation, Harvard University's Berkman Center for Internet and Society and others, tracking rapidly changing habits in media and technology usage and spotlighting hot-button issues ranging from cyber-safety to social media's role in domestic and global conflict. Qualitative research tends to deploy case study and ethnographic methods to examine implications of media practices within and beyond schools for key dimensions of youth development, social organization and the formation of multiliteracies, sometimes grounding analysis in up-close study of individual organizations and projects within which researchers play various roles (e.g., Chavez and Soep, 2005; Fleetwood, 2005; Hull, 2003).

A recent wave of research arising from the MacArthur Foundation's Digital Media and Learning initiative offers the category of 'genres of participation' as one way to organize research data and locate young people's everyday media practices within broader social and cultural 'ecologies' that have significant implications for learning and the production of both opportunity and inequality, even when these activities take place outside environments centred on explicit instruction (Davidson and Goldberg, 2009; Ito, 2010; Seiter, 2008). While it points to digital media's promising potential for literacy development and new modes of participatory politics, this research also warns of the dangers of overstating young people's digital sophistication and underestimating the importance of sustained digital equity efforts, opportunities for youth–adult collaboration and programming that fosters analysis and critique (Buckingham, 2011; Livingstone, 2008; Watkins, 2011). Overall, it's a growing literature that creates a foundation for further efforts to apply the very insights that have emerged from analysis of our research subjects' media ecologies – for example, the implications of the Internet's permanence and searchability on youth identity and literacy – to understanding our own methods for gathering data and generating knowledge about youth culture in a global context.

Production cycle remixed

Youth media researchers often time both fieldwork and analysis to coincide with a four-part production process. Typically, creative media projects start with preproduction (researching, preparing and planning). Next comes production, when participants collect the materials they need to tell their stories, followed by post-production organizing, editing, crafting and polishing the finished product. Finally, data collection will sometimes extend to a phase of distribution, tracking how media products circulate among audiences, whether goals were met and desired impacts achieved.

Shifts in digital technology and media culture have already reconfigured the order, pacing and gatekeeping mechanisms that have traditionally governed these four production phases. These changes convert the production process from a predictable sequence of steps into a cycle without a given starting or stopping point, or fixed pathway from start to finish.

For example, due to the proliferation of user-generated media outlets, a producer might start with the fourth phase, distribution, by curating existing digital content and reposting it with a bit of added context on a website's front page – turning dissemination into an act of creation. A video game player or writer of 'fan fiction' might start at number three, essentially post-producing someone else's media by hacking into an existing game's code, or retooling another author's narrative, thus transforming the media experience into something new. The widespread availability of 'everyday media' (e.g., home videos and digital photos, archived voicemail recordings) can launch a creative project at number two, mid-production, with recordings in hand, around which the maker only later frames a narrative. These and other examples show that media production doesn't necessarily start at the beginning, if we imagine the beginning as a process of pulling an original idea out of the air, or from the inner resources of an individual's mind. Rarely does the process march forward without lots of stopping short, reversing course and circling back to start again. Such shifts are not determined by digital technology: artists have long experimented with collage, appropriation and found object installation, reordering creative cycles that assume starting with the (metaphorical) blank canvas. That said, digital tools and practices seem to make these activities more accessible, available and visible to youth producers.

These shifts in the production cycle have serious implications for how we frame and thus study youth cultural production. By now it is commonplace to argue against a view of culture as a group to which an individual belongs. We know that culture, like literacy, is generated, again and again, through moment-to-moment interactions within social contexts (Gee, 2000; Street, 1984). The advent of social media, which brought us blogs like Finnegan's, takes the interactivity behind creative production to a whole new level – and pulls that participatory dimension to the front and centre. Now it's not just the author, delivering a fixed and polished message. Rather, expressing oneself through social media means launching and sustaining a conversation with various 'networked publics', members of which the originator of the work may know and even admire, but never control. danah boyd (2007) has argued that young people use social media platforms to write themselves and their communities into being. They are doing more than authoring their own lives and identities. They are creating contexts in which others can respond to, repurpose and sometimes subvert their messages. That online community can take the original creative content in entirely new directions, whether the 'first author' likes it or not. This has always been the case for artists and producers who send their work into the world and surrender control over its interpretation and use. What's different as a result of social media is that the feedback loops are coded directly into the original product, through comment streams and search engine algorithms.

Recycling research

Just as the boundary between the creator's expression and the public's uptake is disappearing, so too is the conventional ethnographic compartmentalization of research sites. Ethnographic methods have always heavily invested in the demarcation of proper field sites, so much so that tales of entering and exiting the field are a full-blown subgenre within ethnographic writing (Pratt, 1986). 'Stories of entry and exit usually appear on the margins of texts,' according to Gupta and Ferguson (1997, p. 12), 'providing the narrative with uncertainty and expectation at the beginning and closure at the end.' They imbue ethnographic texts with an aura of authenticity – an 'I was there' quality – and bestow authority by highlighting the difference and distance between researcher and researched considered necessary for the ethnographer to maintain analytical perspective. He or she typically 'writes up' the study after separating from the field, and '[t]emporal succession therefore traces the natural sequence of sites that completes a spatial journey into Otherness' (Gupta and Ferguson, 1997, p. 12).

Gupta and Ferguson's emphasis on temporality is especially germane to the ways in which digital culture interrupts research protocols. Johannes Fabian (1983) argues that time in ethnography is never neutral, but an instrument to impose order that can deny 'coevalness' between researcher and researched. Fabian bases his argument on a critique of traditional ethnographies, wherein anthropologists live with their research subjects for an extended but finite period of time: 'the ethnographer will be an ethnographer only if he outlives them, i.e., if he moves *through* the Time he may have shared with them into a level on which he finds anthropology' (Fabian, 1983, p. 61).

'Finding anthropology' is, in Fabian's sense, about enclosing research subjects in their own time-frame, using ethnographic writing and analysis as a way to rise above the everyday rhythms, clocks and calendars of the people who animate our research. The concept of 'rising above' is key here, pointing to the implicit (though unsubtle) hierarchy that sets in when research relationships are so fundamentally out of sync, as if time stands still for research subjects, who are caught in an everlasting present, while researchers move forward, marking progress even in the act of taking leave. With these critiques in mind, I want to apply Fabian's argument to contemporary ethnographies of digital culture, which, likewise, can be faulted for containing our subjects in time-frames of their own. If my initial characterization of *Emails from Kosovo* depended on a separation between the time of Finnegan's production and my own analysis, his blog post pulled the two of us face to face within the same temporality. This kind of activity will happen increasingly in youth media research, as 'subjects' publicly author their own accounts of the very same experiences we describe, and as they find themselves engaged and sometimes embroiled in conversations with online interlocutors long after they thought they'd moved on – even 'aged out' – of their media production assignments. It behooves us as researchers not to wait for individual young people to pull us back into 'coevalness', but to craft methods and strategies of analysis that follow projects across digital space and time.

Web two dot whoa?

Fast forward exactly ten years from the time when the *Emails from Kosovo* series hit big, and Youth Radio once again was at work on a story touching on transnational themes of war. This time, a newsroom reporter from Oakland, Pendarvis Harshaw, produced a story from Northern Ireland for National Public Radio's *All Things Considered*, on relations between young Catholics and Protestants living on either side of the 'peace wall' in western Belfast. The story opened like this:

Pendarvis Harshaw:	Inside a Belfast classroom, a group of girls giggles and paints pictures of American celebrities. It feels like a teenager's bedroom.
Unidentified Girl #1:	I want to be a lawyer when I grow up, and I want to go to Harvard University.
–	
Unidentified Girl #2:	I just want to be a pop star.
Harshaw:	This working-class part of Belfast has the same problems as any inner city: a high rate of teen pregnancy, and young people at the risk of drug abuse. The classroom windows are covered by bomb-proof bars. They're left over from the constant violence in this area only 10 years ago, Catholic-Protestant violence known as The Troubles.
	Murals are painted on almost every corner building. The murals show war heroes and battle slogans, telling the story of why West Belfast is divided by what's called the Peace Wall.

Pendarvis's story goes on to explore the enduring effects of The Troubles in this region for a generation whose parents rioted in the streets, and now send their offspring to programmes aimed at Catholic–Protestant reconciliation. The story closes on an image reflecting how things have changed:

Harshaw: Our guide stopped at a red light and pointed out a fully armored Range Rover. He said 10 years ago, this was the only kind of police car in the city. We only saw one bulletproof SUV our entire trip.
For NPR News, I'm Pendarvis Harshaw.

Hours after Pendarvis's broadcast, tensions surfaced in the first two comments on National Public Radio's website – tensions surrounding what constitutes 'proper English' and who deserves a prominent place in the national media. The comments read:

I don't mind the 'youth' part of youth radio ... today's story on Belfast had interesting information, and the reporter sounded engaged in the subject ... HOWEVER I cringed each time he said 'belfass' 'behrum' (bedroom) ETC. ETC. PLEASE! PLEASE! Standard American English for ALL American reporters!

Four things make me change stations: (1) Pledge breaks. (2) This I believe. (3) Story Corps. and (4) Youth Radio.[1] Sorry, but I tune to NPR for reports from professional adult journalists. But NPR seems to want to keep reverting to amateur hour. Maybe these kids would be better off spending their time on real academic subjects.

Youth Radio stories in general, and Pendarvis's in particular, often receive major accolades: these two critical comments are not therefore typical. However, they do show how tricky it is to anticipate how any given project will be received and to determine the best course of action once that conversation gets under way.

The assumptions in these criticisms say more, of course, about US linguistic, racial and academic ideologies than they do about Pendarvis's actual story, but I asked him what went through his head when he read them. Seven months had passed, and he laughed, 'What is the "standard English" between an African American man and a group of Irish people? No one speaks the queen's English in that conversation!' But still, at the time of the broadcast, he was discouraged. He had a long talk with Youth Radio's News Director, Nishat Kurwa, who'd been with him in Ireland, about his frustration. What was the point, he wondered, of doing journalism, if this was the reaction he was going to get? It was further evidence of something he already knew: that in reporting for public broadcasting audiences, he wasn't reaching 'his demographic': 'I'm not talking to an audience I care about.'

After that conversation, Nishat emailed the newsroom's production team with the subject line, 'Web 2.0 – when it's personal'. She included the two comments, noting that the 'personal' nature of such unregulated responses are part of what Youth Radio has to wrestle with more than other production companies, given the organization's positive youth development goals, in its efforts to engage online audiences.

There followed some email discussions about whether Youth Radio or Pendarvis himself should respond. One of the defining principles of what is known as 'Web 2.0' is the idea that you need to trust your users: website publishers should create the space for others to bury or argue down the comments they disagree with, and to reinforce the material that resonates.

The problem with this logic is what happens when there's a significant gap between the author's social values and identities (what Pendarvis calls 'my demographic') and the 'community' he or she reaches through any given media outlet. Will a community 'self regulate', in Web 2.0 terminology, automatically, or do they require intentional intervention?

Two days after Nishat's email, three more comments appeared:

[...]Mr Harshaw did an incredible job on his report. If I recall correctly any individual could contribute to National Public Radio, not just professional adult journalist. Perhaps, if listeners spent more time listening to the content of his report, as opposed to trying to create alleged word mispronounciations, they would have grasped the effectiveness of the story.

[....] Do you honestly mean to tell me that learning about world history and current events is not a 'real' academic subject?!?!?! In an age where the youth would rather be watching MTV and playing video games you want to cut down a young man who is trying to expand his boundaries? ... I have had the blessing to meet Mr Harshaw and he is THE MOST knowledgeable and insightful people I have met on Howard's campus. Keep up the good work Pen :)

[...] Bigotry with the tagline 'Standard American English for ALL American Reporters!' is a shameful slogan designed by someone with a blind spot about who creates the 'standard' American English in our country. And if someone does not care for [...] Youth Radio, why not just move along? Why be so bitter about it [...] Thank you, Mr Harshaw. I for one loved your piece on Belfast.

The adult production staff was pleased by these comments. Look, the community regulated itself, the Web 2.0 logic worked! Except, there was more to the story than we realized. Pendarvis had taken matters into his own hands.

'Why are they coming at my neck on NPR?' paraphrases the status update Pendarvis remembers posting on his Facebook profile after his Ireland story aired, with a link to the piece. 'My friends don't listen to NPR,' he explains, 'but [if] I put up something with an interesting, juicy heading, they'll click on it, and if they feel so inclined, they'll respond to it.' Pendarvis had more than 2000 Facebook friends and says he got lots of support from that network, mostly telling him to 'keep doing your work', and not to 'trip off the haters'. It reversed the crushing experience of reading the initial negative comments. He adds, 'It's a tremendous feeling that you can connect your friends, knowing their habits, they receive their news from TMZ or allhiphop.com, and I can connect them to a story on National Public Radio.' Crucially, he's making that connection via content he had created, highlighting the importance of enabling young people otherwise marginalized from digital and media privilege to participate as producers and not just audiences in these contexts, no matter how active and vocal those audiences can now be.

A case for multi-sitedness

What's striking in this account is that so much of the action took place after the piece was technically finished. Researchers who study creativity and literacy have a strong set of tools to draw from in analysing the work involved in making dispatches like Pendarvis's. We need to build up new repertoires for examining the digital afterlives of these stories, methods to investigate how 'post–post-production' activities relate not only to the initial production process but also to larger questions about imagination, agency and identity as social achievements. There are new political, organizational and even legal considerations involved in creating work that generates 'participation' among audiences and online communities. How do youth media producers and their collaborators monitor, navigate and create momentum behind the content they generate, even when comments get ugly? Even when organizational missions are at stake? Even when laws protecting intellectual property, privacy and safety are sometimes violated through digital manifestations of everything from content appropriation to hate speech?

To address such questions requires 'a mode of study that cares about, and pays attention to, the interlocking of multiple social–political sites and locations' (Gupta and Ferguson, 1997, p. 37). It calls for research strategies that can sense movements and ripple effects across on- and offline activities and can notice creative and cultural practices that defy that dichotomization. We need methods that acknowledge the connections that interlock our varied research 'sites and locations' within architectures young people navigate in the course of their daily lives.

One resource for developing that mode of study lies in the methodological approach of 'multi-sited ethnography'. This approach rejects the still dominant (though widely critiqued) conception of culture as a phenomenon contained within a single place, a kind of inherited membership possessed by a defined group of people (for critique see Varenne and McDermott, 1998; Pratt, 1986). Ethnography practiced the old-fashioned way has been governed by a principle of immersion followed by departure and writing up. While 'we learn a great deal from such studies,' argue Dimitriadis and Weis (2006, p. 478), 'what we do not know is what happens to them after they leave these specific locations.' Multi-sited ethnography, according to Marcus (1998), operates instead on a principle of migration, 'following' people, objects, metaphors, conflicts, tensions, plotlines, across time and space.

And so we have a real methodological opportunity, to treat even our studies of individual field sites or circumscribed media projects as 'multi-sited' investigations. Pendarvis's original production of the Ireland story was set in Belfast itself. A second site was Youth Radio's newsroom, where he collaboratively crafted the story's script and audio mix. A third site could be defined transactionally, via the editorial process between Youth Radio and National Public Radio. And then there is the site of the online conversation described here, the afterlife of his broadcast that constituted its own context for creative expression and contestation deploying digital tools. Each of these sites is driven by its own histories, cognitive and aesthetic demands, politics and opportunities for hope and disappointment. The timeline that runs through these varied sites is considerably more prolonged than a conventional framing of creative production confined to the work that goes into generating a piece of media in the first place. And crucially, it's a timeline that never truly ends, even after the comments stop and Pendarvis has moved on, because the material is permanently available as part of an ever-moving digital culture and structure.

The same conditions transforming research methods also force us to reimagine some key dimensions of youth culture in the age of global media. Youth culture scholars including myself have for some time now argued that 'youth' is not a fixed category but contingent and dynamic; that agency is not a thing to obtain but an uneven, often fleeting social act; that cosmopolitan or transnational citizenship is not a permanent assignation but a mode of interacting and belonging that emerges through gestures and moments of connection (Fisherkeller, 2011; Maira and Soep, 2004). Certainly, activities in the digital afterlife keep youth media dynamic, in the sense that its meanings are continually reworked through public uptake. But one must now ask what happens to all this fluidity when young people's media expressions are rendered permanent and hard-coded through algorithms that determine how content is discovered, searched and circulated?

The afterlife creates records that are difficult if not impossible to undo, including searchable artefacts that never used to exist. And the means by which those records are ordered and presented – through, for example, Google search engine results – are determined by institutional forces and engineering and business decisions into which young people can have little insight, and over which they can exercise little power.

Cathy Davidson (2011) has made the case that thinking 'algorithmically' belongs right up there alongside 'reading, writing and 'rithmetic' as a key dimension of literacy today. The writer Teju Cole (2012) critiques the failure of some producers and audiences to think 'constellationally' in the face of global media projects that reduce enormously complex social conditions to neat narratives appealing uncritically to the popular desire to feel like a saviour. Thinking algorithmically means understanding how codes structure information. Thinking constellationally means connecting the dots, and refusing to reach for the simplest and most self-satisfying explanation or course of action. In the story of Pendarvis's reporting project and its digital afterlife, we start to see some of the concrete literacy practices that underlie these interconnected modes of thinking. Rather than rely on one-way distribution, Pendarvis mobilized allies to bring reception of his story back on track. In so doing, he activated 'latent publics', meaning associates whose connection to Pendarvis might have little to do with the themes of his Ireland story, but who can be skilfully engaged and provoked into action (Soep, forthcoming; Zuckerman, 2011). Finally, Pendarvis knew how to nurture his network as evident in those follow-up comments challenging the initial two harsh ones. Media makers call it 'link love'. It's an often tacit and nuanced system of circulating attention for media content by promoting the work of peers and thereby setting oneself up for that same kind of support when you need it the most.

These dimensions of literacy are not the activities we most often use to describe what it takes for young people to participate fully in digital media and learning. And yet I would argue that just as we need new methods for understanding our joint activities in this realm, so too do we need ways to recognize and support the many incarnations of literacy in youth media's global digital afterlife.

Acknowledgements

I am grateful for the support given to the Youth and Participatory Politics research network by the John D. and Catherine T. MacArthur Foundation. This chapter is adapted from Soep (2010), with permission from Taylor and Francis Books.

Note

1. 'Pledge drives' are the periods of time public broadcasting stations set aside by interrupting programming to solicit donations from audiences. 'This I Believe' and 'Story Corps' are both independent public radio projects that invite listeners to submit content for radio broadcast.

References

boyd, d. (2007). Friends, friendsters, and top 8: Writing community into being on social networking sites. *First Monday*. www.firstmonday.org/issues/issue11_12/boyd/ date accessed 15 January 2008.

Buckingham, D. (2011). Youth media production in the digital age: Some reflections – and a few provocations. In J. Fisherkeller (ed.) *International perspectives on youth media: Cultures of production and education* (pp. 375–380). New York: Peter Lang.

Buckingham, D. (2003). *Media education: Literacy, learning and contemporary culture*. Cambridge: Polity Press.

Buckingham, D., Burn, A. and Willett, R. (2005). *The media literacy of children and young people*. London: Ofcom.

Chávez V. and Soep, E. (2005). Youth radio and the pedagogy of collegiality. *Harvard Educational Review*. 75(4), 409–434.

Cole, T. (2012). The white savior industrial complex. *The Atlantic Monthly*. http://www.theatlantic.com/international/archive/2012/03/the-white-savior-industrial-complex/254843/, date accessed 5 May 2012.

Davidson, C. (2011). *Now you see it*. New York: Viking.

Davidson, C. and Goldberg, D. (2009). *The future of learning institutions in a digital age*. Cambridge: MIT Press.

Dimitriadis, G. and Weis, L. (2006). Multisited ethnographic approaches in urban education today. In J. Kinchelo (Ed.). *The Praeger handbook of urban education* (pp. 451–460). Westport: Greenwood Press.

Fabian, J. (1983). *Time and the other: How anthropology makes its object*. New York: Columbia University Press.

Fisherkeller, J. (ed.). (2011). *International perspectives on youth media: Cultures of production and education*. New York: Peter Lang.

Fleetwood, N. (2005). Authenticating practices: Producing realness, performing youth. In S. Maira and E. Soep (eds), *Youthscapes: The popular, the national, the global* (pp. 155–172). Philadelphia: University of Pennsylvania Press.

Fleetwood, N. R. (2005) 'Mediating youth: community-based video production and the politics of race and authenticity' *Social Text* 23(1): 83–109.

Gee, J. (2000). The new literacy studies: From 'socially situated' to the work of the social. In D. Barton and M. Hamilton (eds). *Situated literacies* (pp. 180–196). London: Routledge.

Goldfarb, B. (2002). *Visual pedagogy: Media cultures in and beyond the classroom*. Durham: Duke University Press.

Gupta, A. and Ferguson, J. (eds) (1997). *Anthropological locations: Boundaries and grounds of a field science* (pp. 1–46). Berkeley: University of California Press.

Hull, G. (2003). Youth culture and digital media: New literacies for new times. *Research in the Teaching of English*, *38*(2), 229–233.

Ito, M. (2010). *Hanging out, messing around, geeking out: Kids living and learning with new media*. Cambridge, MA: MIT Press.

Jenkins, H., Ford, S. and Green, J. (2013). *Spreadable media: Creating value and meaning in a networked culture*. New York: NYU Press.

Karaganis, J. and Jeremijenko, N. (2007). (eds) *Structures of participation in digital culture*. Durham: Duke University Press.

Kirwan, T., Learmonth, J., Sayer, M. and Williams, R. (2003). *Mapping media literacy*, http://www.ofcom.org.uk/static/archive/itc/uploads/Mapping_media_literacy1.pdf, accessed 17 January 2008.

Livingstone, S. (2008). Taking risky opportunities in youthful content creation: Teenagers' use of social networking sites for intimacy, privacy and self-expression. *New Media & Society*, *10*(3), 393–411.

Maira, S. and Soep, E. (eds) (2004). *Youthscapes: The popular, the national, the global*. Philadelphia: University of Pennsylvania Press.

Marcus, G. (1998). *Ethnography through thick and thin*. Princeton: Princeton University Press.

Morrell, E. (2004). *Becoming critical researchers: Literacy and empowerment for urban youth*. New York: Peter Lang.

Pratt, M. L. (1986). Linguistic Utopias. In N. Fabb, D. Attridge, A. Durant, and C. McCabe (eds) *The linguistics of writing* (pp. 48–66). New York: Methuen.

Sefton-Green, J. (2005). Timelines, timeframes, and special effects: Software and creative media production. *Education, Communication, and Information*, *4*(1), 99–110.

Seiter, E. (2008). Revisiting 'old' media: Learning from media histories. In T. McPherson (Ed.), *Digital youth, innovation, and the unexpected* (pp. 27–52). Cambridge: MIT Press.

Soep, E. (2007). Working the crowd: Youth media interactivity. In S. B. Heath and D. Lapp (eds), *Handbook of literacy research: Visual, communicative and performative arts* (pp. 271–278). Mahwah, NJ: Lawrence Erlbaum.

Soep, E. (2010). Research methods for web two dot whoa. In P. Thompson and J. Sefton-Green (eds), *Researching creative learning: Methods and approaches* (pp. 185–196). London: Routledge.

Soep, E. (forthcoming). Participatory politics: Next-generation tactics for remaking public spheres. MIT Reports.

Soep, E. and Chávez, V. (2010). *Drop that knowledge: Youth Radio stories*. Berkeley: University of California Press.

Street, B. (1984). *Literacy in theory and practice*. Cambridge: Cambridge University Press.

Torre, M. and Fine, M. (2006). Researching and resisting: Democratic policy research by and for youth. In S. Ginwright, P. Noguera, and J. Cammarota (eds), *Beyond resistance! Youth activism and community change* (pp. 269–286). New York: Routledge.

Varenne, H. and McDermott, R. (1998). *Successful failure: The school America builds*. Boulder: Westview Press.

Watkins, C. (2011). Digital divide: Navigating the digital edge. *International Journal of Learning and Media*, *3*(2), 1–12.

Zuckerman, E. (2011). What if Tunisia had a revolution and nobody watched? http://www.ethanzuckerman.com/blog/topics/global-voices/page/2/, accessed 5 May 2012.

11
Claiming Content and Constructing Users: User-generated Content and BBC Blast

Helen Thornham and Angela McFarlane

Introduction: interrogating the individualized, autonomous new media 'user'

This chapter utilizes key findings from a research project investigating teenage user-generated content, creativity and learning on 'Blast', an initiative by the BBC, the UK's public service broadcaster, which ran between 2004 and 2010. It was an on- and offline resource for teenagers, encompassing a range of creative strands (film, music, dance, games, writing, fashion, art and design). The website allowed teenagers to view, comment on and upload creative material: it included a showcase section, message boards, blogs and short instructive clips from professionals in the field. In addition, the project included an eight-month touring workshop, links with local educational and creative groups, televisual output, film and videomaking competitions in conjunction with Media Trust, work placements and work experience for young people. Sustained by user-generated content and with the notion of creative autonomy at its heart, BBC Blast was both inherently flawed and truly exciting. As John Millner, the Executive Producer, noted in the foreword to our 2008 report:

> Blast is the BBC's most ambitious and sustained experiment to date in user-generated content ... Blast aims to be a catalyst and incubator of teenagers' creative skills in the fields of art and design, music, dance, video, gaming, writing and fashion ... by the beginning of 2007 Blast was growing fast, mounting a nationwide roadshow of creative workshops, attracting tens of thousands of uploads of young creatives' work to its online galleries, and generating real excitement from everyone who came into contact with the project. (McFarlane and Thornham, 2008, p. 3)

This chapter draws on our research in order to critique three key issues in relation to new media. The first is the widely constructed conception of the user of new media in individualized terms (for instance in Rheingold, 1992, 1994, 2002; Castells, 2009 and Jenkins, 2006; as critiqued by Fenton and Barassi, 2011; Prensky, 2011), a construction that is doubly exacerbated by the discourse of the digital native found in youth studies and beyond (for critical analyses of this notion see Bennett *et al.*, 2008; Lange and Ito, 2010; Thomas, 2011; Thornham and McFarlane, 2011). The second issue relates to the value placed on uploaded content, which is often taken as evidence or affirmation of what Castells calls 'the practices of [creative] autonomy' (Castells, 2009, p. 129), thereby resonating with the construction of the user of new media noted above. Both these notions rely on a dichotomous understanding of 'new' media and their users as 'more' active, representative and interactive than 'old' media and their audiences. Consequently, our third argument is that these constructions offer a blanket approach to both content and users, one that tends to conceptualize new media in singular terms, where uploading becomes a linear action into and onto the technology. None of them represent what are complex, plural and iterative processes of mediation (a point made by many media and cultural theorists such as Bassett, 2001; Barker and Petley, 2001; Thornham, 2011b; Walkerdine, 2007). Interrogating these constructions through the lens of our research data, we argue that uploaded content and the new media user should be conceptualized in relation to a much wider iterative, dialogic process rather than, for example, in accordance with Castells's notion of creative 'autonomy'. Here we draw on José van Dijck (2009, 2011) and Jodi Dean (2008) who argue for the need to contextualize online content 'itself' and to interrogate the claims made about such content in terms of impact and interaction.

Such arguments move beyond the context of youth online engagement. Thus, although BBC Blast was a digital resource aimed at teenagers, and despite the clear connection in discourses emanating from youth studies and users of new media, we position our research within the much broader field of new media studies. Primarily this is because our findings resonate beyond the perforated edges of youth studies and beyond a specific focus on creative work. Moreover, when positioned within the wider framework of new media *per se*, these findings highlight a need for engagement with *how* we value online content. This is an increasingly pertinent issue for a digital age as we see key media and government institutions assuming that making material accessible, transparent and searchable online will allow individuals to create and co-create content and show that government is empowering its citizens; and as social media content is claimed as evidence of participation or engagement.[1] Before addressing the central issues of the chapter outlined above, we offer a brief synopsis of our research into Blast, which was much broader in terms of scope and length than can be detailed here (more comprehensive accounts can be found in Thornham and McFarlane (2011) and on www.bbc.co.uk/blogs/knowledgeexchange/bristol.pdf).

Researching teenage media creativity and learning

Our research into Blast began in 2007 and involved two distinct projects,[2] connected by the overall need to understand engagement and mediation with and within the initiative. The first project (2007–9) investigated the potentials for creative learning dialogue on Blast – identifying creative learning as iterative, dialogic, *supported* and to a certain extent tied to the creative 'affordances' of technology and in particular Web 2.0. These conceptions of creativity were firmly embedded in the ethos of the resource (Blast described itself as aiming to 'inspire' and 'equip' young people to be creative[3]) and in the various modes of engagement that were supported through mentoring systems and technological facilities. The second project (2009–10) investigated authorship, motivations, quality and values of creativity from the perspective of both the teenage users and the Blast team. The rationale for the second project was partly related to our central concern that creativity as a process was rarely evidenced in the final uploaded and showcased work. Indeed, if we were really interested in creativity, we needed to understand the process of engagement with – and beyond – Blast. Consequently we interviewed and observed teenagers in relation to their motivations and use of the resource, and considerations about their work. It is on these findings that we draw here. We also surveyed comparable websites, most of which, we found, also operated within the creative learning parameter (with the emphasis on the latter), and tended to separate learning (as tied to school curriculum) from creativity (as a reward for learning).

Subsequently in 2011, to address the changing landscape of the BBC and reflect on our research, we interviewed a number of people involved with Blast, many of whom continue to work within the Future Media remit of the BBC. These interviews revealed an understanding of broadcaster–audience relationship as more dialogic and less one way than before; a wider move towards what the BBC call the Digital Public Space;[4] and an increasing insistence on the inadequacy of the concept of 'user-generated content' for understanding audiences/users. Nonetheless, there were still no appropriate frameworks or tools with which to understand (young) people's creative online content and how it might be valued, or to substantiate the claims that we make about it. The need for such a framework is even more pressing when, as we suggested above, digital content is increasingly being taken as evidentiary for user engagement and creativity, and the increasing accessibility of previously 'owned' content proclaimed as a participatory, creative and even a democratic act.

In what follows, we outline the notions of user-generated content as they relate to Blast and bleed into the construction of young people as digital users. We address some of the problematic slippages and assumptions entwined in these conceptions before arguing that rather than assume that online content is evidence of individual intention, creative expression or autonomy, we understand it as something else – something that, when located in a context of motivations, of users, of iterative interaction may be more akin to what Dean has called (drawing on Žižek, 1997) a 'culture of interpassivity' and 'fetish of connectivity' (2008, p. 109), where the technological potential has overtaken, and even replaced, a more complex and contextually specific (sociocultural, economic, personal, relational) understanding of mediation or interaction.

Individualism and the digital native

In 2007, when the research project began, user-generated content seemed to encapsulate the attempt by the BBC to engage more dialogically with its audience. The authored nature of content, the speed and immediacy of uploads, the range of opinions that could be collated and expressed were all met with enthusiasm by the BBC and indeed prompted the research funding call on which this chapter is based. As the Executive Producer quoted above noted, Blast was an 'ambitious' and 'sustained experiment' in user-generated content, potentially 'transformational' in 'harnessing a creative community of young people'. User-generated content seemed truly exciting, for creative and interactive reasons. It appeared to meet the 'widening participation' agenda of the BBC's public service remit, whereby the notion that the BBC should appeal to as wide a demographic as possible is taken as a central ethos of its remit. User-generated content seemed to offer audiences an accessible arena for expression, opinion and thought, in which anyone could participate regardless of gender, age, class, ethnicity, disability (etc.). In turn the audience was reconceptualized as active, engaged, individual, autonomous and, most importantly, *in control.* It was no longer adequate to talk about audiences – these were users: they were active, vocal and participatory.

For van Dijck (2009), it is this conceptualization of the user that demonstrates the significant value of user-generated content. However problematic and oversimplified the term, user-generated content marks a change in attitude towards media audiences from being tradition- ally seen as 'passive' to active, vocal and participatory. These shifts are explained on the one hand through recourse to the *user,* and on the other hand, through recourse to the *technology.* Indeed, if the user is now (and by comparison with the 'audience') active, participatory and creatively engaged, it is the technology that supports this transition. For many scholars writing about new media, emphasizing the autonomy of the individual, and constructing the technology as a support for this use, shifts power almost completely from the media to the user thereby reversing conceptions of mass media. As she acknowledges, these popular conceptions of new media 'audiences' are oversimplified and perhaps inherently problematic: a body of work within media and cultural studies has long argued that audiences were never passive (e.g., Barker and Petley, 1997).

Nonetheless, negating the complexities of interaction, and maintain- ing the dichotomy between user/audience–media/technology, this shift also feeds into and exacerbates an increasingly prolific rhetoric of neo- liberalism and individualism; the user becomes variously constructed as the powerful agent able to direct or navigate through the technologies on offer (Fenton and Barassi, 2011, p. 191, Castells, 2009, p. 129). In turn, the technology, as a supportive facilitator of the users' needs (see, for example, Jenkins, 2006; Rheingold, 1992), is constructed in relation to the *possibilities* on offer in Web 2.0 (see, for example, Östman, 2012; O'Reilly, 2005) and perhaps best encapsulated through the particu- lar rhetoric of the 'platform'. As Gillespie argues, the term 'platform' constructs new media as a technological support, ultimately working to 'empower the individual' and 'fits neatly with the long-standing rhetoric about the democratizing potential of the internet, and with the more recent enthusiasm for user-generated content' (2010, p. 352). This not only feeds into the construction of the technology as the agent of improved interaction or creativity (Thornham and McFarlane, 2011, p. 262), it also doubly emphasizes the *user,* who is, to use Prensky's term, digitally 'enhanced' (2011, p. 20).

Such representations relate not just to users of new media in general, but specifically to young users of new media as they are constructed both in wider literature on youth studies and through our research into BBC Blast. In case of the latter, these conceptions of user-generated content, autonomous users and empowering technologies were embedded in the design of the resource, in its ethos and working practices, in the language used by the adults working on the resource and in their assumptions about young people. The (adult) Blast team repeatedly referred to the 'natural' creativity or drive of young people, arguing that Blast was a resource that spoke 'the same language' as young people because it allowed self-expression through creative means. Indeed, the entire resource was underpinned by the notion that young people were routinely creating material, and also wanting to showcase it. Such presuppositions are not of course unique to the Blast resource, but are very common, particularly in the discourse of the digital native.

Although widely critiqued (see, for example, Buckingham, 2008; Livingstone, 2002; Thomas, 2011), the notion of the digital native remains prevalent in discussions of young people and new media. This may be because it resonates with, and taps into, the discourses of the individual and neoliberal user discussed above. Indeed, it is easy to see these similarities when we consider the terms in which the digital native is described: as 'digitally enhanced' (Prensky, 2011, p. 20), 'techno-savvy' (Bennett and Maton, 2011, p. 172), 'immersed' in the technology (Bennett *et al.*, 2008, p. 776), an active author or agent of their (here, technological) journey (Gadlin, 1978, p. 236; Bennett, 2007, p. 24), whose autonomy is bound up in singular relations with technology. Further, the concept of the digital native works to construct the young person as the natural and obvious 'explorer' of new technology and media (Rheingold, 1992, p. 191), a metaphor loaded with colonial connotations as Grosz (2001, pp. 41–7) and others have remarked. We might note in this respect that youth itself is often constructed as a particular kind of journey towards adulthood, as the young person navigates and directs their 'routes' (Evans and Furlong, 1997) or 'pathway' (Jeffrey, 2010) (see also Bennett, 2007; Myers and Thornham, 2012). The digital native also claims this agency, navigating the terrain of new media in their journey through technology.

Sonia Livingstone has argued that work on young people and new media should be located within a 'long-term historical trend towards individualisation' (2009, p. 12) and is conflated with a set of further anxieties around media, public spaces and control (ibid.). Lange and Ito also emphasize these connections when they suggest that the notion of a competent and creative agent is further enhanced through an emphasis on activity and creation that is taken as evidence of (individual) self-expression (2010, pp. 245–251). What emerges from both these discussions is the centrality of individualism, doubly entrenched and celebrated through a discourse of creative expression/activity in which the technology plays a formative and supportive role. Further, as all three authors suggest, such constructions are heavily loaded with value signifiers, enmeshed with wider fears around the damaging potential of media on young people and notions of young people as 'at risk' (Lange and Ito, 2010, p. 246).

There are three issues we want to take from these arguments: the first is the positive correlation between individualism, action and control, and the negative correlation between a collective and passivity, which feed into and exacerbate the discourse of the active digital native and the individual user of new media. Even as these positions are increasingly critiqued (see, for example, Fenton and Barassi, 2011; Dean, 2008; van Dijck, 2011), they, nevertheless, continue to emerge as powerful claims about new media use where value is located either with the *user* or with the *potentials* of technology. What is of course absent, as many new media theorists have noted, is a generative understanding of mediation – which is not simply theorized by actions onto the technology or vice versa (see Bassett, 2001, Thornham, 2011b). This brings us to our second issue: that such conceptions of new media use ultimately serve to mask, rather than elucidate, any real understandings of engagement, use, meaning or motivations not only for young people, but for users *per se*. The third issue is that value is located in the *act* of production insofar as it constructs the user as a creative agent. This generates a crucial slippage both for Blast and for online work more widely, as evidence of creativity is searched for – and found – in the content itself (rather than, for example, the value judgements of the users).

Evidencing individual autonomy: claiming and valuing content

For Blast there was always a real danger of overvaluing the online content as evidence of creativity or individual self-expression. This was partly because the resource depended on user-generated content – it would not be sustained without users contributing and creating content. Indeed, Blast's Executive Producer suggested when we interviewed him in 2011 that its lack of content (along with wider financial issues) was one reason for its closure in 2010. For Blast, the amount and diversity of content was taken to signify both need and interest in/for the resource. However, as we explain below, when we investigated online content further, we found that young people posted content on Blast *and elsewhere* (Bebo, MySpace, Facebook) suggesting that the content online on Blast was only ever a partial account of a wider on- and offline creative activity. This raises interesting questions for how we should value and contextualize the work on Blast (and any other single site). Young people posted elsewhere for valid and serious reasons that related to their perception of the quality and value of their work. For teenage users, Blast did not signify in the same way as other websites.

The second reason Blast overvalued the online content as evidence of creativity or individual self-expression was because of the pervasive and embedded discourse of the digital native. The construction of the user as a technologically proficient, self-motivated producer and creator of content meant that it was assumed that Blast was responding to an existing need, and that technological provision would automatically ensure take-up. The Executive Producer reflected in an interview:

> The Blast project was posited on the assumption (especially the social online part of it) that just throwing young people who were engaged in creating stuff together in an environment that felt amenable and caring ... had enormous potential. (interview with Thornham, 2011a, MediaCity UK)

As our research found, however, the numbers of people who selected and submitted content to Blast was miniscule, particularly when we compared the site to Bebo or MySpace. Instead, the majority of content came from the workshops, and was uploaded by the Blast team, with little awareness or agreement from the delegates. Indeed, retrospectively we would suggest that the assumption that young people were digital natives ultimately undermined the resource, which had to work very hard to sustain interest on- and offline. Comments such as 'it's their language' and 'they know how to use [the technology]' unhelpfully shifted attention away from understanding young people's motivations for engagement or existing online (creative) activities, and onto the content itself, which was touted as evidence of individual intention, creative expression or autonomy. In other words, the user-generated content was not only being taken as evidence of interest, participation and engagement – and even in some instances, learning – it was also being taken as evidence of creativity, digital literacy as well as of the need for and success of such a resource in the first place.

Assuming that content is evidence of creative expression, autonomy or interest is a widespread, if unsurprising, consequence of the discourses discussed above. Fenton and Barassi (2011), discussing political participation, argue that (over)valuing online content is part of an 'automatic syllogism that sees social media as enabling creative autonomy; creative autonomy as a positive democratic process, and thus social media as sites of transformation and social change' (p. 189). As suggested above, this is a crucial issue not only for Blast, but for new media *per se* if individual agency is becoming 'evidenced' through the practices of creating and uploading work, and then further 'evidenced' in the (creative) content online. Indeed, Dean (2008) has cautioned that 'emphasis on the fact that one can contribute to a discussion and make one's opinion known misdirects attention from the larger system of communication in which contribution is embedded' (pp. 108–9). And more recently, van Dijck (2011) has also argued that meaning and impact is complexly arrived at through a range of relations that are both technological and human:

> Individual uploads only acquire meaning and impact through the collective work of human contributors, networked technologies and institutional protocols (e.g., selection mechanisms) – which are in turn already prefigured by the institution's and project's *modus operandi*. (p. 411)

In this context, and in a similar vein to Dean's suggestion, the so-called autonomy of the individual 'evidenced' in the act of uploading work and the content uploaded are only partial and incomplete accounts of new media and mis-locate value onto the user and content – rather than in the relationship between institutional protocols, networked technologies and human contributors (as van Dijck would argue, for example).

Rather than an expression of creativity or debate, interaction or participation, we are witnessing what Dean (2008) terms a culture of contribution, of circulation, or even of 'interpassivity' (p. 109), where the fantasy of participation enacted through the production of created work (and the emphasis on the ability to create as a sign of autonomy, participation and individualism) is little more than a fetish produced in part by the technology: a fetish of freedom of expression, agency, authorship and creativity. It is a fetish that works, in the end, 'to prevent something from really happening' (Dean, 2008, p. 109). Indeed, if the emphasis is on *volume* over participation or quality, user-generated content may well be visible, but, as Dean suggests, it is rarely *meaningful*.

The issues discussed above, then, relate to the value accorded online content – as evidence of interaction, creativity and participation – and the slippage through which this content is taken as a mark of similar qualities in the creator of uploaded work. However, our research suggests that young people's online work rarely evidences creativity or indeed autonomy in the way it is imagined in the discourses detailed above. In what follows, we consider these judgements highlighted through interviews with young people about their online content, before addressing the crucial question for this chapter, which is, given these considerations, how *should* we value online content?

(Not) articulating value

When we discussed with teenagers their motivations for uploading work, we found that it was neither the linear nor the singular experience assumed by many of the discourses above. Our interviews revealed three key interlinked issues. The first relates to the motivations teenagers offer for uploading their creative work, which contrast with the constructions of user-generated content discussed above. The second relates to *where* teenagers upload material, which further elucidates their rationales for uploading work. Finally, we discuss their perceptions of quality in relation to their work. The data demonstrates that considerations of quality and value relate to young people's perceptions of what their work is (about) and where it is located online.

Our questions about what participants would do (if anything) with the content they created during a workshop occasionally, as in the extracts below, led onto a different discussion of other creative practices in which the teenagers were engaged. The fifteen-year-old below, for example, discussed mixing and creating music in his own time (not at a Blast workshop). He describes his process of creating and uploading music as one that is embedded in stages of peer validation:

B1:   I show it to me mates and then they tell me whether to upload it or not. Otherwise I never know whether it's good enough to go up on Bebo ... I mean I would just keep doing stuff to it. So say I do summat [something] else to it, if they say 'enough, it's all right' then I put it up.
Interviewer: And always to Bebo?
B1:   Yeah, Bebo is the only place I put it up.
                                        (Blast on Tour, Portrush, 2009)

The process described above is one that is not solely facilitated by the ubiquity or possibilities of the technology. It is a process that is made possible through long-standing practices of peer review, and (perhaps less articulate) notions of quality in terms of the work itself. Further, while the teenager does clearly remain the creator of the work, he is not singular or isolated in the way suggested by the discourse of the user of new media. Instead, he is social, dialogic and collective, sourcing and drawing upon expertise in friendship circles during the process of creation. The extract below also relates to work created away from the Blast workshop, and as with the extract above, discusses notions of quality and the work as reflecting something about themselves. While the fifteen-year-old interviewee cited above articulated this more overtly, claiming that created work was 'a part of you', it is more implicit in the quote below, particularly in relation to the negative connotations associated with 'showing off':

G1:   I don't upload [photos], I just have them on Bebo so people just come and look and say things about them, but I don't upload them.

G2:   Bebo is uploading them!

G1:   No but she means seriously. I only upload them for my friends, for them to say things ... otherwise it's a bit showing off isn't it? Bebo is just my friends.

(Blast on Tour, Portrush, 2009)

This sixteen-year-old clearly distinguishes between uploading work to Bebo and uploading work *per se*. In both cases, their rationale for uploading work elsewhere (not to Blast) is valid and serious, and relates to their perception of the quality and purpose of their work. For feedback and comments, social groups are used, whereas other sites suggest a serious showcasing ('showing off') of work for a different purpose. This suggests to us that at a very basic level, different sites have different purposes for users, and a blanket approach to online content that does not take this into consideration is inadequate. The final extract also demonstrates attempts to articulate quality, and the teenagers distinguish between the work created during a workshop and work they create themselves:

G3:   It's ok, but not good enough to go on Bebo or YouTube.

I: So you think Bebo or YouTube has good stuff on it?

Both: yeah.

I: So what is 'good stuff' then?

G3:   No not like 'good' maybe. Funny, and, I dunno, something that like *you've* done for something.

G4:   And stuff that everyone's into. Not like this.

G3:   No I mean, something that your friends are into.
G4:   And comes from you.
G3:   Not this.
            (Fourteen and fifteen year olds, Blast on Tour Telford, 2009)

Taken together, the comments above demonstrate that the meaning or value of created work is clear to the teenagers even if difficult to express. Further, such meaning and value is arrived at through a non-linear and iterative process of peer evaluation. For us, this suggests, at the very least, that the uploaded content should not be interpreted as a final isolated product, but should be seen as embedded in a complex process, in which pleasure, desire and quality also play a part. (We could add van Dijck's (2011) considerations here too and include institutional protocols and networked technologies to the relations between human contributors, pleasure, desire and quality, p. 411). Secondly, the teenagers are clear that uploaded content needs to be good. *How* they understand and value the notion of 'good' work may be complex and difficult to articulate, but is, nevertheless, clear to them. The comments highlight that peer evaluation is an important process of validating quality. Peer validation, in turn, undermines the notion of singular relationship either with the technology or with the created work. Uploading content is much more than an act of (one way) creation (into/onto the technology): it is a negotiation, a process of refinement and development; it is iterative and deeply personal. Third, if content is being uploaded to a variety of sites, each understood in different way, then our contextual framework for interpreting online content needs to be much wider: it needs to go beyond a single website. Similarly, this raises questions around the value of that content, if we locate the content as further embedded in a process extending beyond its immediate (spatial, temporal, technological) context.

Indeed, valuing a singular act of uploading, which demonstrates action onto or into the technology, rather than, as van Dijck (2011) and Dean (2008) suggest, understanding value as an outcome of contextually specific and negotiated relations, is clearly problematic here. The accounts above that emphasize mediation, context and shifting power relations locate content as a partial element of a much bigger process, and therefore undermine claims that content evidences certain characteristics such as creative autonomy or digital nativism. Seen here, while we could perhaps claim that technology 'empowers' the users to create and upload work, the meaning and value of that work, and the evidentiary claims made about it regarding the user, are more complex, nuanced and embedded in the wider media ecology of online content flow, than a singular or linear account of new media allow for.

Finally, if work is 'showcased' on some sites, and responded to on others, this suggests that a blanket approach to online content as always indicative of participation/creativity is misguided. 'Showcased' work, with little discussion or comments around it, may simply be 'there' as Dean suggests, but it may 'simply be there' on purpose. Incorporating articulated motivations into accounts of online content immediately problematizes a number of notions, related to constructions of the user, to claims made about content in relation to the user, and to accounts that understand new media as something occurring or circulating wholly online.

Conclusion: user-generated content in context

While we take Dean's assertions more cautiously than she intends, she does, nevertheless, warn against overvaluing or mis-valuing online content. The Blast resource is now closed, but many of the initiatives spearheaded by Blast have been transported to Bitesize, the educational resource aimed at younger children. In Blast, then, we see the discourses of user-generated content at work, doubly articulated through discourses of youth, new media and creativity. For Bitesize, the discourses of user-generated content take on an educational hue, where learning replaces 'creativity', but new media remains the natural tool to demonstrate (educational) participation. Such claims about online content and new media users intensify the prevalent discourse of neoliberalism and individualism, which, as Jeffrey (2010) reminds us, has infiltrated many constructions of young people (including in education, civic society and employment) (p. 499). It is these same discourses and accompanying dichotomies that we see reproduced in the construction of the user of new media and the digital native. And in the digital age for the BBC, where increasing attention is being directed towards the Digital Public Space and content is being freed up for users to create, use and reproduce, the question of how we *could* and *should* value this content, and of what we should take it as evidence, is increasingly significant.

Online (created) content needs to be contextually located – not just online, but in relation to a much bigger process of negotiated production. Even then, online content needs to be further interpreted in relation to those negotiations, and context – not taken to indicate participation, creative or intention and still less as evidence of these. Seen in this context, Jodi Dean's warning that such approaches do more than simply misrepresent online content – they serve to mask rather than elucidate practices, power relations, and even interaction – is a warning we should all heed.

Notes

1. For examples of this rhetoric, see http://www.bbc.co.uk/blogs/bbcinter net/2011/10/digital_public_space_idea.html; http://opendata.leeds.gov.uk/ Default.aspx or http://data.gov.uk/about. The Executive Producer for Blast, during the interview in 2011, suggested that in relation to the Digital Public Space, 'the idea of broadcasters giving away their content in a completely free and non-reciprocal way with no copyright issues: giving it away on the basis that they expect and allow users to do with it what they want ... is so much more exciting than you know, broadcasters inviting users to send in their pictures.'
2. The research was made possible by a joint grant from the BBC and the Arts and Humanities Research Council no AH/H500065/1 & AH/F006748/1.
3. See www.bbc.co.uk/Blast
4. see http://www.bbc.co.uk/blogs/bbcinternet/2011/10/digital_public_space_ idea.html

References

Barker, M. and Petley, J. (eds) (2001). *Ill effects: The media/violence debate 2nd edition*. London: Routledge.

Bassett, C. (2001). *The arc and the machine*. Manchester: Manchester University Press.

Bennett, A. (2007). As young as you feel: Youth as a discursive construct. In P. Hodkinson W. Diecke (eds). *Youth cultures: Scenes, subcultures and tribes* (pp. 23–37). London: Routledge.

Bennett, S. and Maton, K. (2011). Intellectual field or faith-based religion: Moving on from the idea of "digital natives". In M. Thomas (ed.) *Deconstructing digital natives: Young people, technology and the new literacies* (pp. 169–186). London; Routledge.

Bennett, S., Maton, K. and Kervin, L. (2008). The "digital natives" debate: A critical review of the evidence. *British Journal of Educational Technology, 39*(5), 775–786.

Buckingham, D. (ed.) (2008). *Youth, identity, and digital media*. Cambridge, MA: MIT Press.

Castells, M. (2009). *Communication power*. Oxford: Oxford University Press.

Dean, J. (2008). Communicative capitalism: Circulation and the foreclosure of politics. In M. Boler (ed.). *Digital media and democracy: Tactics in hard times* (pp. 101–123). Cambridge, MA: MIT Press,

Evans, K. and Furlong, A. (1997). Metaphors of youth transitions: Niches, pathways, trajectories or navigations. In J. Bynner, L. Chisholm and A. Furlong (eds) *Youth, citizenship and social change in a European context* (pp. 54–78). Aldershot: Avebury.

Fenton, N. and Barassi, V. (2011). Alternative media and social networking sites: The politics of individuation and political participation. *The Communication Review, 14*(3), 149–196.

Gadlin, H. (1978). Child discipline and the pursuit of the self: an historical interpretation. In Reese and Lipsitt (eds). *Advances in child development and behavior,* vol. 12 (pp. 231–291). San Diego, CA: Academic Press.

Gillespie, T. (2010). The politics of "platforms". *New Media & Society, 12*(3), 347–364.

Grosz, E. (2001). *Architecture from the outside: Essays on virtual and real space.* Cambridge, MA: MIT Press.

Jeffrey, C. (2010). Geographies of children and youth: Eroding maps of life. *Progress in Human Geography, 34*(4), 496–505.

Jenkins, H. (2006). *Convergence cultures: Where old and new media collide.* New York: New York University Press.

Lange, P.G. and Ito, M. (2010). Creative production. In M. Ito et al. (eds). *Hanging about, messing around, and geeking out: Kids learning and living with new media* (pp. 243–295). Cambridge, MA: MIT Press.

Livingstone, S. (2002). *Young people and new media.* London: Sage.

Livingstone, S. (2009). *Children and the Internet.* Cambridge: Polity.

McFarlane, A. and Thornham, H. (2008). *Alone together? Social learning in BBC Blast (Report).* Bristol: Graduate School of Education, University of Bristol. Online: www.bbc.co.uk/blogs/knowledgeexchange/bristol.pdf (retrieved 17/12/2012).

Myers, C. and Thornham, H. (2012). Youthful 'fictions', creative 'journeys' and potential strategies of resistance. *Media, Culture and Society, 32*(2), 228–237.

O'Reilly, T. (2005). *What is Web 2.0? Design patterns and business models for the next generation of software.* Retrieved 17/12/2012 from http://oreilly.com/web2/archive/what-is-web-20.html

Östman, J. (2012). Information, expression, participation: How involvement in user-generated content relates to democratic engagement among young people. *New Media & Society, 14*(6), 1004–1021.

Prensky, M. (2011). Digital wisdom and *Homo sapiens* digital. In Thomas, M. (ed.) *Deconstructing digital natives: Young people, technology and the new literacies* (pp. 15–30). London. Routledge.

Rheingold, H. (1992). *Virtual reality: The revolutionary technology of computer-generated artificial worlds – and how it promises to transform society.* New York: Simon & Schuster.

Rheingold, H. (1994). *The virtual community.* Melbourne: Secker and Warburg.

Rheingold, H. (2002). *Smart mobs: The next social revolution. Transforming cultures and communities in the age of instant access.* Cambridge: Basic Books.

Thomas, M. (ed.) (2011). *Deconstructing digital natives: Young people, technology and the new literacies.* London. Routledge.

Thornham, H. (2011a). Interview with the Executive Producer of Blast, Media City UK, audio recording.

Thornham, H. (2011b). *Ethnographies of the videogame: Gender, narrative and praxis.* Surrey: Ashgate.

Thornham, H. and McFarlane, A. (2011). Discourses of the digital native: Use, non-use and perceptions of use in BBC blast. *Information, Communication and Society, 14*(2), 258–279.

Van Dijck, J. (2009). Users like you? Theorizing agency in user-generated content. *Media, Culture & Society, 31*(1), 41–58.

Van Dijck, J. (2011) .Flickr and the culture of connectivity: Sharing views, experiences, memories. *Memory Studies, 4*(4), 401–415.

Walkerdine, V. (2007). *Children, gender, videogames: Towards a relational approach to multimedia.* Basingstoke: Palgrave Macmillan.

Žižek, S (1997). *The plague of fantasies.* London: Verso.

12
Selling Youth: The Paradoxical Empowerment of the Young Consumer

David Buckingham

The narrative of the 'sell-out' is one of the foundational myths of youth culture. It is a story that is frequently told by academic researchers, popular commentators and youthful participants themselves. The charge of selling out is especially prevalent in the world of popular music: while particular instances – such as the appearance of John Lydon (formerly Johnny Rotten of the Sex Pistols) on butter commercials or Iggy Pop promoting car insurance – carry a distinct air of ironic absurdity, the accusation is routinely laid against supposedly 'alternative' performers who achieve mainstream commercial success. This is a story in which youth culture arises spontaneously, 'from the streets', automatically and necessarily in opposition to the operations and motives of the commercial market. Yet once it enters the marketplace, its pristine authenticity and political challenge are deemed to be inevitably corrupted and recuperated.

While Cultural Studies in particular has often been accused of romanticizing youthful resistance, it has generally recognized that youth culture in capitalist societies is also inevitably a form of consumer culture: it is constructed through and in relation to acts of consumption. Over the years a great deal of work has pointed to the complex and ambivalent relationships between youth culture and the commercial market (see, for example, McRobbie, 1991; Miles, 2000; Thornton, 1995). However, academic debates in this field have often displayed an uneasy relationship with the kind of research that is the primary focus of this chapter – that is, the practice of market or consumer research.

Market research could be seen to construct a 'regime of truth' about consumers. In providing the means whereby marketers can 'know' their target market, it also defines the consumer, and by extension the subject or the individual, in particular ways. Academic discourse does something similar, of course; but marketing discourse undoubtedly has a greater illocutionary force – it can actively conjure into being the market of which it speaks. As Daniel Cook (2000) has argued in relation to children, these 'commercial epistemologies' are often presented as a matter of neutral description, or of revealing truths about consumers that would otherwise be hidden from view: marketers and advertisers present their work as disinterested, a matter of 'nurturing or directing a natural process, not inventing a social one' (p. 487). Yet, on the contrary, Cook argues:

> Market research is a particularly interested form of disciplined knowing. Information must be gathered and organized in ways that make it useful to 'know' the subject differently than it knows itself. (op. cit., p. 499)

Cook shows how, since the early decades of the last century, marketing discourses have increasingly emphasized the agency and autonomy of young consumers, and their right to self-expression and self-determination. Far from being artificially produced by the manipulations of the market, young consumers' desires are represented as somehow authentic and innate. In constructing the young consumer as active, discriminating and sophisticated – and hence as somebody who cannot easily be 'known' – market researchers also implicitly emphasize the need for, and the (financial) value of, their own work.

This phenomenon has been well documented and debated in relation to gender, but it also applies to the construction of age identities (or what Alexander in this volume calls 'age imaginaries'). Cook's historical research (2004) has shown how the market has repeatedly constructed new age-defined categories of children, from toddlers to pre-teens, and most recently 'tweens' (see Mitchell and Reid-Walsh, 2005). The most well-documented instance of this is perhaps the teenager – a category that originally emerged from market research in the late 1940s (Palladino, 1996; Savage, 2007). As Bill Osgerby (2004) has shown, the 'invention' of the teenager was made possible by broader social developments in the immediate post-war period – such as rising affluence, the extension of education and changing philosophies of child-rearing – but it was primarily a commercial phenomenon.

This chapter will begin by looking historically at how the category of the teenage or youth consumer was constructed and understood both in market research and in the academic field at this early stage. It will then leap forward to the present, examining how this category is currently being redefined around notions such as 'Generation Y'. It will also explore the range of new participatory marketing practices that are being targeted particularly (though by no means exclusively) at the young, including various forms of peer-to-peer marketing, social networking and 'co-creation'. It will explore how these new practices are legitimated through new forms of market research discourse that represent young people not as 'passive consumers' but as active agents and participants; and it will point to some paradoxical similarities and overlaps between the avant-garde rhetoric of marketing practitioners and the work of contemporary cultural theorists who have enthusiastically proclaimed the imminent democratization of the media.

Discovering the teenage consumer

Mark Abrams's short report *The Teenage Consumer* (1959) is often cited as an early indication of the 'discovery' of the youth market in Britain – a discovery (or indeed an invention) that seems to have taken place some years later than in the United States (cf. Palladino, 1996, pp. 96–116). Published by the London Press Exchange, a major advertising agency, and based on market research conducted by his own company, Research Services Ltd., Abrams's report maps the emergence of what he describes as a 'newly enfranchised' consumer group. Abrams adopts an extended definition of the teenager, as those aged between 15 (the point of leaving school) and 25, although he excludes those who are married; and on this basis, he estimates that they represent around 5 million people, approximately 13% of the British population. According to Abrams's research, the spending power of this group had doubled in real terms between 1938 and 1958, as young people had moved into what he terms 'modern jobs' – engineering and building for young men, and retail, nursing and secretarial work for young women.

Abrams notes that the expenditure patterns of this group were dominated by media and leisure (cinema admissions, records, popular magazines, clothing, soft drinks). As he puts it:

> The quite large amount of money at the disposal of Britain's average teenager is spent mainly on dressing up in order to impress other teenagers and on goods which form the nexus of teenage gregariousness outside the home. In other words, this is distinctive teenage spending for distinctive teenage ends in a distinctive teenage world. (Abrams, 1959, p. 10)

Despite this insistence on age-defined identities, Abrams's account is principally concerned with *working-class* youth – a characteristic that differentiates it from the more class-blind approach of early research on the youth market undertaken in the United States (e.g., Gilbert, 1957; see Palladino 1996, p. 110). Middle-class youth and the small minority then in full-time education are explicitly ignored: Abrams suggests that 'not far short of 90 per cent of all teenage spending is conditioned by working class taste and values' (Abrams, 1959, p. 13).

Abrams argues that the distinctiveness of this market in terms of both age and class poses a significant new challenge for marketers and manufacturers. The teenage years, he argues, are 'a period of intense preoccupation with discovering one's identity', and teenagers are looking for products that are 'highly charged emotionally' – something that will be difficult for the 'middle-aged industrialist' to understand. Despite the relative stability of its basic needs, this market is seen as volatile and unpredictable: 'the manufacturer must gear himself [*sic*] both temperamentally and productively to accept, even to welcome and stimulate, frequent change' (p. 20). Likewise, in terms of class, Abrams argues, 'post-War British society has little experience in providing for prosperous working-class teenagers' (p. 19):

> The aesthetic of the teenage market is essentially a working-class aesthetic and probably only entrepreneurs of working class origin will have a 'natural' understanding of the needs of this market. (ibid, pp. 13–14)

The influence of American culture on working-class youth is seen as a further problem in this respect: 'it is difficult', Abrams argues, 'for the middle-aged British manufacturer to adopt the styles and language and appeals of American manufacturers concerned with the teenage market' (p. 19).

In a 1961 follow-up report, Abrams notes the 'marked bias' of working-class young readers towards new weekly magazines (such as *Reveille* and *Valentine*) that were largely ignored by their middle-class counterparts; and he calls for research to explore why they 'stand in such acute psychological need of what is provided by these publications' (Abrams, 1961, p. 16). Yet aside from this slightly awkward pathological note, his account of this market is generally neutral and non-judgmental, even defending young people against adults' negative perceptions. The economic enfranchisement of the teenager, he argues, has provided

> the chance to be himself and show himself, and has misled a number of people, especially some elderly ones, into the belief that the young of mid-twentieth-century Britain are something new and perhaps ominous. We ourselves see no cause for alarm, and not much for

diagnosing novelty except in the new levels of spending power and their commercial effects. There remains the ancient need for the older to understand the younger, and we now confront a business necessity for this understanding, as well as the older moral and psychological imperatives. (Abrams, 1959, p. 3)

Cultural Studies reads the youth market

By comparison, the response of academics to this emergent youth market was much less sanguine. Richard Hoggart's notorious description in *The Uses of Literacy* (1958) of the 'juke box boys', the working-class youth he saw loitering in a 'milk bar' in a Northern town, is a case in point. Hoggart is scathing both about the bars themselves – 'the nastiness of their modernistic knick-knacks, their glaring showiness' – and the young men who frequent them, 'with drape-suits, picture ties, and an American slouch':

> Compared even with the pub around the corner, this is all a peculiarly thin and pallid form of dissipation, a sort of spiritual dry-rot amid the odour of boiled milk. Many of the customers ... are living to a large extent in a myth-world compounded of a few simple elements which they take to be those of American life. (Hoggart, 1958, p. 248)

Hoggart's account reflects his wider suspicion of the influence of American commercial culture, and might even exemplify the 'elderly' response described by Abrams: it is shot through with a patrician condescension that makes it difficult to stomach today.

Interestingly, Abrams's report was briefly reviewed in an article in *New Left Review* by an emerging scholar from the second generation of Cultural Studies, Stuart Hall (1959). Hall professes to be 'shocked' and even 'staggered' by Abrams's account; but unlike Hoggart, he also perceives a latent radicalism in this emergent youth culture – albeit one that operates at the level of 'style' rather than anything close to overt politics (Bentley, 2005). However, he locates this radicalism not so much in working-class youth, but in the more middle class bohemian identity that he finds best expressed in Colin MacInnes's novel *Absolute Beginners*:

> A fast-talking, smooth-running, hustling generation with an ad-lib gift of the gab, quick sensitivities and responses and an acquired taste for the Modern Jazz Quartet. (op. cit., p. 23)

Unlike the 'depressing group' portrayed by Hoggart, these hip young people do not appear to be wholly duped by consumerism:

> They know that the teenage market is a racket, but they are subtly adjusted to it nonetheless. They seem culturally exploited rather than socially deprived. (ibid.)

Both Nick Bentley (2005) and Joe Moran (2006) have offered reassessments of these early Cultural Studies (or 'New Left') responses to commercial youth culture. Both argue that the writings of Hoggart and Hall need to be viewed in their historical context, as responses to the increasing affluence and commercialization of British society in the post-War period. As Bentley argues, the Left's responses to this emerging commercial youth culture were diverse, and reflected the 'seemingly paradoxical duality of the teenager – both a cultural manifestation of emerging post-industrial consumerism and a point of resistance to that economy' (Bentley, 2005, p. 68). Somewhat more questionably, Moran seeks to rescue Hoggart from the charge of mere condescension, arguing that he focuses on questions of cultural literacy, class and education that have been marginalized in subsequent responses to consumer culture.

Yet while Hall is ultimately less judgmental than Hoggart, both writers implicate youth culture within a grander narrative about the cultural disintegration of contemporary capitalism. For Hoggart, this is essentially about the 'massification' wrought by commercialism and Americanization, and its destruction of the authentic values of the industrial working class. Hall is also prone to similarly grandiose laments about cultural decline: 'the truth is that we live in an age in which the very flow between human beings – a truly human and personal thing – has become distorted, part of a total crisis which eats through into the family life, and personal relationships as well' (ibid., p. 21). Both implicitly regard young people (and especially working-class young people) as 'other', and as the most prominent victims and harbingers of these changes; and both accounts reflect the problematic assumptions about age and social class that are frequently made by academic critiques of consumer culture.

Reconstructing the teen consumer

As we leap forward more than 50 years from this early moment to the present, we can identify some abiding continuities in the construction of the young consumer, but also some significant differences. In the following sections of this chapter, I discuss some of the rationales and practices of contemporary marketing to youth, with a particular focus on market research. I draw on the websites of leading British youth marketing, consultancy and market research companies,[1] on sources in the trade press and on observations and personal contacts made during and after the production of a major UK government report (Buckingham et al., 2009). To begin, however, I focus on a range of books written by and for youth marketers (mainly in North America), including Kit Yarrow and Jane O'Donnell's *Gen Buy* (2009), Tina Wells's *Chasing Youth Culture and Getting It Right* (2011), Lisa Johnson's *Mind your X's and Y's* (2006), Aiden Livingston's *The Secrets of Advertising to Gen Y Consumers* (2010) and Freddie Benjamin et al.'s *The Youth Marketing Handbook* (2011).[2]

These books provide a discourse *about* marketing, but one that is itself designed to market the services of those who produce it. Their authors repeatedly insist that the world is dramatically changing, and that today's young people are radically different from their predecessors. In this context, they argue, young consumers have become more difficult for marketers to know, and hence to reach: a fundamental 'revolution' in thinking, and in marketing practice, is thus required. Both explicitly and implicitly, these texts make the case for the new, specialized knowledge that their authors are uniquely able to provide, as consultants, researchers and youth 'experts'. They claim to have privileged access to the new 'laws of cool' (Livingston, 2010) that are indispensible if companies are to engage with this new generation.

These 'commercial epistemologies' therefore entail a particular set of appeals to truth and authority, and particular kinds of rhetoric. The tone is frequently evangelical, conveying a breathless urgency through relentless absolutes and imperatives. 'Inspirational' brands are eulogized, creating a delirium of name-checking that begins to resemble the parody of Bret Easton Ellis's *American Psycho* (1991). The texts are replete with snappy slogans, lists of bullet points and keywords. Many create their own technical terminology and neologisms – Wells (2011), for example, offers 'tweenebes' (adults who want to be tweens), 'instanity' and 'authenticitude' – that appear to imply new forms of quasi-scientific knowledge.

Yet despite the insistence on understanding the 'secrets' of reaching this apparently elusive age group, the amount of hard data here is minimal: rather than providing unprecedented or novel insights, these books provide copious amounts of sweeping generalization, much of it repetitive, self-confirming and banal. Most of the evidence provided is anecdotal, taken from journalistic sources, or simply unsupported – perhaps most clearly in the case of Livingston (2010), whose primary point of reference (and source of authority) is his own experiences and preferences as a self-declared member of 'Generation Y'.

Both the titles and the subtitles or cover straplines of these books reflect what I have termed elsewhere a new 'generational rhetoric' (Buckingham, 1998): *How Tweens, Teens, and Twenty-Somethings Are Revolutionizing Retail* (Yarrow and O'Donnell); *How Your Business Can Profit by Tapping Today's Most Powerful Trendsetters and Tastemakers* (Wells); or *Satisfying the 10 Cravings of a New Generation of Consumers* (Johnson). All these books draw dividing lines between generations in the process of defining them, but they do so in different ways. A range of labels is applied – Generation X, Generation Y, Millennials, Boomers – and categories constructed, such as tweens, teens, young adults, tweenebes, and while some of these distinctions are quite forcefully drawn, others are very blurred. Thus, while Johnson (2006) frequently combines Generations X and Y, Yarrow and O'Donnell (2009) distinguish between younger and older members of Generation Y and Wells (2011) differentiates between teens, tweens and young adults within the same generation. In some instances, the authors appear to be identifying characteristics and practices that are described as specific to youth, while in others they seem to be much more widely applicable. As this suggests, this process of 'generationing' often appears distinctly arbitrary (Buckingham, 2006): contemporary academic research suggests that generations are much more internally fragmented and diverse than these accounts tend to imply (e.g., Henderson et al., 2007).

As I have noted, much of the discussion here emphasizes the new and unprecedented nature of these emerging generations; and as in so many popular accounts, it is technology in particular that is seen to be driving this process of generational division and change (see Buckingham, 1998, 2006; Herring, 2008). The latest emerging generation – the Millennials or Generation Y – is described as 'entirely wired', the 'microwave' or 'connected' generation, one essentially defined through its relationship with technology. While this generation is seen to be 'empowered' by technology, it is also being pressured to live at an increasingly fast pace. Yet, for both good and ill, technology is seen to have an all-encompassing neurological impact: it is 'changing how our brains operate' (Johnson, 2006).

For the most part, these different generational groups are characterized in psychological rather than sociological terms. By contrast with

Mark Abrams's analysis, social class differences – and even simple inequalities of income – are almost entirely missing from these accounts. Even where (as in several of these texts) there is mention of global recession, there is no sense that it might impact differentially on different social groups. In place of demographics, we find a psychographic account of youth in terms of psychologically defined 'tribes' – techies, preppies, alternatives, independents and so on (Wells, 2011).

Although most of these accounts are driven by a need to proclaim the new, there is a recurring sense of the timelessness of young people's fundamental psychological preoccupations. Thus, according to Wells (2011), tweens are characterized by aspiration, security and acceptance; teens by inspiration, disruption and value; and young adults by reflection, commitment and self-fulfilment. Likewise, Yarrow and O'Donnell (2009) present a very familiar account of Generation Y as preoccupied with exploring new roles and identities, beset by raging hormones and mood swings, and characterized by needs and insecurities that are part of 'being human'. Unlike those in other age groups, young people apparently suffer immense 'physiological, cognitive and psychological upheaval', as they desperately seek 'to figure out who they are'.

Even Benjamin et al. (2011), who are probably the most avant-garde of these authors in their approach to marketing, insist that in many respects young people 'are no different from previous generations': teenagers are seen to be driven by a fundamental need for 'social proof' or esteem among the peer group – an argument that aligns with long-established adult concerns about 'peer pressure', and yet never seems to be applied to adults themselves (see Buckingham, 2011). While there are some superficial references here to the currently fashionable discipline of neuroscience, this popular wisdom mostly relies on well-established developmental stage theories (such as those of Piaget and Erikson) as well as broader theories like Maslow's perennial hierarchy of needs – theories that remain extremely popular in market research, especially in relation to young people, even though they have been widely challenged in academic research.

Marketing to the new generations

For these authors, the primary reasons for tracing these generational differences and changes are of course to do with marketing. Different generations, it would seem, consume products and relate to marketing in different ways, and therefore need to be approached using different techniques. These differences are partly defined here in terms of psychological dispositions. Generations X and Y (or their correlates) apparently represent a particular challenge to marketers because of their intense pursuit of individuality. For example, Johnson (2006) argues that contemporary consumers' key motivations are to do with autonomy, confidence, identity, self-expression and self-esteem, and they expect brands to become partners in their search for 'personal growth'. Yarrow and O'Donnell (2009) trace this sense of individualism to the non-authoritarian child-rearing style of their baby-boomer parents and the wider influence of the 'self-esteem movement'. Modern marketing therefore needs to be 'personalized' or 'customized' in ways that reflect consumers' individual needs: old-style 'mass marketing' is bound to fail.

Indeed, these authors argue that young people are now highly resistant towards overt marketing techniques – although there is some disagreement here as to when this resistance is manifested. Johnson (2006), for instance, argues that Generation X (born 1965–1979) was more hostile towards marketing, while Generation Y (born 1980–1997) apparently 'embraces the marketing process' – although she offers no evidence to support this, or indeed any historical explanation of why it might be the case. Nevertheless, all these authors agree that contemporary young people are likely to reject the authoritarian approach of the 'hard sell', and are especially suspicious of marketers' vain attempts to appear 'cool' or to cash in on youth trends. They argue that young consumers now value honesty, integrity and authenticity on the part of companies and brands, and are innately suspicious of what they see as corporate business values.

In some instances, this resistance is seen to extend to a more overtly political critique of marketing and commercialism. These authors argue that young people are inclined to subscribe to social 'causes', and that appealing to this can be a powerful means of building a positive brand image. 'Ethical consumption' – especially defined in terms of ecological sustainability – is seen to be a key imperative for this generation (see Banaji and Buckingham, 2009). For example, Johnson (2006) argues that companies should address young people's desire to be 'giving something back', 'making a difference', 'connecting to our communities' and 'finding meaning' or even 'our true calling' – although this desire is one that she accounts for in individualistic (rather than political) terms.

Of course, this is not a new argument: marketers' attempts to engage with consumers' ambivalence and resistance towards 'mass culture' have a long history, dating back at least to the late 1950s (see Frank, 1997).

Heath and Potter (2005) argue that the boundaries between consumer culture and the so-called 'counterculture' were always very fluid; and they go so far as to assert that the counterculture itself is merely a logical extension of the individualistic ideology of consumer capitalism. Certainly, there are reasons to doubt whether 'mass marketing' was ever as monolithic or as crude as some of these commentators suggest. Nevertheless, young consumers in particular are now predominantly defined and addressed, not as vulnerable and open to manipulation, but as 'savvy', sophisticated and discriminating. They do not want to be told what to do, but to make their own choices. They expect dialogue and collaboration with brands, rather than the hard sell. They want to be valued and respected, and to be in control. The aim of marketing in this context, therefore, is not so much to sell specific products but rather to engage with consumers' sense of personal agency, and to create more intense forms of intimacy and 'bonding' in the relations between consumers and brands (Arvidsson, 2006).

Here again, technology is regarded as both a key definer and an enabler. Its proliferation results in a fragmentation of attention, such that marketers have to work much harder to reach their audience. The members of Generation Y are fast-thinking, interactive and visually oriented, and they live in an accelerating world (Yarrow and O'Donnell, 2009). According to Benjamin et al. (2011), traditional marketing was born in an era in which 'youth trust and attention were abundant', whereas in the new attention economy, brands have to earn young people's attention and respect through mobilizing deep, long-term identification and participation.

The use of technology is also seen as both a manifestation and a cause of one of the fundamental characteristics of the new generation: its sense of connectedness. While this emphasis would seem to contradict the focus on individualism identified above, all these authors identify it as a significant new dimension of contemporary young people's lives. Involvements in social networking sites, mobile communications, 'user-generated content' and online sharing are seen to be creating new opportunities for collaboration and dialogue, and leading to an intensification of peer group relationships.

According to Benjamin et al. (2011), it is this sense of connection with fellow enthusiasts, as much as the qualities of products themselves, which motivates the emotional attachment of the strongest consumers or fans. 'Word of mouth' or personal recommendation has long been recognized by marketers as significantly more influential than mass advertising; and technologies such as social networking and mobile communications are seen to create new arenas in which this can occur, and which marketers can employ for their advantage. According to this rhetoric, connection leads to 'empowerment'. It enables people to choose and customize products according to their own needs, and to communicate more effectively with their peers and with companies. Contemporary consumers, Johnson (2006) argues, require a 'dialogue' with their favoured brands: they want active participation, cooperation and interaction.

New techniques

For all these reasons, traditional forms of advertising and marketing – using television, radio and print media – are now widely declared to be redundant, especially as far as young people are concerned. Generation Y is apparently now 'immune' to them, and new approaches are required (Livingston, 2010). A full account of these techniques is beyond the scope of this chapter, but they include integrated, cross-media, '360 degree' or 'synergistic' marketing; product placement and 'embedded' marketing; advergaming and 'immersive' marketing, for example, in online social worlds; viral marketing, for instance, via mobile phones and online sharing sites; branded 'applications' on social networking sites; and 'experiential marketing', which has moved beyond the sponsorship of existing events (such as music festivals) to create brand-defined live experiences in public spaces, often tied in with the use of social media.

Likewise, new market research practices typically draw on creative and ethnographic tools for accessing young people's 'voices' that have recently become popular within academic disciplines such as anthropology and Cultural Studies (see Gauntlett, 2007; and for a critical account, Buckingham, 2009). For instance, researchers may visit young people repeatedly in their homes, spending extended periods observing them in their most private spaces, such as bedrooms and bathrooms (Quart, 2003). They may invite young people to create video diaries, blogs, visual displays, websites or other forms of 'auto-ethnography' as means of representing intimate aspects of their identity and consumption.

These forms of research often blur into more promotional practices, such as 'cool hunting', the recruitment of young people as 'consultants', who are paid to supply their views on products and advertisements, and to track trends among their peer groups. This may elide with peer-to-peer marketing, whereby opinion leaders are recruited and paid as brand 'champions' or 'ambassadors' who will actively display and advocate the use of particular products within their contact group (the ubiquitous display of logos on branded clothing might be seen as a 'softer' form of this practice). 'Guerrilla marketing' likewise entails embedding marketing practices within peer group interactions, often using low-cost and unexpected methods such as 'flash mobs' or demonstrations led by 'street teams' of young people.

Most of these approaches make use of digital technology, albeit often combined with face-to-face methods. Even a cursory reading of contemporary marketing publications should be sufficient to dispel any utopian view of new social media as inherently democratic or politically radicalizing. Facebook, Twitter, YouTube and other services are seen here in primarily commercial terms, as providers of a new universe of exciting marketing opportunities.

These new techniques are typically much less overt and much more pervasive than traditional marketing. They appear to be 'personalized', in the sense that they seem to appeal and respond to the individual's wants and needs, rather than addressing them as a member of a mass market. They are tightly locked into, and symbiotically dependent upon, the social dynamics of young people's friendship groups. Many of them are primarily about branding – creating a set of values or emotions associated with the brand – rather than specific products. Indeed, they often depend upon erasing distinctions between marketing and 'content'.

As such, these techniques may offer a greater potential for deception: they are often accused by critics of being 'stealthy', in the sense that their persuasive intentions are rarely made apparent (see Mayo and Nairn, 2009). However, marketers typically claim that, on the contrary, such techniques are 'empowering'. Young people themselves appear to be involved as active participants, rather than mere consumers or target markets. Such techniques are frequently described as 'participatory' or 'interactive', or as part of a 'brand conversation': they require the positive engagement of the consumer, who may be called upon to contribute actively to the communication (as in social networking applications or advergames), to pass it on to others (as in the case of viral marketing) or even to help create the message (as in user-generated campaigns). In respect of the latter, marketers are now extensively involved in the commercial cultivation of 'fan cultures', especially those that involve collecting commodities (often with a market-induced 'rarity' value), or creating forms of fan 'art' (e.g., through re-editing video material). There is growing use of so-called user-generated content, in which companies recruit (or themselves masquerade as) 'ordinary' consumers to create blogs or online videos promoting particular brands or products.

The use of digital media also creates many new opportunities for marketers to gather personal information about consumers. The practice of 'data mining' involves the gathering, aggregation and analysis of data about consumers, based on either their responses to online requests or questionnaires or (more covertly) on 'cookies' that track their movements online. Such practices are widely used, not only in online shopping or commercially branded sites, but also in social networking sites and online social worlds. They are frequently justified on the grounds that they make the experience of consumption – as well as the practice of marketing – more efficient: marketing communications can be 'personalized', to some extent reducing the redundancy of old-style mass marketing. Yet the media that are often celebrated for their ability to 'empower' consumers clearly also provide powerful means of surveillance.

The rise of co-creation

The work of the UK agencies Mobile Youth and Face Group represents what might be seen as the next logical step in this respect. The former's *Youth Marketing Handbook* (Benjamin et al., 2011) shares the broader argument identified above about the importance of consumers' emotional relationships with brands: in their terms, the important thing is not the content (the product) but the 'context' or the 'social package' that surrounds it – the images and values, and the motivational and social factors, that are associated with the brand. However, these authors propose that this context is now created not by marketers but by consumers. They argue that marketers and creative agencies may lose credibility if they attempt merely to co-opt trends or 'memes' that they see emerging in youth culture. Rather, they need to 'let go' and engage in a more equal dialogue with consumers. The success of brands like Apple, they argue, is a result of their ability to 'build grass-roots activism' and to mobilize 'an army of fans'.

In this environment, advertising as such is effectively finished: the energies of marketers need to focus on 'social thinking' – on creating 'context' and 'social currency'. The elusive but indispensible values of authenticity, trust and credibility will not be achieved through crass promotional techniques, campaigns or gimmicks, or even through careful brand management. As noted above, word of mouth – generated, crucially, by fans – is seen to possess much greater influence than traditional marketing techniques. The best approach for marketers is therefore to foster connection and dialogue between consumers – a 'brand democracy' that is built from the grass roots, rather than a 'brand bureaucracy' that promulgates a monolithic marketing message. Companies may create or curate the platforms for dialogue and seek to 'set the tone', but they need to step back and let fans do the rest. Marketers need to 'stop advertising, [and] start activating the fans'.

In this situation, the boundaries between marketing and market research, and ultimately between consumption and production, appear increasingly blurred. According to Benjamin et al. (2011), researchers will not gain access to the all-important 'social and emotional context' through conventional focus groups, or indeed through online advertising. Rather, they need to work on building relationships over time, especially offline, if they are to obtain more honest and reliable responses. In particular, they need to cultivate fans, who apparently act as opinion leaders or gatekeepers for other consumers: fans need to be encouraged to share information about how they are appropriating and customizing products for their own purposes. In this context, 'deviant' forms of consumption are not to be suppressed, but considered as forms of bottom-up innovation that will provide guidance as to companies' future strategies.

This approach to market research blurs into what is often termed 'co-creation' – an approach espoused by both of the agencies mentioned here. Initially promulgated by Prahalad and Ramaswamy (2004), co-creation refers to the active involvement of consumers or users in the design of products or services. While there is a good deal of somewhat mystificatory rhetoric in this field, this approach is seen to enable companies to become more responsive to consumer demand and more collaborative in their approach, and to result in products that are more appropriately 'personalized' to consumer needs. A more sceptical view would suggest that (even though they are generally paid or incentivized for their work), participants in co-creation activities are simply enabling companies to appropriate their intellectual property on the cheap.

The Face Group, for example, makes extensive use of co-creation through its online youth community Headbox, which it employs for research with a variety of mainstream commercial clients including Coca-Cola, Nokia and Google.[3] On one level, Headbox functions as a kind of online market research panel, in which data mining and cybermetric techniques enable the company to conduct quite fine-grained quantitative analysis. Participants can also take part in more extensive tasks or projects that relate to particular brands, involving in-depth qualitative approaches, such as 'netnography', gaming techniques and forms of 'life logging' such as video diaries.

However, groups of participants also attend face-to-face co-creation workshops, in which they engage in dialogue with researchers, product designers and company representatives. Crucially, these workshops do not simply involve consumers in talking about their needs, or about existing products, but also in identifying 'seed ideas' for new product developments. They are also likely to involve collaborative, creative approaches, rather than traditional focus group discussion. Face Group research director Francesco d'Orazio (2009) argues that these practices are more appropriate to a context in which outdated models of 'mass consumption' no longer apply. Consumers, he argues, are being connected and empowered by their use of technology to the point where consumption has become personalized. He argues that we are living in a 'post-consumer era' – 'we should just drop the word consumer'.

Conclusion: what price participatory culture?

Readers familiar with recent debates in Cultural Studies about the emergence of so-called 'participatory culture' will perceive many echoes in these accounts. Market researchers may well be acquainted with the work of academic proponents of this approach, such as Henry Jenkins (2006) and David Gauntlett (2011): the celebratory emphasis on connectivity, creativity, fandom and democratization cuts across both domains. Some market researchers also draw on recent academic work on youth culture. For example, *The Youth Marketing Handbook* and the work of Face Group staff such as Needham (2008) and d'Orazio (2009) both make use of the notion of 'youth tribes', originally drawn from the work of Maffesoli. Both also proclaim what they regard as the 'democratization' of media through services such as YouTube and Facebook, which according to Benjamin et al. (2011) will represent the 'nemesis' of 'oppressive and stifling regimes'. Meanwhile, academics such as Jenkins are explicitly aware of the commercial dimensions of participatory strategies, although they rarely address them in their writing. As I have noted, there are also some interesting connections between the cutting-edge participatory methodologies espoused by some more avant-garde market research companies and those enthusiastically promoted by academic advocates of 'creative' methods – although in many respects the marketers appear to be more adventurous.

Overall, there appears to be a striking convergence here between the academy and the marketplace (or at least some elements of them), not merely on the level of superficial rhetoric, but also of fundamental cultural and political values. Yet should this necessarily surprise us, or give us cause for concern? Some critics might regard this as the final apotheosis of the misguided 'populism' of Cultural Studies – as evidence that it has become indistinguishable from a neoliberal celebration of the 'free' market. Some recent academic critiques of ideas about 'participatory culture' and 'media 2.0' certainly tend in this direction, but they seem to lead back only to a reassertion of gloomy cultural pessimism and to a kind of economistic 'vulgar Marxism' (there are strong indications of this in the work of Fuchs (2012), although Turner (2011) and Curran et al. (2012) offer rather more balanced assessments).

The economic, social and technological landscape of the twenty-first century is obviously vastly different from that of the 1950s, where my account began. Yet the problem of how academic researchers might understand and respond to young people's immersion in consumer culture remains. We clearly need more than the disdain of Richard Hoggart, or even the more qualified surprise of Stuart Hall; but the responses of contemporary academics are often no more useful. The new discourses and practices I have discussed here appear to represent a new paradigm in terms of how the market both imagines and constructs the young consumer. The diversity and the detail of these phenomena are important, and they are in need of much further empirical research: they are by no means all the same. Yet, when taken together, they suggest that the narrative of the 'sell-out', of recuperation and manipulation, is merely a caricature. Easy oppositions between youth culture and consumer culture, between the authentic and the fake or indeed between culture and the economy are in need of some substantial rethinking.

The materials I have discussed in this chapter are by no means a neutral revelation of the facts – or indeed the 'secrets' – of youthful consumption. As such, they should be subjected to continuing critical analysis. Yet academic research on youth culture needs to address the complexities of these discourses and practices more seriously than it has tended to do in the past; and it needs to update its theories and methods in order to take account of contemporary change. We need more than simple-minded celebrations of the power of 'creative consumers' or ritualistic denunciations of 'neoliberalism' – or indeed sentimental myths about 'selling out'. We know that youth culture is inevitably a form of consumer culture: it is the precise contradictions and consequences of that fact, and the changes that are currently under way in this domain, that are in need of much more sustained investigation.

Notes

1. These are mainly based in the United Kingdom, and have included Force 7 (www.force-7.co.uk), The Lounge Group (www.theloungegroup.com), Reach Students (www.reachstudents.co.uk), Cake Group (www.cakegroup.com), Mobile Youth (www.mobileyouth.org), Dubit (www.dubitlimited.com), Face Group (www.facegroup.com) and The Eleven (www.theeleven.co.uk). I have also accessed some US sites via Ypulse, which acts as a portal for a range of US youth marketing companies (http://www.ypulse.com/). All sites were accessed at various times between January and June 2012.
2. The book by Benjamin et al. is from the United Kingdom (the authors are staff of Mobile Youth).
3. See http://www.headbox.com.

References

Abrams, M. (1959). *The teenage consumer.* London: London Press Exchange.

Abrams, M. (1961). *Teenage consumer spending in 1959: Part 2.* London: London Press Exchange.

Arvidsson, A. (2006). *Brands: Meaning and value in media culture.* London: Routledge.

Banaji, S. and Buckingham, D. (2009). The civic sell: young people, the Internet and ethical consumption. *Information, Communication and Society, 26*(8), 1197–1223.

Benjamin, F., Dhalwal, J., Brown, G. and Kunto, G. (2011). *The youth marketing handbook.* London: Mobile Youth.

Bentley, N. (2005). The young ones: A reassessment of the British New Left's representation of 1950's youth subcultures. *European Journal of Cultural Studies, 8*(1), 65–83.

Buckingham, D. (1998). Children of the electronic age? Digital media and the new generational rhetoric. *European Journal of Communication, 13*(4), 557–565.

Buckingham, D. (2006). Is there a digital generation? In D. Buckingham and R. Willett (eds) *Digital generations: Children, young people and new media* (pp. 1–17). Mahwah, NJ: Erlbaum.

Buckingham, D. (2009). "Creative" visual methods in media research: Possibilities, problems and proposals. *Media, Culture and Society, 31*(4), 633–652.

Buckingham, D. (2011). *The material child: Growing up in consumer culture.* Cambridge: Polity.

Buckingham, D. et al. (2009). *The impact of the commercial world on children's wellbeing: Report of an independent assessment.* London: Department of Children, Schools and Families and Department of Media, Culture and Sport.

Cook, D.T. (2000). The other 'child study': Figuring children as consumers in market research, 1910s–1990s, *Sociological Quarterly, 41*(3): 487–507.

Cook, D.T. (2004). *The commodification of childhood: The children's clothing industry and the rise of the child consumer.* Durham, NC: Duke University Press.

Curran, J., Freedman, D. and Fenton, N. (2012). *Misunderstanding the Internet.* London: Routledge.

D'Orazio, F. (2009). Presentation at 'Rethinking Youth Cultures in the Age of Global Media' seminar, Open University, February.

Easton Ellis, B. (1991). *American psycho.* New York: Vintage.

Frank, T. (1997). *The conquest of cool: Business culture, counter culture and the rise of hip consumerism.* Chicago: University of Chicago Press.

Fuchs, C. (2012). *Foundations of critical media and information studies.* London: Routledge.

Gauntlett, D. (2007). *Creative explorations.* London: Routledge.

Gauntlett, D. (2011). *Making is connecting.* Cambridge: Polity.

Gilbert, E. (1957). *Advertising and marketing to young people.* New York: Printers' Ink Books.

Hall, S. (1959). Absolute beginnings: Reflections on the secondary modern generation. *Universities and New Left Review, 7,* 17–25.

Heath, J. and Potter, A. (2005). *The rebel sell: How the counterculture became consumer culture.* Sussex: Capstone.

Henderson, S., Holland, J, McGrellis, S. and Thomson, R. (2007). *Inventing adulthoods: A biographical approach to youth transitions.* London: Sage.

Herring, S. (2008). Questioning the generational divide: Technological exoticism and adult constructions of youth online identity. In D. Buckingham (ed.), *Youth, Identity and Digital Media* (pp. 71–92). Cambridge, MA: MIT Press.

Hoggart, R. (1958). *The uses of literacy.* Harmondsworth: Penguin.

Jenkins, H. (2006). *Convergence culture.* New York: New York University Press.

Johnson, L. (2006). *Mind your X's and Y's: Satisfying the cravings of a new generation of consumers.* New York: Free Press.

Livingston, A. (2010). *The secrets of advertising to Gen Y consumers.* Bellingham, WA: Self-Counsel Press.

Mayo, E. and Nairn, A. (2009). *Consumer kids: How big business is grooming our children for profit.* London: Constable.

McRobbie, A. (1991). *Gender and youth culture.* London: Macmillan.

Miles, S. (2000). *Youth lifestyles in a changing world.* Milton Keynes: Open University Press.

Mitchell, C. and Reid-Walsh, J. (2005). *Seven going on seventeen: Tween studies in the culture of girlhood.* New York: Peter Lang.

Moran, J. (2006). Milk bars, Starbucks and the uses of literacy. *Cultural Studies, 20*(6), 552–573.

Needham, A. (2008). Word of mouth, youth and their brands. *Young Consumers, 9*(1), 60–62.

Osgerby, B. (2004). *Youth media.* London: Routledge.

Palladino, G. (1996). *Teenagers: An American history.* New York: Basic Books.

Prahalad, C.K. and Ramaswamy, V. (2004). Co-creation experiences: The next practice in value creation. *Journal of Interactive Marketing, 18*(3), 5–14.

Quart, A. (2003). *Branded: The buying and selling of teenagers.* London: Arrow.

Savage, J. (2007). *Teenage: The creation of youth 1875–1945.* London: Chatto and Windus.

Thornton, S. (1995). *Club cultures: Music, media and subcultural capital.* Cambridge: Polity.

Turner, G. (2011). *What's become of cultural studies?* London: Sage.

Wells, T. (2011). *Chasing youth culture and getting it right: How your business can profit by tapping today's most powerful trendsetters and tastemakers.* Hoboken, NJ: John Wiley.

Yarrow, K. and O'Donnell, J. (2009). *Gen buy: How tweens, teens, and twenty-somethings are revolutionizing retail.* San Francisco: Jossey-Bass.

Part V
Politics

13
Youth Citizenship beyond Consensus: Examining the Role of Satire and Humour for Critical Engagements in Citizenship Education

Kathrin Hörschelmann and Elisabeth El Refaie

A key aim of youth citizenship programmes over the last 20 years has been the realization of participation rights enshrined in the UN Declaration of the Rights of the Child, enabling young people to contribute to decision-making on issues that directly affect them. While one of the positive outcomes of this has been greater recognition amongst policymakers of young people's rights to be consulted, there has been a tendency to concentrate on 'local' or 'national' issues and to continue treating young people as apprentices who still have to *achieve* the status of citizens (see Lawy and Biesta, 2006; Skelton, 2010), assuming that in order to *become* 'good' citizens, they need to adopt a ready-made set of civil values, as outlined, for instance, by Crick (2000), in his recommendations for British citizenship education. Young people have been positioned as waiting and learning rather than as active members of society who already practice citizenship at a range of scales in their everyday lives (Kallio and Häkli, 2011; Skelton, 2010; Buckingham, 2000). As Lawy and Biesta (2006, p. 42) argue:

> Current policy and educational practice have been informed by the idea of citizenship-as-achievement [...] The major problem with the idea of citizenship-as-achievement – a status that is achieved only after one has traversed a particular developmental and educational trajectory – is that it does not recognize the claims to citizenship of young people.

While research on youth cultures has long demonstrated the political nature of young people's everyday practices, showing for instance how social and cultural inequalities are contested and negotiated in youth subcultures (Thornton, 1995; McRobbie, 1993; Hebdige, 1979; Willis, 1977), citizenship education and public discourses on youth continue to construct such cultural practices as a risk to 'mainstream' society, emphasizing instead the need to inculcate 'good' civil values and to achieve consensus rather than articulate conflict and dissent. The images of homogenous national community that are entailed in such constructions, however, empty citizenship of much *political* content and do little to enable young people to engage with differences in perspective that arise from their positioning in diverse power relations, stretching often beyond the local and national (El Haj, 2007).

Based on analysis of qualitative interviews that we conducted with 16–19-year old school and college students in Bradford, UK, in 2005 and 2006, we show in this chapter how a more thorough engagement with issues of conflict and dissent can invigorate campaigns for democratic youth citizenship, respond better to the diversity of young people's political positions, actions and perspectives in a globalizing world and provide routes for belonging *through*, rather than despite, dissent (also see Maira, 2004, and this volume).

Agonism and political humour

Citizenship inevitably entails exclusions and marginalizations that make it open to contestation (Laclau and Mouffe, 1985/2001). The conflicts that arise from this are, argues Mouffe (2005), inalienable features of pluralism:

> A well-functioning democracy calls for a vibrant clash of democratic political positions. If this is missing there is the danger that this democratic confrontation will be replaced by a confrontation among other forms of collective identification, as is the case with identity politics. Too much emphasis on consensus and the refusal of confrontation lead to apathy and disaffection with political participation. Worse still, the result can be the crystallization of collective passions around issues which cannot be managed by the democratic process and an explosion of antagonisms that can tear up the very basis of civility. (p. 104)

Mouffe contends that it is impossible to reach a consensus that somehow dissolves power; and that assuming otherwise is dangerous for democracy and ultimately leads to antagonistic political struggles. A similar argument is advanced by Rancière (2010), who disputes that consensus is an expression of democracy and of politics. His argument that consensus 'consists in the attempt to dismiss politics by expelling surplus subjects and replacing them with real partners, social and identity groups and so on' (p. 71) is particularly relevant for our discussion of youth politics. For not only are young people's conflicts with the state and between themselves 'turned into problems to be resolved by learned expertise and the negotiated adjustment of interests' (ibid.), but their representation as 'youth issues' denies the existence of multiple subject positions and political opinions amongst young people, meaning that, so long as 'young people's interests' are sufficiently understood by 'experts' (e.g., after having been agreed upon in participatory, yet consensus-driven political arenas), they can be represented by those 'experts' without any further need for young people's engagement.

The potential for becoming political subjects, however, rests not so much with the identification of common 'youth interests', which would in fact foreclose the possibility of politics, but with finding forms of political engagement that enable the articulation of the frequently 'unspeakable', of divergent, power-related views through agonistic rather than antagonistic struggles. While it is important to challenge the exclusion of young people *as* youth from formal political realms, *politics* only begins with greater youth participation and has little to do with finding a consensual, generational position.

What we are advocating here is not a simple reversal of power relations, but a more sincere effort to enable dissenting voices to be expressed in ways that enhance rather than undermine democratic decision-making. We argue that this is important not just in the context of local or national decision-making, but equally, and perhaps more so, in the context of international relations and transnational politics, since the consequences of decisions taken in this sphere can be far-reaching, even for young people's personal lives. Not only do they bear the primary burden of building societal futures out of the rubble of contemporary political conflicts, economic crises and environmental destruction, but, as we have shown elsewhere (Hörschelmann, 2008 and Hörschelmann and El Refaie, forthcoming), young people's hybrid identities and social relations, together with a sense of global connectedness (Nilan, 2006), mean that they often feel highly affected by the plight of people in apparently distant places.

In the following sections, we show how and why engagement with satire and political humour in citizenship education can contribute to this aim of encouraging the articulation of dissenting voices, through a medium that is by definition open to multiple interpretations and that provokes critical assessments of political decisions and actors (Dodds, 1996; Matthews, 2005). While cartoons are frequently dismissed as 'silly distractions' that are 'meant to be glanced over rather than considered seriously' (Dodds, 1996, p. 575; also see El Refaie and Hörschelmann, 2010), their value for the articulation of dissent is increasingly being recognized. Thus, in relation to Steve Bell's cartoons about the Malvinas-Falklands war of 1982, Dodds (1996), argues that cartoons can help develop critical perspectives that challenge dominant ways of seeing (p. 588) and 'hegemonic ways of representing international politics and geopolitics' (p. 575). Matthews (2005), likewise, advocates using visuals and humour in debating the issues thrown up by the 'War on Terror', since 'visuals and quite often humour do the preliminary work necessary to set students outside conventional ways of seeking and engage critically with processes of truth and knowledge production' (p. 207).

That said, satire and political humour can also encourage the kind of cynicism that already leads many people, not just the young, to adopt a distanced stance on (government) politics and thus potentially encourage a further withdrawal from political participation (cf. Baumgartner and Morris, 2006). They should also not be seen as a substitute for other forms of political information, as a sense of being un- or misinformed or ignorant likewise reduces (young) people's confidence in taking political action on issues and can be a major obstacle to their engagement with politics. They can quickly become insecure and discouraged by fears of giving the 'wrong' answers and not being knowledgeable enough. While, as we show here, humour can be a means of countering this insecurity because of the diverse ways in which it can be read and interpreted, it can likewise lead to further uncertainty over the truth value of political media representations.

Further, as Caswell (2004), and Cooper and Holman (2008), have pointed out, cartoons and other visual media can, and often are, used for propagandistic reasons. There is no essential link between satire and a critique of state power. Particularly in the context of war, humour can be used to confirm simple oppositions between 'the nation' and its 'enemies'. It can reify cultural stereotypes and entrench existing power hierarchies that are particularly difficult to challenge if humour is given a free license, because 'it's just funny'.

We consider the benefits and drawbacks of using cartoons in citizenship education within this context of contradictory possibilities. Starting with a brief discussion of participants' own explanations for the scepticism that many shared towards politics, we discuss how they responded to our use of cartoons as a different entry point to political discourses, focusing on the different literacies, levels of information, confidence and political positions that our participants brought to them. The chapter concludes with a discussion of the contradictory effects of humour as it is received by diverse audiences.

Methods

The material on which this chapter is based stems from a small research project conducted with 37 young people in the UK city of Bradford in 2005 and 2006. We recruited students from a range of cultural backgrounds, many with dual heritage and family relations in other parts of the world. Nineteen participants identified themselves as Muslim with family links to Pakistan, Afghanistan and Bangladesh, while nine participants identified as white British-born (Christian or atheist), four as Hindu, three as Caribbean, two as Sikh and one as British Indian. In describing their identities, students frequently chose hyphenated titles, mixing national, 'ethnic' and religious identities, showing the complex positioning of young people in a multicultural, globalizing society. They were evenly split by gender and between 16 to 19 years old. The majority were studying for higher-level school qualifications (A/AS levels) that allow access to university education, while others were taking a vocational course. We chose schools and colleges in different areas of the city to reflect a range of socio-economic backgrounds.

The main aim of our research was to explore attitudes of young people to recent geopolitical events through discussions of satirical and political cartoons. We selected cartoons from UK broadsheet newspapers, including some by well-known British cartoonists, Steve Bell and Nicholas Garland.[1] They focused mainly on the connection between the military invasions of Afghanistan and Iraq, and the outcome of the US presidential and mid-term elections in 2004 and 2006. We aimed for diverse representations that did not require expert knowledge of political processes, obscure personalities or complicated allegories and metaphors, which could have prevented students with a self-declared low interest in 'politics' from engaging with the material. Students were asked to interpret five cartoons, using a semi-structured format that moved from open to more specific questions. Since we conducted the research in three phases (July and November 2005, November 2006), the cartoons varied somewhat between groups to allow new issues to be discussed.

In this chapter, we draw mainly on the semi-structured individual interviews, but we also include two examples from follow-up focus groups conducted with the same students, in which participants were asked to reflect on our methodology and to discuss broader issues of the uses and abuses of humour.

'Not really interested' – Understanding young people's attitudes towards 'Politics'

Mirroring findings by O'Toole (2003), Bang (2003) and others, most of our research participants described themselves as 'not really into politics', although some expressed a sense of 'politics' as a part of everyday life and a majority showed high levels of interest in international politics, particularly the wars in Afghanistan and Iraq. When asked how they would define 'politics', participants rarely mentioned international issues, however, and instead described politics in terms of national government, including 'voting' (Lajita), 'elections' (Aaniya), 'the people who run the country ... summat that the government decides on, and not really us' (Alex), and 'all the politicians [that] represent the country, and ... make decisions on behalf of us' (Darshana).

Those students who declared an interest in politics had often been involved in student councils, youth parliaments or similar forums, or came from families with politically active or interested parents. Direct participation in decision-making processes thus enhanced young people's understanding of and willingness to become involved further in formal political arenas.

For the majority of other participants, however, distrust of political institutions and processes, together with a striking lack of confidence in their own factual knowledge, combined to make them sceptical of their ability to become more actively involved in political decision-making. They felt excluded not just by social hierarchies of age and associated power relations, but also by what they perceived to be their own limited understandings of political issues and structures:

Aaniya: I don't really pay much attention to the politics bit! (*laughs*) It's not very appealing to the younger generation [...] Because it's not very self-explanatory, and you have to know bits – you have to know, basically the whole story before you can learn things about it.

Raminder: Talking about politics is easy but actually understanding the right tone of politics from books and stuff I think that would be harder but if you were interested in a lot I think you would be more motivated and you could do it.

Students further commented on their distrust of media representations and of the truth value of party political speeches and programmes, explaining that they were at a loss as to how to develop informed political opinions. This echoes the 'cynical citizen' thesis outlined by Hay (2007), but with an important twist. Students claim to understand – and to distrust – how the media work, but as a result feel poorly informed about political processes. Although some of our participants were old enough in principle to vote, many noted the inability of under-18s to vote and to participate in decision-making processes as a reason for young people's lack of interest in Politics:

Claris: It's like when people are registered to vote, and they don't really know anything about it, 'cos [...] they don't get anything explained to them [...] so you just make your own opinion based on what you've seen on the TV, or what your parents have told you, so, you never really make your own.

Gajrup: We can 'cos we get all these party broadcasts, their conferences and that.

Rob: Yeah, but they're all full of ... like, sheer propaganda.

Darshana: But we're not actually allowed to get involved that much at all, so I don't really see any point for us to vote for anybody that we haven't had part of.

Helen: It's like we had citizenship lessons and we'd do about politics, but that was no good, because when you're younger you don't wanna learn about politics, and now, since you've got an opinion, you can't tell people your opinion about it, because there's nobody there who's listening.

Rob: We're too young to vote, so we can't make a difference.

The issue of trust was developed further by a student who argued that power relations between adults and children may inadvertently lead to disillusionment when young people start to question adult authority and decision-making:

Rob: I don't see how young people can always sift out what's a lie and what's the truth or, you know, politicians – they all lie, so you can't sift out what's a lie and what's the truth. Because as a child you're meant to believe what an adult tells you, but sometimes you can't trust a politician.

The fact that 'not many older people expect us to know about politics' and therefore 'not many of them talk about it to us' (Matt) was also raised, highlighting a potential vicious circle whereby perceptions of children and youth as uninterested, not knowledgeable and possibly too vulnerable for certain aspects of political news constrain the discussions that they can enter, thus limiting further their opportunities for learning about and participating (albeit indirectly) in political decision-making.

Encouraging critical engagement through humour

Political humour can be one route to tackling some of these issues: because the focus is less on giving right or wrong answers than on multiple readings, it allows educators to address, and move beyond, students' insecurities about their own knowledge. Three female participants in one focus group expressed their appreciation of such a non-judgmental approach:

Gajrup: It wasn't what I expected for me personally. It was quite interesting 'cos it did challenge your view of what you thought about the images we were shown. Because usually I wouldn't think that deep about the image. I'd just look at it on the surface, so that helped me think deeper into it really. I thought it was good [...]

Helen: I think I actually thought that the questions would be like: Do you know who the president is of America?

Claris: Like testing our knowledge.

Helen: When I like read that there isn't a correct and a wrong answer I was like, how can that be? But I didn't realise you'd actually look at something and then interpret it yourself. But I was pleased that it was like that because it's more to your own interpretation.

Political humour, including editorial cartoons, can be an excellent means for developing a critical understanding of how power works in political processes, how existing power relations can be challenged, how different views can be articulated and brought to bear on actual political processes and how minimum agreements can be found without silencing *dissensus*, all of which are crucial aspects of exercising citizenship (cf. Baumgartner and Morris, 2006; Jones, 2010). Some of our participants claimed to value this aspect of cartoons. The student below, for instance, commented that although she mainly just flicked through the 'political' stories in the newspapers, cartoons occupied her much longer, demanding decoding and more in-depth reflection:

Sumita: I read the cartoons mostly because they stand out on the page, usually come to my own conclusions about them, even though they are wrong. Yeah, I usually skim through and read them.

Interviewer: So you usually find them funny?

Sumita: The ones I understand I usually find funny. The others I tend to think about for most of the day trying to figure them out.

Several other students commented on the subversive potential of cartoons, which they did not always relate to being 'funny':

Helen: It gets you to think about the situation – rather than just reading the headline and the article, it gets you to think about what is your opinion. If you were for the war, you would see the image very differently.

Rob: On the surface of things it looks pretty funny because [Bush and Kerry] are both trying to fight over the people to get leadership of America ... A very deep and disturbing message to it. The cartoonist has done it very well.

Aspects that appeared to foster critical engagement included comparisons made between figures who were more usually presented in the media as politically opposed (such as Bush and Hussein being depicted in similar ways), the use of exaggeration and the sometimes quite explicit use of symbols of power. One example of the latter, which generated lively discussions, was a cartoon of an oversized boot labelled 'W' pointing in the direction of Iran and North Korea, and the small figure of Tony Blair clinging to the heel and trying to reverse the direction of the boot's step towards Palestine and Israel. The oversized boot with raised tip strongly connoted power and domination for our participants, allowing them to articulate their own opposition to US dominance in world politics:

Hussein: It is showing the power, like, that shoe is a force and when somebody has enough power they think they can just go onto somebody's land you know.

I: So what makes you think it is about power?

Hussein: It is the putting the foot down.

Interviewer: What does the boot mean?

Aamilah: Basically [Bush] is going to cause trouble. He is bigger than that, so he can crush them basically. That's it.

While many of our participants agreed on the meaning of symbols such as the big boot in this cartoon, or matches/fire as signifying 'danger' in another, our analysis revealed a wide range of cultural knowledges and literacies through which cartoons were read and interpreted (see El Refaie and Hörschelmann, 2010; El Refaie, 2009). Symbols such as vultures, peace doves or olive branches, which might have been assumed to be culturally shared signs of decay, threat or peace, were not necessarily interpreted in this way by our participants, while political figures, including Bush, Blair, Hussein and bin Laden, were not recognized by several of the students:

Interviewer: Do any of the characters look like anyone to you do they remind you of someone?

Louisa: Not anybody I know but I said I am not very big on politics so I am guessing somebody else might know who they are. Is that supposed to be Bush?

Interviewer: Yeah it might be. If it is him what makes you think it should be him?

Louisa: Just his face. The cartoon kind of looks like him, but I don't know who he is supposed to be.

How participants approached the cartoons depended in part on their familiarity with the medium, their general exposure to broadsheet newspapers and political information and their cultural repertoires. However, it also reflected their attempts to explain what the cartoonist might have wanted to express, and how they related these ideas to their own opinions. In order to decipher more complex layers of meaning in a cartoon, participants looked to additional information in captions, headlines, subtitles and even accompanying articles, which sometimes confused them. The student in the following quote became increasingly perplexed, however, by the incongruities of meaning between the title of an article placed next to the cartoon and the cartoon itself. Jenny did not suspect that the article may be commenting on a different issue entirely:

Interviewer: On that page what would you say – where would you look first, second, third.

Jenny: Well, I looked at her – she looks better than these men! ... I don't get why her name's more important than this bit.

Interviewer:	Than the subtitle bit?
Jenny:	(*laughs*) That's a bit strange! Something to do with schools ... but isn't a 'P45' something y'get when y'leave a job?!
Interviewer:	Mmm.
Jenny:	I don't get it then (*laughs*).

Emotion and the ambiguities of meaning in political cartoons

Affective responses were a further significant influence on interpretations. The visual language of cartoons relies to a significant extent on exaggerated and generalized facial, and to a lesser extent bodily, features meant to convey and provoke emotional responses. Such affective interpretations may differ widely, nonetheless, as, for instance, tears may convey anger, worry, joy, shock or fear. The meaning of facial or bodily affective states also emerges from interplay with other signs and in relation to the place of the cartoon on the newspaper page.

The simplified, yet at the same time highly open, visual language of cartoons can also disorient the reader in other ways, as we observed in relation to a cartoon on Israel's bombing of Lebanese cities in 2006. We had included this in order to find out whether participants were aware of this more recent military conflict or whether their interpretations were dominated by the wars in Afghanistan and Iraq. The cartoon depicted a derelict city street. Bush and Blair were peering in from the margins as rats, while a speech bubble above the Bush figure read 'Yo, Blair'. For all but one of our participants, this image evoked only associations with the destruction brought upon Iraq and Afghanistan, and occasioned condemnation of the military invasions in these countries:

Rob:	It looks like it's a *bombed street*. It could be Iraq I s'pose, and the tower blocks, all the concrete and everything. 'Yo Blair', it's George W Bush again and Tony Blair as little rats, talking to each other in the bombed out street.
Interviewer:	What makes you think it might be Iraq? What is the setting of the cartoon?
Rob:	Well, it's the only real thing that these two have done – I suppose it could be Afghanistan as well, but I think it is more likely to be Iraq, seeing as that's always in the news, and those two are responsible for everything that's happened.

One young woman was unsure about the setting of the cartoon, but then decided that it must be Iraq, 'because of the war, and like how the buildings – the land structure's been affected by the war ... and the bombing and stuff' (Aaniya). Another student guessed that it depicted a future dystopia:

Jenny: It looks like this city's been abandoned and everything's a wreck, and there's no-one around except for these two rats [...] And I think that's Bush and Blair [...] Maybe it's showing that they've destroyed the country or something. I think it's just a weird picture. It's kind of like futuristic – this is what's gonna happen maybe?

None of the participants who were shown this cartoon in November 2006 associated it with the Israeli attacks on Lebanon which had taken place only a few months earlier, showing not only that the meanings of cartoons are malleable and unfixed, but also how media reporting might contribute to structuring people's sense of politically relevant issues and places (cf. Philo and Berry, 2004). Employing cartoons 'out of context', as we did here, might be useful in political education contexts, stimulating students to consider the unevenness of their/our knowledge about (global) political affairs and how/why certain places are constructed as marginal and others as more central to (Western) political interests. Beyond this, however, educators may wish to provide opportunities for students to research and in other ways explore marginalized or alternative issues, perhaps by drawing on the experiences of students from migrant families whose stories may be little heard in either mainstream media or classrooms (see El Haj, 2007).

Another issue to explore with students is the humorous content of cartoons and other satirical media, and how far, for whom and why certain depictions might be considered humorous. Our research participants had widely different responses in these respects; some felt that they were being made to laugh at issues that, at a different level, they did not feel were funny at all. This occasioned moral ambiguities and ethical dilemmas; these might be productive in exploring the contradictory effects of political rhetoric and the immediacy of images:

Sumita: I always think that when they have Osama bin Laden in cartoons, um, I am a bit uncomfortable with them making light of someone who did something so terrible and put him in cartoons and make jokes. He killed so many

	people, indirectly but he caused a lot of trouble and they just keep using him as a comedy figure and he is not.
Fatima:	There has been loads of people killed in Palestine and all that [...] George Bush is the cause of it all. He seems more powerful and the rest seem powerless.
Interviewer:	And do you agree with that? Do you think it is funny?
Fatima:	I don't find it funny because it is serious. People are dying and that.
Interviewer:	Do you find [the cartoon] funny...?
Alex:	Not really [...] It's related to death.
Interviewer:	So ... how does that ... make you feel?
Alex:	Not happy, but not really sad neither, 'cos it's just a cartoon.

Our research points to the complexities of using cartoons and other satirical or humorous media in political and citizenship education. While their ambiguity can be valuable in stimulating debate, it can also contribute further to students' uncertainties over the truth value of news media and political discourses, and move them right to the edges of what they find ethically defensible. For one female student, a cartoon on the issue of gay marriage rights that depicted two bearded men at the altar being turned away by a priest with the line 'sorry guys' thus felt 'offensive':

Sumita:	I think it is quite offensive. I don't honestly know if he is mocking them or not and if he is, I find it very offensive. I don't think he should be making fun out of it because it is not fair that gay people don't have equal marriage rights as it is.

Further, while on the one hand enabling plural interpretations, cartoons may on the other hand be seen as simplifying, ignoring or even intentionally 'covering up' aspects of an issue that may be significant to a differently positioned reader. The student below, for instance, criticized a cartoon for failing to reveal enough about the extent and reasons for opposition to US foreign politics:

Vandana:	[The cartoon] is showing what is happening in America but it is like different branches to it as well. It doesn't show people's opinions to it as well [...] it doesn't show the reason [Uncle Sam] is worried.

Without appreciating students' diverse multicultural positionings and cultural sensitivities, humour and satire can further become yet another means of silencing critique and of excluding certain voices. This risk became particularly apparent in one group, when one of the interviewers raised the issue of the Mohammed cartoons that had been published by a Danish newspaper in 2005. Up to this point, students in the group had agreed that the portrayal of cultural stereotypes in humorous media was permissible and should not cause offence. However, a Muslim student then introduced some nuances into this discussion, showing why satirizing certain subjects was not unproblematic:

Interviewer B: I don't know if you guys remember there was cartoons – some Dutch [*sic*] cartoons ...
Alex: Oh yeah [...]
Interviewer A: Mohammed.
Interviewer B: [...] What do you think about those? Did you think those were funny? [...]
Mundhir: About the prophet? [...] That was offensive though weren't it Miss. I found that offensive.
Alex: I think they took that too serious; it won't really a laugh was it?
Mundhir: It's like, no, that was out of order. It wasn't like comedy was it.

Without the interviewer's intervention, the Muslim student's departure from the group consensus could easily have been missed, potentially reinforcing power relations that would have placed views such as his on the margins, discounting them as 'overly sensitive'. While humour and political satire can be employed to expose and critique some relations of power, they can also reinforce stereotypes and marginalize those who feel they are the 'butt of the joke'. Yet why or how certain types of humour offend and marginalize can be a fruitful question to explore with students in citizenship education.

Conclusion: agonistic education?

In this chapter, we have drawn on the work of Chantal Mouffe and Jacques Rancière to develop an agonistic approach to youth citizenship that regards dissent as crucial to politics and that responds more adequately to differences in young people's political positions as they inevitably arise from their differential locations in social relations, within and across national borders. We have shown the need to recognize dissent as a claim towards citizenship and belonging rather than as yet another expression of rebellious youth in need of educating to *become* 'good' citizens. One route to developing the critical muscle required to exercise dissent, we have argued, is political satire and humour. Drawing on the responses of young people to cartoons of the US presidential and mid-term elections in 2004 and 2006, we have sought to demonstrate that cartoons, as one form of political humour, can be a valuable resource for citizenship education, enabling engagement with, and the articulation of, political differences and dissent. Participants themselves evaluated cartoons as a resource for developing critical insight into state politics, especially on the international political issues that most of them cared strongly about; and, as we have shown, the multilayered meanings that emerge from readers' diverse engagements with cartoons are useful for engaging young people who are otherwise sceptical not only of politicians, political institutions and political media, but also of their own knowledge and competence. The different literacies, knowledges and understandings which come into play in reading cartoons can become the basis for a deeper exploration of differences in young people's opinions and experiences. Using political humour sensitively can therefore be one way in which citizenship education can promote 'the skills and dispositions needed to listen across differences' (El Haj, 2007, p. 309), enabling young people to develop a sense of belonging *through* rather than despite dissent (Maira, 2004).

Humour can, however, also have the opposite effect of reinforcing rather than challenging existing power relations, further marginalizing those who feel targeted by it. Used in the classroom, it therefore requires not an automatic censoring of particular materials, but critical and sensitive discussion, ensuring that more marginal or unanticipated opinions are not silenced by a dominant consensus, or by those who are still 'sitting comfortably', that is, not (yet) the 'butt of the joke'. Humour and satire should also not replace other forms of engagement with political media, since young people need a variety of resources at their disposal to challenge preconceived ideas and to develop a greater sense of competence and knowledge without which their ability to critique and to construct diverse interpretations will be limited.

Note

1. For further information on these artists' work see http://www.guardian.co.uk/ profile/stevebell, Bell (2004), http://www.telegraph.co.uk/comment/cartoon/ archive/garland/ and http://www.cartoons.ac.uk/.

References

Bang, H. (2003). A new ruler meeting a new citizen: Culture governance and everyday making. In H. Bang (Ed.) *Governance as social and political communication* (pp. 241–266). Manchester: Manchester University Press.

Baumgartner, J. C. and Morris, J. S. (2006). The *Daily Show* effect: Candidate affiliations, efficacy and American youth. *American Politics Research, 34*(3): 341–367.

Bell, S. (2004). *Apes of wrath*. York: Methuen.

Buckingham, D. (2000). *The making of citizens: Young people, news, and politics*. London: Routledge.

Caswell, L. S. (2004). Drawing swords: War in American editorial cartoons. *American Journalism, 21*, 13–45.

Copper, N. and Holman, V. (2008). War and visual culture since 1900. *Journal of War and Culture Studies, 1*, 219–222.

Crick, B. (2000). *Essays on citizenship*. London: Continuum.

Dodds, K. (1996). The 1982 Falklands War and a critical geopolitical eye: Steve Bell and the If... cartoons. *Political Geography, 15*, 571–592.

El Haj, T. R. A. (2007). "I was born here, but my home, it's not here": Educating for democratic citizenship in an era of transnational migration and global conflict. *Harvard Educational Review, 77*, 285–316.

El Refaie, E. and Hörschelmann, K. (2010). Young people's readings of a political cartoon and the concept of multimodal literacy. *Discourse: Studies in the Cultural Politics of Education, 31*, 195–207.

El Refaie, E. (2009). Multiliteracies: How readers interpret political cartoons. *Visual Communication, 8*, 181–205.

Hay, C. (2007). *Why we hate politics*. Cambridge: Polity Press.

Hebdige, D. (1979). *Subculture: The meaning of style*. New York: Methuen.

Hörschelmann, K. (2008). Populating the landscapes of critical geopolitics: Young people's responses to the war in Iraq (2003). *Political Geography, 27*, 587–609.

Hörschelmann, K. and El Refaie, L. (forthcoming) Relational citizenship: Political geographies of youth at times of war. *Transactions of the Institute of British Geographers*.

Jones, J.P. (2010). *Entertaining politics: Satiric television and political engagement*. Latham, MD: Rowman & Littlefield.

Kallio, K. P. and Häkli, J. (2011). Tracing children's politics. *Political Geography, 30*, 99–109.

Laclau, E. and Mouffe, C. (1985/2001). *Hegemony and socialist strategy: Towards a radical democratic politics*. London, New York: Verso.

Lawy, R. and Biesta, G. (2006). Citizenship-as-practice: The educational implications of an inclusive and relational understanding of citizenship. *British Journal of Educational Studies, 54*, 34–50.

Maira, S. (2004). Imperial feelings: Youth culture, citizenship, and globalization. In M. M. Suarez-Orozco and D. B. Qin-Hilliard (eds) *Globalization: Culture and education in the new millennium* (pp. 203–234). Berkeley: University of California Press.

Maira, S. (this volume) Citizenship and dissent: South Asian Muslim youth in the US after 9/11.

Matthews, J. (2005). Visual culture and critical pedagogy in 'terrorist times'. *Discourse: Studies in the Cultural Politics of Education, 26*, 203–224.

McRobbie, A. (1993). Shut up and dance: Youth culture and changing modes of femininity. *Cultural Studies*, *7*, 406–426.

Mouffe, C. (2005). *On the political*. London: Routledge.

Nilan, P. (ed.). (2006). *Hybrid youth? Hybrid identities, plural worlds*. London: Routledge.

O'Toole, T. (2003). Engaging with young people's conceptions of the political. *Children's Geographies*, 1, 71–90.

Philo, G., and Berry, M. (2004) *Bad News from Israel*. Pluto Press, London

Rancière, J. (2010). *Dissensus: On politics and aesthetics*. London: Continuum.

Skelton, T. (2010). Taking young people as political actors seriously: Opening the borders of political geography. *Area*, *42*, 145–151.

Thornton, S. (1995). *Club cultures*. Cambridge: Polity Press.

Willis, P. (1977). *Learning to labour: How working class kids get working class jobs*. Farnborough: Ashgate.

14
'I Matter and so Does She': Girl Power, (Post)feminism and the Girl Effect

Ofra Koffman and Rosalind Gill

> 'Girl Effect, noun. The unique potential of 600 million adolescent girls to end poverty for themselves and the world.'
>
> (Nike Foundation, 2011)

This chapter looks critically at the 'Girl Effect', a new trend in global development policy and practice that involves a focus on and address to young women. The idea of the Girl Effect was coined by the corporate giant Nike in the mid-noughties, and had at its heart a bold claim: that girls hold the key to ending world poverty and transforming health and life expectancy in the developing world. It was proposed that a radical new approach was needed to problems of poverty and ill health that seemed intractable, foregrounding the simple injunction to 'invest in a girl and she'll do the rest'.

The notion of the Girl Effect has fast become a prominent feature of global development discourse and practice, representing a shift in which key organizations (including the UN and the WHO) change their investment strategies in order to target girls in developing countries. However, the significance of the Girl Effect does not end here. It also constitutes a marked shift in the neoliberalization of development, an explicit attempt to mobilize a notion of girls as 'agents' rather than victims (Wilson, 2011), and a clear example of the 'feminization of responsibility' (Chant, 2006). Moreover, it represents a new and distinctive form of address to girls in the global North and West. Via an extensive range of social media campaigns, 'roadshows' and merchandising promotions, girls in affluent societies, particularly the United States, are hailed variously as the allies and saviours of their Southern 'sisters', using discourses of girl power and popular feminism. The Girl

Effect, then, is not a singular entity, but an assemblage of transnational policy discourses, novel corporate investment priorities, bio-political interventions, branding and marketing campaigns, charitable events designed to produce a social movement for change and designer goods that invite young women in the North/West to express pride in 'being a girl' – an act that Girl Effect marketing suggests will contribute to efforts to improve the lives of girls in other parts of the world.

In this chapter we sketch out the contours of the Girl Effect and its key features, not in order to evaluate its truth or value as a development strategy, but rather to explore it as a set of discourses and practices, interrogating its constructions of girlhood, power and development. Our focus on 'youth culture' is two-fold. On the one hand, we are interested in attempts to *construct* youth – specifically to create or bring into being a distinctively marked-out sphere and time of 'girlhood' among young women in developing countries. On the other, we examine the interpellation and mobilization of girls in the United States and Europe around a particular notion of gendered 'girlie' identification and 'friendship'. The analysis presented here is a poststructuralist, postcolonial and feminist one that seeks to perform a 'double reading' of the Girl Effect as it materializes in multiple forms of address to and about girls in the North and South. To do this, we will move dynamically back and forth between the language of development policies targeted at the global South, and discourses of the Girl Effect that are designed to interpellate young women in the North/West.[1]

The chapter is organized around three themes and divided into corresponding sections. First, we examine the 'turn to girls' in policy and popular discourses, highlighting the Girl Effect's contrasting constructions of girls in the global North or South as, respectively, empowered, postfeminist subjects and downtrodden victims of patriarchal values. Second, we discuss the depiction of girls in developing countries as entrepreneurial 'subjects in waiting', for whom extreme poverty is regarded as having the potential to stimulate entrepreneurial capacities, and we juxtapose this with a discussion of the iconic role played by successful global female entrepreneurs involved in sponsoring and promoting the Girl Effect. In the third section of the chapter, we discuss the Girl Effect's address to North American and (to a lesser extent) European young women and its very particular form of 'commodity feminism' (Goldman, 1992). In our conclusion, we pull together the threads of the argument, bringing a postcolonial feminist analysis to bear upon the Girl Effect as a discursive object. We discuss its selective uptake of feminism and how it yokes discourses of girl power, individualism, entrepreneurial subjectivity and consumerism together with rhetorics of 'revolution' in a way that – perhaps paradoxically – renders invisible the inequalities, uneven power relations and structural features of neo-liberal capitalism that produce the very global injustices that the Girl Effect purports to challenge.

The turn to girls and the 'girl-powering' of development

The speed with which a majority of the key global players in the field of health and development have signed up to a 'Girl Effect' agenda is remarkable. In 2007 UNICEF, UNIFEM and WHO established the UN Interagency Task Force on adolescent girls (UNESCO, 2011). In 2008 the World Bank founded its Adolescent Girl Initiative, aimed at improving girls' and young women's economic opportunities (World Bank, 2008). By 2009 girls' role in development was being discussed at Davos, and the following year, the UK government announced that it would focus its development aid on girls and women (DFID, 2010; House of Commons International Development Committee, 2011). Taken together, these shifts constitute a 'girl-powering' of development, the latest in a succession of 'waves' of development policy that have included Women In Development (WID), Women and Development (WAD) and Gender and Development (GAD). This 'girl-powering', how-ever, does not replace policy preoccupation with gender, but instead represents a prominent theme within it. To a certain extent the focus on girls has much deeper roots within development work and within concerns about the girl child (Bunting, 2005, Burman, 1995, Switzer, 2010). Attention to adolescent girls has also been increasing within the work of the UN from the late 1990s (UNICEF, WHO and UNFPA, 2003; Croll, 2006), although it is only in recent years that these earlier themes have come to constitute a broader policy 'turn'.

One of the things that makes the Girl Effect different from previous initiatives is its explicit borrowing and mobilization of discourses of 'girl power' that have been circulating in the West (and increasingly elsewhere) over the last two decades. As has been well-documented by gender and youth scholars, in the late twentieth century and early twenty-first century, girls have become increasingly visible in con-temporary popular culture and in governmental literature. Girls are depicted as educationally successful, economically independent and in control of their sexuality and their reproductive capacities (Aapola et al., 2005; Walkerdine et al., 2001; McRobbie, 2007; Ringrose, 2007; Driscoll, 2002). Notions of choice, agency, independence and empowerment have taken prominence in discussions of girlhood, and this is sometimes contrasted with constructions of young men, particularly in those media discourses that paint masculinity as 'in crisis'. Young women have become 'luminous' (McRobbie, 2009), they are depicted as 'can do girls' (Harris, 2004) and middle-class girls in particular are often presented as the ideal subjects of neoliberalism: hardworking, entrepreneurial authors of their own 'choice biographies'.

However, alongside this depiction of girls as empowered and successful, another significant construction has been the representation of girls as vulnerable. Anita Harris (2004) analyses how discussions of girlhood are structured by movement between discourses of 'can do' girls and 'at risk' girls. To some extent these discourses might be said to map onto different girls – that is, girls who are differently located in relation to class and race – but the oscillation between these constructions of girls constitutes the discursive field for talking about *all* girls. Even the most privileged, the 'top girls' (McRobbie, 2007) who succeed in becoming high-earning celebrities in the worlds of TV, fashion or pop music, are often constructed as fragile and troubled – marked by struggles with weight and eating disorders, alcoholism or drug addiction. Girlhood is thus an unstable category – marked both by 'trouble' and risk *and* by the suggestion of extraordinary capacity.

The promotion of the Girl Effect draws on both these discourses of girlhood, but with a particular, novel inflection. Whilst girls in the United States are portrayed as active, empowered free agents, girls in the global South are depicted as inhabiting a patriarchal order, where their freedoms – such as the right to vote and to own or inherit property – are constrained. In a familiar neo-imperialist move, Girl Effect campaigns suggest that the barriers to girls are constituted by 'cultural' beliefs and practices – such as the failure by families in developing countries to view girls as future economic actors and therefore to invest in their education (Levine et al., 2009; Nike Foundation, 2009). Girls, it is argued, are kept away from the public sphere by the burden of domestic chores, required by their families to be 'the water carrier, the wood gatherer and the caretaker of the young, old and sick' (Nike Foundation, 2009, p. 8). The cumulative effects of these practices, it is suggested, mean that girls' life chances are more limited than those of boys.

It is this gender inequality that the Girl Effect aims to tackle, primarily by exporting a very specific idea of girlhood from the global North to South. The Girl Effect promotes a notion of female adolescence as a time free from and prior to marriage and child-bearing, to be spent instead in education. This is captured by one of the initiative's most bold and powerful claims that the 'revolution will be led by a 12 year old girl' – a girl who has been 'reached' and 'helped' before 'the ticking clock' has seen her married and pregnant (see www.girleffect.org), and thus can go on to transform her life chances and those of her community and nation. Or, as the Girl Effect website puts it: 'Girl Effect, noun. The unique potential of 600 million adolescent girls to end poverty for themselves and the world' (Nike Foundation, 2011).

The Girl Effect literature describes girls in the South as victims of patriarchal culture, but as in the slogans above, also describes them as subjects of extraordinary potential. Indeed, the contrast between girls' powerlessness and their exceptional capacity is a rhetorical device permeating 'Girl Effect' media outputs. The Nike Foundation repeatedly deploys the slogan 'invest in a girl and she'll do the rest', while the UN Foundation proclaims that '[w]here there's a girl, there's a way' (UN Foundation, 2011b). Similarly, one of Nike's promotional animation clips playfully asserts that the solution to the world's problems is not to be found in 'money', 'science' or 'the government' but in 'a girl' (http://www.girleffect.org, accessed 30.8.11).

Moreover, this rhetoric is not confined to media texts for popular consumption, but is found throughout policy and political interventions. As we have analysed more closely elsewhere (Gill and Koffman, forthcoming), the rhetoric of the Girl Effect is strikingly different from the usual discursive register of policy documents, characterized by linguistic styles that are much more familiar from advertising and marketing – bold claims, hyperbole, rhetorical contrasts, emotional appeals, and so on – indicating what Andrew Wernick (Wernick, 1991) has called the spread of 'promotional culture' throughout the polity. We would argue that this reflects the pivotal role Nike plays in the initiative, with its commitment to girls now formally a central part of its global brand image. For example, normally sober and cautious UN bodies call to 'Unleash the Power of Girls' (UN Interagency Taskforce on Adolescent Girls n.d.) and claim that deprived adolescent girls are 'the unexpected solution to many of the world's most pressing problems' (UNFPA 2/3/2011). Thus, claims regarding the extraordinary capacity and potency of adolescent girls permeate the policy literature. We want to suggest that this is not simply the 'girling' of development but its '*girl-powering*': it seeks to export the particular fusion of agency, independence, consumerism and entrepreneurialism that have become the hallmark of Western discourses of girlhood in ways that raise problematic questions about the erasure of cultural differences, and the failure to address questions of power.

'Girls Mean Business'

A striking feature of the Girl Effect is the way it creates novel alliances between large transnational corporations, national development agencies, charities and bodies such as the UN and the World Bank. As mentioned earlier, the term 'Girl Effect' was coined by the Nike Foundation and it can be seen not simply as a development initiative (and way to channel tax dollars) but also a significant part of Nike's global branding and corporate strategy – designed to extend its markets (particularly in Africa) by materializing or bringing into being the category of 'feminine adolescence' as a period free of reproductive responsibility (and therefore potentially as providing opportunities to consume; see Koffman and Gill, forthcoming). Moreover, it rehabilitates the image of US/European manufacturers, which has been tarnished by accusations of relying on sweatshops and other unfair labour practices. Much could be said about this new alliance of development actors and Nike's distinctive role within it, but here we focus on two elements of the Girl Effect discourse: the construction of girls in developing countries as 'entrepreneurial subjects' and the way in which 'success stories' from 'global' female entrepreneurs are mobilized.

A key feature of these constructions is the notion that 'girls mean business' – as the international NGO Plan put it (Plan, 2009, p. 137). In terms that echo the portrayal of US and European girls, the Girl Effect describes young women in the global South as competent neoliberal subjects who, whilst oppressed by their 'culture', have the capacity, with help, to throw off its shackles and to become successful entrepreneurs. In the original Girl Effect video, the viewer is asked to imagine a girl in poverty, and then to replace the image of 'hunger', 'HIV' and 'babies' which it assumes will characterize this, with a girl who has been given a loan to buy a cow:

> She uses the profits from the milk to help her family. Pretty soon the cow becomes a herd. And she becomes the business owner who brings clean water to the village, which makes men respect her good sense and invite her to the village council, where she convinces everyone that all girls are valuable. Soon more girls have a chance and the village is thriving. Healthier babies, peace, lower HIV, food, education, commerce, sanitation, stability. Which means the economy of the entire country improves and the whole world is better off. (http://www.girleffect.org, accessed 30.8.11)

In this simple narrative, told and retold across multiple iterations of the Girl Effect, small businesses are the solution, and at their heart are girls whose entrepreneurial spirits can magically overturn hundreds of years of patriarchy and transform the economic fortunes of the whole world. In accordance with this view, many of the schemes aimed at assisting young women focus on providing 'business-skills' education and helping women start up businesses (TechnoServe 5/8/2009).

Whether or not these schemes do actually help young women is not our concern here. Rather, we are interested in what is produced ideologically, discursively or performatively by the distinctive yoking of neoliberal discourses of entrepreneurialism with others that draw on 'girl power'. Consider, for example, a Nike Foundation report that claims: 'A girl living in poverty is already an entrepreneur-in-training. To simply survive, she has already learned to be resourceful. A negotiator. A networker ... [s]he could be further down the path of economic possibility than she – or anyone else – realizes' (Nike Foundation, 2009, p. 34). Here, a struggle with extreme poverty is cast in terms of empowerment and even celebrated for the entrepreneurial capacities it stimulates. Both the structural dimensions of poverty and the role of First World institutions such as the IMF in bringing about that poverty remain unacknowledged and unexamined (Mohanty, 2003; Hartsock, 2006).

As Kalpana Wilson (2011) has argued, these kinds of constructions are notable for the way they break with older depictions of 'Third World woman' as a passive victim (Mohanty, 1988). The shift to more 'positive images' of women in the global South by international NGOs, donor governments and other development institutions is partly a response to feminist, anti-racist and anti-imperialist critiques of this figure, and has led to an almost ubiquitous stress in development materials upon women's 'agency'. What is at issue, however, as Wilson argues, is how 'agency' becomes linked to a specific modality of neoliberal entrepreneurialism. Moreover, she notes the continuities between contemporary racialized representations of women and girls in the global South with earlier representations of '"productive and contented" workers in colonial enterprises' (Wilson, 2011, p.316), and how girls' and women's own collective struggles for social transformation are occluded in this focus upon idealized, ahistorical and apolitical individual agency and microenterprise.

A similar mixture of neoliberal, entrepreneurial and postfeminist discourse can be found in the narratives of the 'girls who made business', the successful women who are corporate executives involved in sponsoring or implementing Girl Effect initiatives – which form the perfect complement to the microfinance strategies promoted. These executives include their own personal narratives in the reports they help fund, and these play a pivotal role in the Girl Effect's impact. They represent the success stories that 'prove' that entrepreneurialism is the solution to global injustice, and present a picture of neoliberal capitalism as a benign and benevolent force – *especially in the hands of women*. Furthermore, these high-earning professional women describe their work as being driven by a strong sense of gender solidarity. For example, Maria Eitel, then the Nike Foundation's president, writes that '[a]s a woman and a mother, I couldn't help but consider the accident of geography and imagine my life (and my daughter's) if I had grown up in Addis instead of Seattle' (Plan, 2009, p. 138).

Similar claims can be found in an opinion piece by Indra K. Nooyi, Chair and CEO of Pepsico. Nooyi draws attention to the fact that she was brought up in India and highlights the role her mother played in her success. Her climb to the top of a large multinational corporation is described as being enabled by an ambitious and competitive approach cultivated by a mother who did not herself enjoy similar job opportunities. By highlighting her relationship with her mother, Nooyi recasts the familiar neoliberal story of competition and success as a narrative of female solidarity and empowerment – a solidarity and empowerment that is now to be extended to other women in developing countries who are, by dint of being women, 'just like' her. It is an impressive rhetorical accomplishment when the CEO of a multinational corporation can claim solidarity with the world's poorest and most dispossessed people. Nooyi reveals that a specifically gendered solidarity is at the heart of this when she concludes her account with a pledge to 'keep working toward a world in which girls ... can look to the future with the same sense of possibility my mother instilled in me' (Plan, 2009, p. 145). Here, shared 'girlhood' seemingly erases all other differences and divisions.

'Unite for girls'

Key features of the 'Girl Effect' campaign include its address to Northern/Western publics and its endorsement by high-profile public figures including Sarah Brown and Cherie Blair (wives of British former Prime Ministers Gordon Brown and Tony Blair), Mary Robinson (former Irish Prime Minister) and Madeleine Albright (the former US Secretary of State). In 2010 the UN Foundation launched a campaign, titled 'Girl Up', which aims to ignite a grass-roots social movement among girls (UN Foundation 30/9/2010). Its supporters are public figures, mostly women, located at the nexus of celebrity, charity and public life, such as Queen Rania of Jordan, Judy McGrath, the chairperson and CEO of MTV networks, Nickelodeon's teen star Victoria Justice and Ivanka Trump, daughter of entrepreneur and reality TV personality Donald Trump (UN Foundation, 2011b).

The Girl Up campaign particularly encourages North American girls to take on the cause of girls in the Global South and to render their support through their activity in social networks, through financial donations and through fundraising. As part of the campaign a 'Unite for Girls Tour' was launched with motivational rallies, featuring celebrity advocates, taking place in several large American cities including New York, Los Angeles, Seattle, Denver and Washington, DC (UN Foundation, n.d.). Girl Up events and promotional materials articulate the relationship between Western girls and girls in the Global South in ways that are claimed to transcend North/South differences. American teenage girls are portrayed as 'more educated, socially connected and empowered today than ever before in history' (UN Foundation, 30/9/2010). The vast discrepancy between American girls and girls in the global South is highlighted while evoking a universal notion of girlhood as the basis for solidarity. The website states: 'With Girl Up, you can join the fight for every girl's right to be respected, educated, healthy, safe and ready to rule the future. Just like you' (UN Foundation, 2011d). Western girls are already 'ready to rule the future' and are now alleged to be in a position to try to ensure that girls in developing countries enjoy similar privileges.

The 'oneness' of girls is evoked repeatedly through Girl Up campaigns, disavowing the tensions and power differences between girls in the North and in the global South. While US girls are hailed as donors and girls in Africa as recipients, the campaign stresses that the latter are girls 'just like you'. The Girl Up website is suffused with the familiar language of girl power, organized around pride in *being* a girl and being part of a social movement '*for* girls, *by* girls'. Slogans such as 'I am her, she is me' reinforce this sense of unproblematic identification and solidarity, whilst necessarily obscuring discussion of differences, power, history or social transformation. Indeed, these are further elided by the use of American slang phrases such as 'BFF' with which accolade US girls are invited to nominate themselves if they believe they have made an 'extraordinary contribution'. Charitable giving, then, is systematically recast as an act of identity, friendship and girlie solidarity, and expressed through consumption and display.

The Girl Up website features a 'Girlafesto' which is downloadable as a poster. It can also be purchased in the form of bag and a magnetic sticker. A sense of 'cheekiness' and resistance to power runs through this text. The Girlafesto states:

> I AM A GIRL. bright, able, outspoken, soft-spoken, serious, spirited, adventurous, curious and strong ... I am me. I follow. I lead. I learn. I teach. I change my clothes, my hair, my music and my mind. I have a voice that speaks, ideas to stand on, and a world to step up to. I matter. And so does she. She may look different and talk different, but she is like me. SHE IS A GIRL. And together, we will rise up. (UN Foundation n.d.)

The American girl is interpellated as empowered, 'outspoken' and 'spirited'. This empowerment manifests itself, among other things, in her freedom to change her clothes and her hair. The disempowered girl in the developing world cannot do these things, yet through the solidarity of American girls and their joint 'rising up', she too will become free (to change her hair!).

The Girlafesto, which was put together with the advice of market researchers, resembles many contemporary postfeminist style adverts aimed at girls, with its defiant tone, assertion of individuality, and pride in being female (Gill, 2007). Indeed it bears strong resemblances to a lip gloss advert described by Anita Harris, which included several 'tick-box' statements: 'I have a brain, I have lip-gloss, I have a plan, I have a choice, I can change my mind, I am a girl' (Harris, 2004, pp. 21–22). The tone and character of the 'Girlafesto' speaks to the 'igeneration' shaped by postfeminist culture, immersion in information and communication technologies – particularly social networking sites – and individualism. The 'rights' being championed are not social or collective but relate to consumption, personal growth and individual conduct – including the much-vaunted 'right' to be contradictory (Dobson, 2011).

In line with this, young women are invited to participate in Girl Up through engaging in appropriately feminine consumption. As the website puts it: 'support Girl Up with style – buy a Girl Up tee or tote and fill your bag with a water bottle, pen, magnet and stickers!' (UN Foundation, 2010). Girls are then encouraged to celebrate these choices by posting pictures of themselves wearing or carrying Girl Up products. Social networking sites have been established specifically to display these examples of stylish consumption and media-savvy girlhood. Girls are told 'We ... want to see you in your Girl Up gear. So, send us a photo of you wearing your shirt, drinking from your water bottle ... or post it on our Facebook page!' (UN Foundation, 2011c).

Joining the Girl Up movement is thus not merely an exercise in altruism. It is also promoted as a form of identity work that will benefit US girls directly – as well as those girls in the global South it is ostensibly designed to support. The promotional material describes the campaign as an opportunity for American girls to further their career opportunities, promising that a Girl Up rally will be 'a globetrotting experience that will turn you and your friends into global leaders' (UN Foundation, 2011a). In this way, participation in Girl Up seamlessly blends stylish consumption, networking and social media visibility, with opportunities to enhance one's CV, whilst also – almost incidentally – working to empower girls from the global South who are 'just like you'.

Conclusion: Girl Power as a travelling concept

In this chapter we have discussed the Girl Effect as it materializes in development policy discourses, changed investment priorities for national and international development institutions and as a distinct form of address to publics in the United States and Europe whose support is sought. The Girl Effect, we have suggested, marks or consolidates a number of ongoing shifts that include the neoliberalization of development, the growing role of corporate players such as the Nike Foundation or the Bill and Melinda Gates Foundation, and, above all, the uptake of popular feminist ideas to create what we have called 'the girl-powering of development' – significantly facilitated through social media. This emphasis on girl power can be seen to operate in constructions of those in need of 'aid', in the kinds of projects supported and, crucially, in the modes of address directed towards governments and potential donors in the global North. Taken together, these construct 'girl power' as a new 'globalized' common sense, whilst ushering in a very specific bio-political objective: control of young women's fertility (see Koffman, 2012 and Koffman and Gill, 2013 for longer discussions).

As we have noted, the significant role played by corporate bodies in the Girl Effect is profound, apparent in the shift in the very language of development policy, and the uptake of rhetorics from marketing and branding. The place of celebrity culture, and the role of social media (e.g., in the use of viral web campaigns and 'spoof' online videos such as The Boy Effect and The Idiot Effect) are also very important features, which indicate its significance as a cultural, not simply development, phenomenon. In concluding, however, we wish to highlight a number of points that connect the Girl Effect with current debates around youth culture.

We would argue that the Girl Effect should be understood in the context of shifts towards neoliberalism, postfeminism and the growing interest in girls (cf. Griffin, this volume) within youth studies. Our analysis suggests that concepts such as 'agency', 'empowerment' and 'girl power' have to be read performatively rather than being taken at face value. Thus, whilst we might see agency as a quality that characterizes some acts, it is also worth looking at how notions such as agency and empowerment are deliberately and systematically marketed to young people, and are mobilized for particular purposes. Our research also points to the need for a much more thoroughly transnational youth studies – not simply because of 'global media' including social media and peer-to-peer communication on the Internet, but also, crucially, because of global politics, global development and global war. It is imperative that our accounts of the global and the transnational remain critical and politicized, and keep at their heart an understanding of how (post)colonial flows of power shape the experiences of young (and old) people everywhere.

In this chapter we have situated ourselves in this wider project by looking at how the concept of 'girl power' is mobilized and made to travel – examining how a set of ideas, practices, affects and technologies of selfhood that arose in a particular time and place are now being deliberately exported to the global South. The Girl Effect is a feel-good campaign that breaks in significant ways with earlier forms of address to young people and potential donors in the United States and the developed world more generally. Nevertheless, it effects a number of acts of cultural violence – including (but not limited to) the symbolic erasure of differences between women; the depoliticization of feminism to become an individualistic programme, cut off from collective histories and struggles; the unproblematized deployment of a colonial 'rescue fantasy' by which 'empowered' young women in the North are invited to 'save' girls in developing countries; and the oversimplified 'solidarities' that proclaim 'I am her, she is me'.

At this particular moment Girl Effect can be seen as feeding into the 'Othering' of the global South. As is well documented, the post-9/11 era saw Western societies becoming increasingly preoccupied with Muslim women and this became a key pretext for xenophobic political mobilizations against the Muslim minorities in the West (Bhattacharyya, 2008) as well as the invasion of Afghanistan (Hirschkind and Mahmood, 2002; Abu-Lughod, 2002). Within public discourse, gender equality gained salience as a marker distinguishing the (civilized) North from the oppressive cultures of the South (Scharff,

2011; Razack, 2004, Lewis, 2006; Pedwell, 2010), a trope that has deep historical roots (Abu-Lughod, 2002).

The Girl Effect reinforces these discourses by depicting the global South as a homogenous sphere plagued by patriarchy and 'harmful cultural practices'. Furthermore, while Western girls are depicted as empowered agents who *have* culture, girls in the global South *are* (subjected to) 'culture' (Lowe and Lloyd, 1997). In this sense, whilst trying to 'make a difference', the Girl Effect does little to challenge a global world order marked by profound injustices relating to power, money, resources, gender, 'race', class and nation.

Note

Aspects of the analysis presented here have also appeared in Koffman, O. & Gill, R (2013) 'The revolution will be led by a 12 year old girl': Girl Power and Global Biopolitics' *Feminist Review* 105, October 2013

1. The notions of the North or West are of course highly problematic – not least because of the growing range and force of discourses of girl power in Asia and Latin America. As with other designations, for example, 'developing' versus 'developed', First/Third World, the notions of Global South and North serve only to attempt to speak of a world characterized by massive geographically patterned injustice and inequality – while failing to capture complexity and specificity.

References

Aapola, S., Gonick, M. and Harris, A. (2005). *Young femininity : Girlhood, power and social change.* Basingstoke: Palgrave Macmillan.

Abu-Lughod, L. (2002). Do Muslim women really need saving? Anthropological reflections on cultural relativism and its others, *American Anthropologist, 104*(3), 783–790.

Arai, L. (2009). *Teenage pregnancy : The making and unmaking of a problem.* Bristol: Policy Press.

Aries, P. (1962). *Centuries of childhood.* New York: Vintage Books.

Arney, W. R. and Bergen, B. J. (1984). Power and visibility: The invention of teenage pregnancy. *Social Science and Medicine, 18,* 11–19.

Barn, R. and Mantovani, N. (2007). Young mothers and the care system: Contextualizing risk and vulnerability. *British Journal of Social Work, 37,* 225–243.

Bhattacharyya, G. (2008). *Dangerous brown men: Exploiting sex, violence and feminism in the 'war on terror'.* London: Zed Books.

Bunting, A. (2005). Stages of development: Marriage of girls and teens as an international human rights issue. *Social & Legal Studies, 14*(1), 17–38.

Burman, E. (1995). The abnormal distribution of development: Policies for southern women and children. *Gender, Place and Culture, 2*(1), 21–36.

Chant, S. (2006). Rethinking the "feminization of poverty" in relation to aggregate gender indices. *Journal of Human Development, 7*(2), 201–220.

Croll, E. J. (2006). From the girl child to girls' rights. *Third World Quarterly, 27*(7), 1285–1297.

DFID (2010). Department for International Development Press Release 14 September 2010 (online): http://www.dfid.gov.uk/Media-Room/Press-releases/2010/UK-to-focus-aid-efforts-on-women (accessed 1 February 2011).

Dobson, A. (2011). Hetero-sexy representation by young women on MySpace: The politics of performing an 'objectified' self. *Outskirts* 25. [Online]: http://www.outskirts.arts.uwa.edu.au/volumes/volume-25/amy-shields-dobson (retrieved 12 December 2011).

Driscoll, C. A. (2002). *Girls: Feminine adolescence in popular culture & cultural theory.* New York: Columbia University Press.

Gill, R. (2007). Postfeminist media culture: Elements of a sensibility. *European Journal of Cultural Studies, 10*(2), 147–166.

Gill, R. and Koffman, O. (forthcoming). Where promotional discourse meets global inequality: the 'empowering' language of the Girl Effect. *Discourse and Society.*

Goldman, R. (1992). *Reading ads socially.* New York: Routledge.

Harris, A. (2004). *Future girl: Young women in the twenty-first century.* London: Routledge.

Hartsock, N. (2006). Globalization and primitive accumulation: The contributions of David Harvey's dialectical Marxism. In N. Castree and D. Gregory, D. (eds). *David Harvey: A critical reader* (pp. 167–190). Oxford: Blackwell.

Hirschkind, C. and Mahmood, S. (2002). Feminism, the Taliban, and politics of counter-insurgency. *Anthropological Quarterly, 75*(2), 339–354.

House of Commons International Development Committee (2011). The 2010 Millennium Development Goals Review Summit: Government Response to the Committee's Second Report of Session 2010–11. Online: http://www.publications.parliament.uk/pa/cm201012/cmselect/cmintdev/959/959.pdf (accessed 1 February 2011).

http://www.girleffect.org (n.d.). The Girl Effect. Online: http://www.girleffect.org/learn/the-big-picture (accessed 30 August 2011).

Koffman, O. (2012). Children having children?: Religion, psychology and the birth of the teenage pregnancy problem. *History of the human sciences.*

Koffman, O. and Gill, R. (forthcoming). Making her up: Nike and the new Rwandan 'teenager'.

Levine, R., Lloyd, C. B. and Grown, C. (2009). Girls Count: A Global Investment & Action Agenda. Online: http://www.cgdev.org/content/publications/detail/15154 (accessed 1 September 2011).

Lewis, G. (2006). Imaginaries of Europe: Technologies of gender, economies of power. *European Journal of Women's Studies, 13*(2), 87–102.

Lowe, L. and Lloyd, D. (1997). Introduction. In L. Lowe and D. Lloyd (eds). *The politics of culture in the shadow of capital.* Durham: Duke University Press, 1–32.

McRobbie, A. (2007). Top girls? *Cultural Studies, 21*(4–5), 718–737.

McRobbie, A. (2009). *The aftermath of feminism : Gender, culture and social change.* London: Sage.

Mohanty, C. T. (1988). Under Western eyes: Feminist scholarship and colonial discourses. *Feminist Review, 30*, 61–88.

Mohanty, C. T. (2003). "Under Western Eyes" revisited: feminist solidarity through anticapitalist struggles. *Signs, 28*(2), 499–535.

Nike Foundation (2009). Girl Effect: Your Move. Online: http://www.girleffect. org/media (accessed 27 September 2010).

Nike Foundation (2011). Girl Effect website. Online: http://www.girleffect.org (accessed 27 September 2010).

Pedwell, C. (2010). *Feminism, culture and embodied practice: The rhetorics of comparison.* London Routledge.

Plan (2009). Because I Am a Girl: The State of the World's Girls 2009; Girls in the Global Economy. Online: http://plan-international.org/about-plan/resources/ publications/campaigns/because-i-am-a-girl-girls-in-the-global-economy-2009 (accessed 23 August 2011).

Razack, S. (2004). Imperilled Muslim women, dangerous Muslim men and civilised Europeans: Legal and social responses to forced marriages. *Feminist Legal Studies, 12*(2), 129–174.

Ringrose, J. (2007). Successful girls? Complicating post-feminist, neoliberal discourses of educational achievement and gender equality. *Gender and Education, 19*(4), 471–489.

Scharff, C. (2011). Disarticulating feminism: Individualization, neoliberalism and the othering of 'Muslim women''. *European Journal of Women's Studies, 18*(2), 119–134.

Scott, J. W. (2007). *The politics of the veil.* Woodstock, UK: Princeton University Press.

Switzer, H. (2010). Disruptive discourses: Kenyan Maasai schoolgirls make themselves. *Girlhood Studies, 3*(1), 137–155.

TechnoServe (5/8/2009). TechnoServe and The Nike Foundation Expand Young Women's Entrepreneurship Training Program (Press Release). Online: http:// www.technoserve.org/resources/press-room/2009-2010-press-releases/ywe-nike.html (accessed 30 August 2011).

UN Foundation (30/9/2010). United Nations Foundation Launches Girl Up (Press Release). Online: http://www.unfoundation.org/press-center/press-releases/2010/united-nations-foundation-launches-girl-up.html (accessed 30 August 2011).

UN Foundation (2010). Girl Up website: Girl Up store. Online: http://store. girlup.org/default.aspx (accessed 30 August 2011).

UN Foundation (2011a). Girl Up Facebook page: "Washington DC Unite for Girls Tour: Pep Rally''. Online: http://www.facebook.com/events/191107120904746/ (accessed 30 August 2011).

UN Foundation (2011b). Girl Up website. Online: http://www.girlup.org/ (accessed 30 August 2011).

UN Foundation (2011c). Girl Up website: Gear Up with Girl Up. Online: http:// www.girlup.org/blog/gear-up-with-girl-up.html (accessed 30 August 2011).

UN Foundation (2011d). Girl Up website: Making an Impact. Online: http:// www.girlup.org/learn/making-an-impact.html (accessed 30 August 2011).

UN Foundation (n.d.). Girlafesto. Online: http://www.girlup.org/get-involved/ girlafesto.html (accessed 30 August 2011).

UN Foundation (n.d.). Girl Up blog: Unite for Girls Tour. Online: http://girlup. org/blog/?category=unite-for-girls-tour (accessed 30 August 2011).

UN Interagency Task Force on Adolescent Girls (2010). Accelerating Efforts to Advance the Rights of Adolescent Girls: A UN Joint Statement. Online: http:// www.unicef.org/media/files/UN_Joint_Statement_Adolescent_Girls_FINAL.pdf (accessed 30 August 2011).

UN Interagency Taskforce on Adolescent Girls (n.d.). Girl Power and Potential leaflet. Online: http://www.unicef.org/adolescence/files/UN_IATF_Girls_post cardFINAL.pdf (accessed 2 February 2012).

UNESCO (2011). Gender Equality theme, Adolescent Girls webpage. Online: http://www.unesco.org/en/gender-equality/themes/adolescent-girls/ (accessed 2 February 2012).

UNFPA (2011). Unleashing the Power and Potential of Adolescent Girls. Online: http://www.unfpa.org/public/cache/offonce/home/news/pid/7324;jsessionid= 1C6B7A464ACBAB326818F4498AE587DA (accessed 30 August 2011).

UNICEF, WHO and UNFPA (2003). Adolescents: Profiles in Empowerment. Online: http://www.unicef.org/adolescence/files/adolescent_profiles_eng.pdf (accessed 30 August 2011).

Walkerdine, V., Lucey, H. and Melody, J. (2001). *Growing up girl : Psychosocial explorations of gender and class.* Basingstoke: Palgrave Macmillan.

Wernick, A. (1991). *Promotional culture: Advertising, ideology and symbolic expression.* London: Sage.

Wilson, K. (2011). 'Race', gender and neoliberalism: Changing visual representations in development. *Third World Quarterly, 32*(2), 315–331.

World Bank (2008). Adolescent Girl Initiative Launch (Press Release). Online: http://web.worldbank.org/WBSITE/EXTERNAL/NEWS/0,,contentMDK:21935 449~pagePK:34370~piPK:34424~theSitePK:4607,00.html (accessed 30 August 2011).

World Economic Forum (2009). World Economic Forum Annual Meeting 2009: Shaping the Post-Crisis World. Online: https://members.weforum.org/pdf/ AnnualReport/2009/social_backlash.htm (accessed 30 August 2011).

15
Politics, Identity, Representation and UK Asian Suburban Youth: Voices from the Margins

Rupa Huq

This chapter shifts away from the more familiar focus on the urban in youth cultural studies to the somewhat neglected category of *suburban* youth: those residing in districts of big cities that are at their edges not their cores. Whilst suburb-dwellers might once have been presumed to be ethnically white, the chapter draws on interviews conducted with young people of Asian origin in the suburban towns of Bury in greater Manchester (North West England) and Kingston in greater London. In this sense it is also a corrective to criticisms that youth culture studies has been 'too white' in outlook, redressing the balance along with others such as Nayak (2010) and Watson and Saha (2012) who have also examined Asian suburbia. From the transcript excerpts included it can be seen that the young people interviewed are fashioning their own narratives of identity and belonging in seeking to encompass multiple cultures, to which their British citizenship, country of origin, faith background and location as suburban all contribute. In this way the chapter presents voices from the margins literally and metaphorically as they reflect on political themes; it also shows how the media were ever-present in their understandings of big and small p politics.

Suburban youth: an under-researched species

Youth culture research has frequently focused on 'spectacular subcultures' that 'express forbidden forms' through 'transgressions of sartorial and behavioural codes, law-breaking etc.' as Dick Hebdige put it in his classic formulation (1979, pp. 91–92). The geographical remit of such studies has frequently been urban. Hebdige, for example, refers to 'the recognisable locales of Britain's inner cities' as wellsprings of youth culture (1979, p. 65). One of the criticisms of the Birmingham Centre for

Contemporary Cultural Studies (see Griffin, this volume) was that ethnic minority youth were a blindspot: gangs of white, working-class males tended to predominate. Among the early well-known US titles rooted in the Chicago school of urban study is Whyte's *Street Corner Society* (1955). In the United Kingdom, 'streets' are a city appellation, unlike the quasi-rural descriptors of 'avenues', 'drives', 'crescents', 'dells' and 'ways' used for suburban roads, with their grass verges and trees. As marketing literature for developments such as the interwar private housing estates of London's 'metro-land' attest, the benefits of suburbia were meant to be better quality of life, cleanliness and a better class of resident. As green-field sites gave way to mock Tudor commuter enclaves and out-of-town council cottage estates, English suburban life attracted criticism from commentators, but became an aspiration for many. Part of the appeal of moving out from the city was about moving up the social ladder, out of the grime of the insalubrious big, bad city and away from 'undesirable' populations, which implicitly included minority ethnic residents – a process known in the United States as 'white flight' (Frey, 1979).

Yet suburbanization has been complicated by urban gentrification: the industrial areas once spurned are now desirable to a city-working demographic seeking period property and a quick commute. In some respects, urban gentrification, often practiced by the children and grandchildren of interwar suburbanizers, is a reaction against what its proponents see as stultifying suburban childhoods, recounted in numerous memoirs (see Boorman, 2003; Collins, 2004; Rhys Jones, 2006).

Meanwhile, it can be argued that the suburban ideal has been desirable to 'Asians' of all backgrounds in the postwar era (and here I acknowledge the reductiveness of the term 'Asian', which in the United Kingdom is replete with colonial hangovers, reducing an entire continent to the peoples of ex-British India – Pakistanis, Bangladeshis, Sri Lankans and Indians, with different languages, religions and social classes). Sukhdev Sandhu (2003, p. 236) refers to the single men working on the factory/foundry floor and living in lodgings of several to a room in inner-city locations before they sent for their wives. For such men, he argues, 'the suburbs [were] a promised land, light at the end of the industrial tunnel'. Woolfs rubber factory in Southall is one example; another is the Vauxhall car-plant in Luton described by the journalist and broadcaster Sarfraz Manzoor (2008), whose father worked there. Counterposed with these memories of initial post-migratory hardship, the spaciousness and clean air of suburbia are what Asian populations have long equated with success.

Suburban populations have tended to be young: one of the principal motivations of the people moving there was that the suburbs offered ample physical space for a growing family. Nonetheless, explicitly *suburban* youth have rarely been seen as subjects worthy of sustained youth cultural research, barring very few exceptions. Willmott and Young (1967) carried out a study of the London suburb of Woodford but did not address young people directly; and this work is far less well-known than their *Family and Kinship in East London* (1957). Asians too have tended only to be addressed selectively by youth cultural studies, in the 1970s as voiceless victims of racism (Pearson, 1976) or in the 1990s as part of a fashionable club culture scene (Sharma et al., 1996).

This chapter draws on interviews with young Asian Muslims and Tamils from the Royal Borough of Kingston-upon-Thames in South London, on the border with the wealthy county of Surrey. As the capital's outermost borough to its southwestern tip, this counts as an unashamedly suburban location. The young people were interviewed for research funded by, firstly, the government's counterterrorist Preventing Violent Extremism initiative which supported Muslim community projects fostering community cohesion and, secondly, a 'knowledge transfer' grant from the Economic and Social Research Council. Additional interviews with Muslim respondents also took place in Bury, Greater Manchester, at an interfaith project that works to build links between Muslim and Jewish communities.

Muslims and politicization

Muslim interviewees were keenly aware of the diversity that characterizes Muslim communities, in terms of ethnicity, language, religious denomination and so on. They also recognized the public demonization of Muslims, or Islamophobia (Runnymede Trust, 1997). Since the fall of state communism, Islam has been constructed as a new threat to the West; and this process has arguably accelerated since the bombings of 11 September 2001 and (in the United Kingdom) the London bombings of 2005. There is a perception of growing numbers of asylum seekers, many of whom are Muslim, in the population at large. In our interviews, localized events were shaped by broader geopolitical happenings, as can be seen in the following exchange with students in their 20s who describe the hostility they as hijab wearers encountered from non-Muslims, even in the once genteel market town of Kingston:

Haneefa: Do you remember 9/11, do you remember the twin towers? – I went to shopping in Kingston, everybody was giving me dirty looks, it was horrible to be Muslim after 9/11.

Iram: The next day everybody was looking at you, I got dirty looks even from Afro-Caribbeans, I got dirty looks, non-Muslims giving me dirty looks, it was horrible and then you had the July bombings – was that 2005? – in London.

Alia: I think I was year 9 at school. We came into school. I specifically remember that morning. They had all come to school and they had newspapers, saying it was ... 'bin Laden', and the only thing they could associate between him and us was that we were Muslims, but it very quickly became 'oh it was your people'. And I was like, 'we don't even know him, who is he?' We were kind of defensive as well, saying 'What are you talking about, why are you trying to accuse us? We haven't done anything. It's just obviously this group, which has nothing to do with us' ... I don't know what they thought. There was definitely friction after that, it was not necessarily racist remarks, but they were a bit distant. They were suddenly a bit wary of 'who are they, what do they think?' It was a bit scary at the time because, the impact it had, we didn't actually realise the impact it had on us, but obviously it did. It was a shock to us as well.

In recounting her experience at school, it is only once she starts talking about the period after 9/11 that this particular respondent distinguishes between 'them' and 'us'. Earlier, when talking about her friends at school she uses the pronoun 'we' (e.g., 'we were all mixed, but we all but got along'). This clearly illustrates the dynamic nature of identity. As well as experiencing an increase in discrimination, various participants also reported a qualitative change in the type of racism they were experiencing. Whereas beforehand racism tended to be focused on their ethnicity, it was now quite clearly focused on religion and its perceived association with terrorism:

Haneefa: Before it was racism, now it's become anti-Muslim ... before it was from, you were from, like, Pakistan [...], about where you're from and the colour of your skin. And now it's about being a Muslim. It's not so much about which country you're from, I think, it's about whether you are Muslim or not.

As particular age groups (especially older teenagers and younger adults) were exposed to prejudice against Muslims, this experience also seemed to politicize them and affect how they could explore their faith. Many young Muslims reported how the constant confrontation with such issues had made them much more politically aware:

Farooq: I think Muslims are now compelled to have an awareness of politics as well, because of the questions we always have to answer. Such as 'why did 9/11 happen, why did July the 7th [2005] happen?' And I feel that if Muslims don't research these questions, and have answers to these questions prepared, it's almost like people are going to continue with the stereotyping, what they've got in their mind.

Mu: You kind of have to become political. I was never political, but people expect me to have an opinion on what happened.

'Suburbia' is not normally associated with 'extremism'. Medhurst (1997, p. 244) has written of 'what one might call the *newslessness* of suburbia ... a cornerstone of the vision of tranquillity that sold the suburban dream'. For our interviewees, recently politicized experiences also intersected with their faith; they voiced a fear of being classed as extremists. Young people and in particular young men tended to self-censor the events they went to or the people they became involved with:

Shenaz: I'm not involved in any of the [Islamic] groups at Kingston [University]. I sometimes go to talks and lectures, and I go to like the Islamic week but I'm not really part of the society ... I think mum would be very worried about extremism, she's always saying don't get too involved with any group, do what you need to do, you know go and pray or, OK, go to some talks if you want to. But even if I go to a talk I have to tell them what it is.

The function of post-compulsory education in recruiting religious fundamentalists was echoed by a former member of Hiz but Tahrir whom I interviewed is a young man of Bangladeshi origin who grew up in Kingston and was initially recruited when a sixth former at Kingston College. He then rose up through the ranks to be a top University of London recruiter when attending one of its constituent universities. He described a pan-Muslim underclass rather than the social standing of individual members who had been implicated in terrorist plots as the reason why people are attracted to such groups:

RH: But why is it suburban people who've been to private school as the media reports it?

Amin: Yeah but there is no class distinction between suburban Muslims and urban Muslims or rural Muslims ... It's less to do with where one is situated in Britain but more to do with Britain, so if you live in the suburbs you'll be radicalised in a different way from what you would be if you were urban, but you'll still be radicalised ... The people that *do* turn to Islamism do it for a multitude of reasons and those are the result of social, economic, political mismanagement by the powers that be, you know ... unintentional mismanagement. Historical process results in their alienation, disenfranchisement. If we take the most extreme example of the [London] Tavistock Square suicide bomb [of 2005]. These guys before they died left a message saying we're doing this for our brothers around the world, we're doing this to fight oppression. This is a profound political message. Their entire endeavour was political and the constituency if you like that they ascribe themselves to was not in England, necessarily. It's this sort of global ummah, global community of Muslims, so they identify themselves as Muslims before anything else and as suffering the consequences of foreign policies of the sort of postcolonial world. They saw these corrupt rulers that the ex-colonies put in place after they left. It's actually quite a sophisticated political critique of the global world as it stands today. They felt that pain to such an extent that they were willing to give up their lives for it and that's where the religion comes and kicks in ... ideas of afterlife and reward. I think all people who are Muslims in the country are immediately underclass. It doesn't matter how rich they are. If you're non-white Muslim in this country you're immediately underclass. You're not even working class, you're less than that. For me class doesn't work on level of affluence per se and I think Muslims, along with asylum seekers and migrant workers, have the lowest social capital.

Other people involved in terror plots have hailed from similarly suburban locations. The *Bucks Herald* newspaper commented: 'When news filtered through that suicide bomber Germaine Lindsay – the deadliest of the four London bombers – was an Aylesbury resident, the town was stunned ... The biggest police operation in Aylesbury's history took place days later when Lindsay's family home was raided by officers led by anti-terror branch officers' (Jackson, 2007). However, it is notable that our interviewee here represents Muslim disaffection as deriving from a form of class inequality.

Suburban settlement, social mobility and politics

Nevertheless, these issues also vary between different ethnic groups. My question 'what would you say were the big issues for the Tamil community, locally or nationally?' prompted a range of responses from the young people I interviewed. This Kingston college student had a vague awareness but coming from the second generation he felt he was not directly involved enough to give a comprehensive answer:

Nihal: I don't take a big interest in the active Tamil community as such but I know that there's a rally to get the council, get like a private institution for Tamils, I know my mum went to a peaceful protest a while ago. My father is against it though, he just thinks it's going to cause more trouble with the government and make them think of us more of a problem than a help ...

His parents speak to him in Tamil but he replies in English and in his youth he has attended Tamil language and culture classes:

Nihal: Yeah I was there [the Tamil Saturday school] until I was about 12 so when I started going to secondary school, I had a lot of work and a lot of extra curricular activities so that I didn't want to do it anymore. At the start I didn't like it but I did like the making friends and everything but some of the things, we had to play Tamil instruments and Tamil songs, things like that and it wasn't my thing. I like some of the aspects of Tamil culture but some of them are not for me, I was forced to do it.

According to Mr Ram of the Tamil Information Centre, an international organization representing Tamil immigrants across Europe, there is a constant in all settlements:

Mr Ram: Everywhere the Tamils go and settle they try to maintain their culture that means their language schools, dance classes, instrumental classes, even in Kingston one school which is one of the oldest [Tamil] schools in London [...]

The research took place at a time when Tamils were prominent in national news media, and protesting in Westminster. However, Mr Ram saw these high-profile demonstrations in Parliament Square as atypical or unrepresentative of the average Tamil:

Mr Ram: The majority of the community are dormant, they are not particularly active, but whenever there is a political require-ment they will join 1000 people marching in London. So as and when there is a need they will join but other than that they are dormant ... the children are the most priorities ... [there is pressure to study] medicine ... so [in response to that] we inform the parents that there are other opportuni-ties they must look for, even the children they don't want to do many things, they are forced so it's conflict within the family as well. There are a number of people, women particu-larly are suffering from domestic violence, it is an issue [but] it's not spoken about.

Many of the issues highlighted here are common to all groups: domestic violence by its nature occurs behind closed doors. Others are relevant to other migrant groups such as the split identified by Tamil elders who migrated to the United Kingdom in the 1970s or 1980s, between previ-ously established, largely professional families who saw themselves as socially superior to the younger, more recent asylum-seeking arrivals – 'you know, the ones who work in Asda [the supermarket]', as one Tamil pensioner of longstanding Kingston residence described them.

My interviews also illustrated different reasons for settlement in Kingston. One 23-year-old Tamil man described how his father arrived in Britain on his own at first, then his parents settled initially further towards central London, but once the children were born, moved as a family unit to Kingston because of the appeal of its selective grammar school system.

Narayan: My father was here since the 70s, late 70s, so yeah ...
RH: And he came straight to Kingston?
Nihal: No he went to Tooting, my mum came about a decade later ...
RH: Was it perceived as a step up to come to Kingston from Tooting?
Nihal: I think they moved because so my sister could go to Tiffin girls and me to Tiffin boys so because we both applied for those I think we moved for that so it would be easier for us.

Meanwhile, the restaurant trade had been a motivating factor in sustaining growth amongst the Bangladeshi community in Kingston. There was a perception voiced that Bangladeshis in Kingston and its environs were those who had 'made it' as compared with more down-at-heel counterparts in the multiple-deprivation blight districts such as East London's borough of Tower Hamlets:

Mohammed: There weren't very many [Bengali] families when I was very young [but] while I was growing up more and more Bengali families came because Surrey is a goldmine for Bangladeshi restaurants and they all do really well because it's a wealthy county and they all like Indian food. So a lot of families started emerging. I'd say from mid 90s onwards there was this kind of rush, they'd say, 'it's too far from east London ... well we work in Surrey, we have a business in Surrey, we might as well move there', so people actually moved out from East London and set up businesses in Byfleet, Weybridge, Tadworth, Epsom, places like that ... sprang up. Bengalis in Epsom are actually growing to a higher more accelerated level than Bengalis in Kingston but the number of Muslims in Kingston has significantly increased since when I was young.

There is an assumption that migrants come to the United Kingdom to better their lifestyle, but some of the interview data shows the reverse. The age-old career path of medicine has long been sought after by middle-aged Asians as the gold standard for their offspring. Mr Ram told us that he had to counsel participants in the Tamil Information Centre's community activities that there are other alternatives. These kinds of variations were also apparent among different 'Asian' communities in the north, to which we turn next.

Politics: at the ballot box and beyond

Bury in the north west of England is more than 200 miles away from Kingston but the two areas have much in common. Bury was once a town in its own right, while Kingston was a market town, although both have effectively become suburbs dependent on Manchester and London, respectively. When interviewing Asian Muslims of Pakistani background there the conversation turned to parliamentary politics as one of the group was at the time a Conservative prospective candidate in a Labour area in the region:

RH: Surely the Asian vote should be Conservative really, given the social conservatism of Asian communities?

Imran: Looking after your family, looking after your community, paying your taxes, contributing to your society ... they're all sort of Asian traits really, aren't they? I think, yes, Labour has taken the Asian vote for granted but things are changing for a number of reasons. I think women within our communities are far more empowered to making their own decisions, that includes who they're voting for. I think families don't vote as a bloc, as a bloc-vote, as it used to in the past. Young people are learning about the democratic system so I think now more than ever before you're finding households that are voting for different parties rather than all voting for one.

Sabba: Before it used to be the inheritance vote, so whatever your father votes, or your parents voted, you'd vote for at the same election, but I think you can see that slowly eroding. I mean in our family household we voted completely different parties. Our parents still voted Labour because they see themselves as staunch supporters, but the rest of us all did our own thing. I think partly that's a reaction against centralised politics anyway because we're seeing that there is no distinction anymore between Labour and Conservative anymore because they are all so centralised, so I think that has played a role but I think people are more polarising their opinions because they want to say 'I'm in this camp or I'm in that camp'. They don't want to be in the middle. In Conservative foreign policy and New Labour foreign policy, there's nothing there to differentiate them.

Evidence suggests that Asian voters have always overwhelmingly backed Labour, in part due to the anti-immigrant rhetoric of Conservative MP Enoch Powell's infamous 'rivers of blood' speech in 1968 predicting social discord as a result of multi-ethnicity, which has left an indelible mark. Sunder Katwala (2012) has argued of this legacy: 'It is hard not to take Enoch Powell's argument personally, for any Briton of black or Asian heritage. He wished that we had never been born. He argued that it would be a matter of national suicide if any significant number of us were [here] ... But that argument is rejected today as strongly on the democratic right as on the liberal-left.' Our interviews conducted in Bury in December 2009 showed the attempts made by the far-right racist British National Party (BNP) to increase their North West representation whereas in South West London the issue did not arise:

Imran: I think there has been a resurgence of BNP over the last couple of years. When it comes to towns like Rochdale, Bury, Bolton … up to 2–3 years ago you'd never find a BNP candidate on the ballot paper but they started off testing the waters I'd say about 2 years ago and at the last election I think they virtually fielded a whole range of candidates, full slate in most of the towns, which is worrying because I think they're attracting 4 to 500 votes in the wards that they're standing in. So it is worrying, but it's difficult times for the country as a whole with the recession, with people losing their jobs, with us having a devastat[ed] economy with the downturn. So people need something to blame.

Shazia: There's a lot of protest voting going on.

Imran: People want to blame government and in addition to that with the MPs' expenses [see below] people are really put off voting for the mainstream parties because they feel they've been let down and quite rightly so … Some changes need to be made in the parliamentary process … to bring those voters back to the mainstream when really I think in the European elections the BNP gained a Parliamentary seat in the north west which I believe is a protest vote. The other thing is I think the mainstream parties have been very scared of having a debate on immigration. I think there is a need for a sensible debate to take place and once that does take place I think people will stop protesting and move away from the BNP.

Usma: I don't really like the way that [then Prime Minister] Gordon Brown for example is pandering towards that, using that tagline 'British jobs for British people', I mean …

RH: What's it protesting for or against then?

Shazia: More the Labour government, just its failures and it hasn't lived up to its promises. Iraq would come into it I'd say.

Usma: The people, instead of channelling the frustrations and energies back into politics, they're channelling it to more areas, towards the environment issues, the green movement, so they're redirecting those energies towards them whereas in the generations before you'd have seen loads of young people really get interested in politics, so Conservative, Labour party, Green party, whatever. You feel them move away from that. I think that's partly due to disaffection with the way in which the political spectrum works and the way in which parties function.

An anti-politics sentiment in popular opinion was rife in the summer of 2009 following media coverage of the 'expenses scandal', in which MPs were accused of overclaiming on their parliamentary allowances. The notion that 'all politicians are as bad as each other' is a powerful argument that frequently resurfaces in everyday political debate. The interviews took place at a time when Labour were in power. Subsequently a by-election in nearby Bradford West was won by a 'Respect Party' candidate with a clear anti-Iraq war message appealing to a large Muslim electorate. Throughout spring 2013 the isolationalist UKIP (UK Independence Party) gained some impressive scores in one-off by-elections, beating government parties and finishing in second place in northern and southern England (South Shields and Eastleigh) on a message that played more to xenophobic fears than the detail of EU legislation. These interviews and recent UK by-elections show a decline in deference and tribal voting patterns and demonstrate that international issues as much as national matters and local factors can influence voting behaviour (Bright, 2005).

Conclusion: In the shadow of the media and the city

The attention commanded by Asian youth in academia and the media has waxed and waned over the years. The 1970s arguably represented a peak in Britain for youth culture studies, although as I have argued, Asian youth barely figured here, except occasionally as victims of 'paki-bashing' (Pearson, 1976). In the 1990s, there was renewed media interest in Asian youth as a new 'Asian underground' club scene emerged from some of the more fashionable spots of central London. However the term 'Asian' itself has unravelled somewhat since. My interviewees did not self-describe with the term and this comment from Amin (the former extremist quoted above) describes the historical period of extremism's emergence and how he stopped attending pan-Asian bhangra music happenings for example:

Amin: I've got sisters [in their late 30s] and I used to hang round with them a lot and with their friends, we'd go to places like

Asian events, loads of events. But it shifted. It shifted with the Rushdie affair [the fatwah issued against author Salman Rushdie]. It shifted with the Gulf war. It shifted with Bosnia. These are all 90s. Bosnian Muslims, they're white but they're Muslims getting annihilated, do you see what I mean? Bang bang bang bang bang. The 90s was the period where radicalisation in Britain prevailed. Now it's been curtailed because there's [anti-terrorism initiatives], think tanks, there's this, there's that. But the 90s was mental, that's when I got sucked in, I got sucked into the wave. So did a lot of these guys.

When, long before 9/11, in summer 2001 northern English towns witnessed riotous friction between British-born Asians, extreme right-wing sympathizers and the police, Hindus were quick to claim that these clashes were not 'Asian riots' (as the police labelled them) but Muslim riots, as those involved were of Pakistani and Bangladeshi origin (Huq, 2004). The underlying causes of these riots were multiple, including the principal driver of structural disadvantage coupled with racist provocation. Subsequent years have seen the rise of a politicized Islam led by charismatic imams and followed by youth such as Amin, who are asserting religious identities that their parents frequently downplayed. Minority communities once seen as passive and quiescent have increasingly flexed their muscle. The government has been keen to downplay any link between domestic events and foreign policy, but the United Kingdom's joining with the United States in the invasion of Iraq in 2003 has not helped New Labour's image amongst Muslims and its inaction over Israel's bombing of Gaza has also reinforced resentment. The government has committed significant funds to a cross-departmental initiative entitled 'Preventing Violent Extremism' which is ostensibly designed at countering international terrorism but tellingly provides funding for Muslim groups providing that they are from the 'correct' (anti-extremist) persuasion.

The 2011 UK census has illustrated what has already been observed in many contemporary cities: that Christian faith is in decline while other religions are rising in popularity, and suburbs (particularly in outer London) are becoming more ethnically mixed. Prior to the census providing 'hard' data on these shifts, the UK population's perception of them was shaped partly by media news reports, televised dramas such as Hanif Kureshi's 1990 novel *The Buddha of Suburbia* or TV comedies such as the BBC's *The Kumars at Number 42*. Some grand claims have been made about such cultural phenomena: for instance, Donnell (2007, p. 47) has declared the successful British Asian themed film *Bend It Like Beckham*, set in the London suburb of Hounslow, to be 'both a feminist and a postcolonial triumph ... [which] ends with a more celebratory and harmonious version of cosmopolitan conviviality than Stuart Hall or Paul Gilroy could have imagined'.

The interviewees in my research were more guarded in their language. Whilst they all refer to their uses of the media to make sense of the world around them, they are mature enough to interrogate media representations rather than accepting them unquestioningly. On the evidence of the above we can make a case for a second-generation, suburban British Asian 'habitus' (utilizing Bourdieu's (1990) concept) that goes wider than physical location. These young people negotiate daily life and display a high degree of media literacy, making them more sophisticated than the official line from the last two governments on 'radicalization' seems to presume. In the process, the identities of UK 'Asians' and of British suburban youth are undergoing a continuing process of social, cultural and political change.

References

Boorman, J. (2003). *Adventures of a suburban boy*. London: Faber and Faber.

Bourdieu, P. (1990). *The logic of practice*. Cambridge: Polity Press.

Bright, M. (2005). Leak shows Blair told of Iraq war terror link. In *The Observer* 28/8/05 at http://www.guardian.co.uk/politics/2005/aug/28/uk.iraq. Also see http://politics.guardian.co.uk/foi/images/0,9069,1558170,00.html

Collins, A. (2006). *Where did it all go right? Growing up normal in the 70s*. London: Erbury Press.

Donnell, A. (2007). Feeling good? Look again! feel good movies and the vanishing points of liberation in Deepa Mehta's *Fire* and Gurinder Chadha's *Bend It Like Beckham*. *Journal of Creative Communications, 2* (1-2), 43–55.

Frey, W. (1979). Central city white flight: Racial and nonracial causes. *American Sociological Review, 44*, 425–448.

Hebdige, D. (1979). *Subculture: The meaning of style*. London: Methuen.

Huq, R. (2004). *Beyond subculture*. London: Routledge.

Jackson, A. (2007). The Bucks Herald 1963 – Present day. 15/3/2007. http://www.bucksherald.co.uk/newspaperhistory/The-Bucks-Herald-1963-.2051918.jp

Katwala, S. (2012). Powell: 'best understood as part of our history'. http://www.britishfuture.org/blog/powell-best-understand-as-part-of-our-history/

Manzoor, S. (2008). *Greetings from Bury Park*. London: Bloomsbury.

Medhurst, A. (1997). Negotiating the gnome zone: Versions of suburbia in British popular culture. In R. Silverstone (ed.). *Visions of Suburbia*. London: Routledge.

Nayak, A. (2010). Race, affect, and emotion: Young people, racism, and graffiti in the postcolonial English suburbs. *Environment and Planning A, 42*(10), 2370–2392.

Pearson, G. (1976). "Paki-Bashing" in a north-east Lancashire cotton town: a case study in its history. In G. Mungham and G. Pearson (eds). *Working class youth culture* (pp. 48–81) London: Routledge & Kegan Paul.

Rhys Jones, G. (2006). *Semi-detached: Pulling up roots in Suburbia*. London: Penguin.

Runnymede Trust (1997). *Islamophobia: A challenge for us all*. London: Runnymede Trust.

Sandhu S. (2003). *London calling: How black and Asian writers imagined a city*. London: HarperCollins.

Sharma S., Sharma, A. and Hutnyk, J. (eds). (1996). *Dis-Orienting rhythms: The politics of the new Asian dance music*. London: Zed Books.

Watson S. and Saha A. (2012). Suburban drifts: Mundane multiculturalism in outer London. *Ethnic and Racial Studies* DOI: 10.1080/01419870.2012.678875.

Whyte, WF. (1955). *Street corner society*. Chicago: Chicago University Press.

Willmott, P. and Young M. (1967). *Family and class in a London suburb*. London: New English Library.

Young, M. and Willmott P. (1957). *Family and kinship in East London*. London: Routledge & Kegan Paul.

Conclusion: Elusive 'Youth'

Sara Bragg and David Buckingham

> My mum said she really wanted me to do it [take part
> in this research] because I've got a really good opinion
> on things and [....] she thinks that I'd be, like, a good
> representative of what people think. [Girl, aged 12,
> interview]
>
> (Buckingham and Bragg, 2004)

For some time, those who would study youth have been enjoined to be
Janus-faced: on the one hand, to remember that 'youth', like 'childhood',
is a social construction; but on the other, never to forget that children
and youth are 'social actors' (James, Jenks and Prout, 1999; Jeffrey, 2010).
As a social construction, 'youth' is to be interrogated, unmasked, exposed
or critiqued; yet as social actors, young people need to be heard, brought
in from the margins, respected, listened to – and even 'empowered'.
These contrasting arguments involve different methodological, analytical
and epistemological approaches, but they also entail different positions
for the researcher. So is it possible to resolve the apparent incompatibility
between these two perspectives – or at least to find some way of theorizing the relationship between them?

Summoning 'youth': the constructionist perspective

As the contributing authors to this volume have shown, 'youth' has
been variously imagined, represented, invoked, deployed, summoned,
assembled, interpellated and addressed, by a range of discourses and
institutions. 'Youth' emerges here as a contingent cultural construction whose reference point is elusive and variable. These contributions
remind us yet again that – like 'childhood' – the term is a site of struggle

over its social meanings, a repository of hopes and fears for the future of the world in times of socioeconomic, technological and cultural change. On the whole, however, 'youth' proves more ambivalent – potentially explosive or negative – than the 'moral rhetoric of childhood' (Meyer, 2007), which retains its gilded aura and its capacity to mobilize sentiment that will add persuasive power to almost any position or policy.

The chapters in this book adduce several examples of the 'naturalizing' discourses about youth that are typically challenged by the social constructionist approach (cf. Lynch, 2001). The marketing manuals David Buckingham discusses, the development policy documents analysed by Ofra Koffman and Ros Gill, the expressed intentions of the BBC initiative explored by Helen Thornham and Angela McFarlane all claim to be simply identifying inherent qualities possessed by youth, yet do so in quite particular and partial ways. In this respect, they might well be compared with other well-known constructions of adolescence as a time of raging hormones and *sturm und drang* (see Lesko, 2001), or more popular representations that identify youth with idealism, independence and creativity.

Against this, we can point to compelling evidence of how 'youth' has signified differently in different times and contexts. In this book, for instance, we have the case of India, discussed in Ritty Lukose's chapter, where 54 per cent of the population is under 25: here, 'youth' can more readily denote a specific age or stage of life, even as it figures in debates about globalization as always more than that. On the other hand, in contemporary Britain, with its ageing population, the term has slipped its temporal anchoring. It has come to refer both to consumption styles and attitudes that people of widely divergent ages may adopt and simultaneously to the extended period of dependency experienced by 'young adults' in a time of socioeconomic downturn. Moreover, the 'youth' who featured in the groundbreaking studies of the Birmingham CCCS in the 1970s are now potentially the grandparents of those under investigation by new generations of researchers – and, as was noted in the Introduction, remote historical curiosities to today's undergraduates. Simply remarking on these facts suggests that 'things could be otherwise' – a broader cultural and historical view that significantly expands our thinking about youth cultural studies.

Yet this idea that 'youth' is a social construction is perhaps a truism these days, especially in contexts where secure categories of social reproduction have become significantly more uncertain for most. In most 'Western' countries at least, the progression from youth to adulthood – defined in terms of acquiring social goods such as a stable job, valuable skills and secure housing (Jeffrey, 2010) – is coming to seem far from inevitable (Cohen, 2003). The social, cultural and historical construction of 'youth' – as it emerged from specific conditions in mid-twentieth-century capitalist societies – is little in dispute. What is more of interest is to discover *how* and *why* this occurs, and what consequences it might have. What qualities are attributed to 'youth' in different discourses, by whom, within which different institutions and with what effects? We also need to consider what is at stake in making this very argument in the first place. As Lynch (2001) asks, what is the meaning, philosophical purpose and political pay-off in arguing that an entity like youth is constructed? Hacking (1999) has noted that social constructionist accounts become more provoking and revealing when they suggest something beyond established, commonsense narratives. Yet does it follow that youth is a cultural category we would be better off without? Do we *need* the idea of 'youth' – and if so, what do we need it for, and why do we need it now?

If we were to place these arguments in their own historical context, we might well conclude that in different ways, all the contributions to this book explore the impact of contemporary processes of neoliberalization and globalization on the construction of youth. In very broad terms, the politics of neoliberalism involve economic policies promoting private accumulation, entrepreneurship and free markets; but they also entail a project of 'governmentality' that assigns individuals increasing responsibility for their own regulation, welfare and enterprise. Young people today are increasingly being addressed, summoned or interpellated, not as 'juveniles' in need of discipline and control, but as active, creative and autonomous subjects who are required to manage their own choices, conduct and risks (Rose, 1999). As such, they become harbingers of 'an emergent, newly global world order', as Ritty Lukose argues.

Thus, Thornham and McFarlane expand on the familiar construction of the 'digital native' by exploring the idea of the youthful user of new media as powerful, individual, creative, self-motivated, active, vocal and participatory, with a natural affinity for technology; while technology in turn is constructed as merely a tool or platform for these users. Koffman and Gill explore how the narrative of youth as a journey through life stages is now taking gendered contours globally, with girlhood brought into being as 'a distinctively marked-out sphere and time among young women in developing countries'; and they contrast the image of girls in the global North as empowered and able with that of girls in the global South as victims but somehow also entrepreneurial.

More broadly, Griffin suggests that in 'late modern' societies, young people must increasingly construct themselves as distinctive, authentic and discerning selves through consumption, and as ethical, responsible moral subjects.

However, some categories of youth seem less able or less disposed to respond to these demands than others – while some are constructed as being inherently incapable of doing so, and continue to be defined in stigmatizing and pejorative ways. Thus, Sunaina Maira, Rupa Huq, and Kathrin Hörschelmann and Elisabeth El Refaie demonstrate how Muslim youth in particular are now being homogenously constructed as culturally alien, even as jihadists or 'the enemy'. Mary Jane Kehily and Anoop Nayak indicate the limited terms of 'charver' and 'pram face' available to many white working-class youth. In addition, several authors refer to constructions of young masculinity as 'in crisis', as less able to fit the demands of neoliberal times. More rarely, it is argued that social constructions are changing for the better – as when Carles Feixa and Oriol Romaní argue that youthful Latino culture is increasingly constructed as a valid model of social organization, or Kyong Yoon shows how in Korea national sentiments towards Japan have shifted in the space of a few years.

Whether positive or negative, it is interesting to note that these are constructions not only of youth, but of youth *and* something else (class, globalization, gender, development, religion). In this sense, the question is not so much about the construction of 'youth' in isolation, but about the motivations and the consequences of mobilizing this category in combination with others – or alternatively, in order to exclude others that for various reasons might prove more difficult to address. When and why, in these neoliberal times, do we speak about 'youth', as distinct from (or in combination with) gender, class, or ethnicity, or any other category of social difference? What kinds of arguments and practices does the addition of 'youth' support or justify – and what does it exclude or prevent?

In some instances, of course, these constructions of youth clearly reflect particular forms of self-interest, as when marketers' images of youth as elusive justify their own special and indispensable expertise (Buckingham), or when Nike depicts entrepreneurialism and consumption opportunities as the solution to global inequalities and poverty (Koffman and Gill). Sometimes an even more sinister agenda is hinted at, as when Koffman and Gill refer to 'ushering in a very specific biopolitical objective: control of young women's fertility'. More blandly, and possibly benignly, it is assumed or implied that summoning young people into enterprising, self-actualizing and self-responsible identities will contribute to national prosperity, competitiveness and well-being. In some cases, these constructions constitute an own goal, as in the case of the BBC initiative Blast, effectively scuppered by the too-ready belief in the image of the autonomous media creator, which then foundered on a lack of user-generated content (as discussed by Thornham and McFarlane). The latter argue that 'such conceptions of new media use ultimately serve to *mask*, rather than elucidate'; and indeed, analysis of these constructions is commonly performed in the language and mode of critique. Attention is drawn to paradoxes, elisions, obfuscations, 'disavowals', to how contradictory concepts such as extreme poverty and enterprise are yoked or drawn together, potentially constituting 'acts of cultural violence' (Koffman and Gill).

Many chapters gesture towards the likely contradictions that these constructions entail for young people living in contemporary society, even if they do not explicitly explore them. Koffman and Gill, for instance, state that they are not concerned with the effectiveness of girl-oriented policies or empirical research with young women, but in 'what is produced ideologically, discursively or performatively by the distinctive yoking of neo-liberal discourses of entrepreneurialism with others which draw on 'girl power'. However, by showing how closely the ideal 'can do' middle-class girl is shadowed by her opposite, the vulnerable 'at risk' girl (Harris, 2004), they gesture towards the potential difficulty of trying to build identities and meanings through and with such notions. At the same time, and perhaps paradoxically, the 'Girl Effect' – sponsored and promulgated as it often is by commercial companies – appears to enact the kinds of approaches advocated by the marketing handbooks discussed by David Buckingham: offering young women social meaning and substance. We return to these dilemmas below.

Taken together, therefore, these chapters suggest that the social construction of 'youth' is a diverse and multifaceted process, whose motivations and consequences are by no means straightforward or guaranteed. Yet to argue that 'youth' (like gender or ethnicity) is a constructed category is by no means to imply that it is therefore dispensable, unnecessary or too politically tainted. Aside from anything else, such a position risks being politically paralysing, stifling any potential for 'youth politics' – or indeed any other kind of politics. Rather, we would argue that the discourses, assumptions and definitions that surround and create the category of 'youth' have material consequences for young people themselves – and indeed for adults – and we need to attend to and engage with their detail and complexity. In this sense, how we (as 'adults') talk *about, with* and *to* young people makes a real difference. In the following section, therefore, we turn to the other side of this debate.

Representing youth: the trouble with 'youth voice'

This volume as a whole does not, of course, set out to offer a comprehensive portrait of all contemporary youth cultures. As Chris Griffin reminds us, the aims of youth studies are multiple; criticism of the Birmingham CCCS school for failing to do the same in its time not only holds it to an impossible standard, but misunderstands the intentions of the work, which was not primarily empirical but a theoretical and political intervention at a particular point in time. Nonetheless, as we have indicated, a more or less explicit justification for a great deal of research on youth is that young people are marginalized, unheard and disempowered; that on key issues that affect their lives, they are more spoken about than speaking up.

A number of the chapters in this book can be read as restoring balance in these respects. The accounts of Youth Radio, as discussed by Lissa Soep, of the girls' media researched by Mary Celeste Kearney and of the teenagers who participated in BBC Blast (Thornham and McFarlane), all point to the potential of young people becoming media makers and the possibilities of amplifying distinct youth perspectives in mainstream media institutions. Some research participants are defined as marginal, whether by virtue of their assumed and assigned (ethnic or religious) identities, as in the case of Rupa Huq and Sunaina Maira's work, or by their media tastes (as in the case of Kyong Yoon's Korean fan subcultures). Some are 'ordinary', as in the case of the students observed and interviewed by Patrick Alexander and Kathrin Hörschelmann and Elisabeth El Refaie. Hilary Pilkington's work, meanwhile, by focusing on the biographies of racist and nationalist skinheads in Russia, draws attention to voices that many would rather not hear or engage with at all.

The conventional narrative of youth cultural studies is one of 'structure and agency'. Typically, for instance, accounts open by setting the scene of 'structure' or 'context' – the larger forces against which young people live out their lives. These might be, as in this book, contemporary youthscapes, dominant media representations of youth or concepts (empire, imperialism, neoliberalism, translocalism). Following this, data from empirical research often demonstrates something gratifying and hopeful: at best resistance or at least difference, excess, that which escapes the determining force of structure and shows that young people have agency or room to manoeuvre. The abstract age category – 'youth', 'childhood' – is contrasted with the 'real', that is, the live, flesh-and-blood subjects (young people, children) to whom these labels are applied and who live in and through them in ways that are – it is implied – more contradictory, messy, yet therefore optimistic, than might be thought. Implicitly or explicitly, many youth culture studies seem to construct this kind of narrative. Moreover, and perhaps ironically, the young people we encounter on their pages often prove to possess similar qualities to those supposedly constructed by neoliberalizing discourses: they are independent, creative, self-fashioning, critical, reflexive and individuated.

However, attending to young people's perspectives is no longer the preserve of a tiny minority of committed researchers and activists. Currently, we are seeing across a broad spectrum of thinking, policy-making and provision in fields such as education, politics, research and governance, a growing movement to promote, engage and listen to 'youth voice'. Multiple agencies and instruments across a range of voluntary sector and membership organizations, social enterprises and networks compel, direct, invite and/or inspire individuals and institutions working with young people to engage with 'voice', or its cognate terms of participation, consultation, choice, leadership, empowerment, agency, democracy, capacity-building, partnership, and co-design or collaboration with young people as 'service users'. In these contexts, the elusive category of youth is once more stabilized, assigned attributes of obviousness and authenticity: such measures imagine a subject that exists prior to the process in which it engages. 'Voice' as a metaphor evokes notions of presence and authenticity, whilst being reified and emptied of substantive content. 'Youth' is abstracted from other social differences, and universalized. Accounts of youth voice often imply that it arises spontaneously, from the desire of young people to be 'heard': yet in practice it often emerges in conditions that are both structured and heavily incentivized. Paradoxically, whilst the expression of views is seen both as a right and as having inherent value, young people are also seen to need training and development if they are to exercise voice in an acceptable or appropriate manner.

The participatory dimensions of new media (such as blogging, social networking and mobile communications) are often celebrated as the transparent means by which youth voice can be accessed, and despots in other nations overthrown, for example, through so-called 'Facebook Revolutions' like the Arab Spring. This of course conveniently forgets how in the United Kingdom, for instance, these very same technologies have been blamed for facilitating looting and riots – and indeed how they are extensively used by the authorities for surveillance and control. It also ignores the continuing inequalities in access to these media, and their extensive commercial dimensions, not least as means for gathering (and then selling) information about consumer behaviour. New media come to be seen here as merely neutral tools, and even as inherently open and democratic – as providing in themselves a guarantee of authentic dialogue and creative self-expression.

These measures often claim moral backing and transparent legitimacy from the 1989 United Nations Convention, which enshrines children's right to have a say in matters that affect them. However, the kinds of critical, reflexive research discussed in this volume encourage us to ask more searching questions. What are the social positions and relationships constructed in the process of enabling 'youth voice'? What material and symbolic resources are needed in order to realize one's voice or to narrate one's story and place in the world? How do existing opportunities and practices serve to produce particular kinds of voice, and constrain or limit others? And what are the relationships between voice and action?

As many commentators have remarked, there are constraints in terms of which kinds of young people are able and disposed to play these kinds of games in the first place. Phil Cohen (2003) claims that in the United Kingdom, the New Labour government (1997–2010) took a 'cultural turn' that set the agenda for youth research, with its idea that the qualities of marginalized youth could help to rejuvenate the economy, revitalize inner cities and so forth. But in the process, he argues, 'new lines of battle were drawn between those youth identities regarded as examples of healthy happy hybridity (and hence both marketable and political) and those which clung to pathological purities (bad for business and civic boosterism)'. As Anita Harris (2006) argues, young people are actively required to exercise their responsibilities as citizens, yet for many the traditional markers of citizenship have become ever more difficult to achieve; and in this context, participation may not be a meaningful practice – and may even prove to be an oppressive imposition. As Harris suggests, there is a risk that the imperative of participation 'serves only to further 'responsibilize' children and youth, and ultimately blame them for their failure to engage'. Furthermore, if 'voices' are not listened to, and if listening does not translate into action, cynicism and disengagement would seem to be an entirely reasonable response.

More broadly, the search for 'youth voice' has been analysed as symptomatic of the same 'neoliberal' shift identified in the first section, away from the notion of a 'welfare' state to a 'pedagogic' (Pykett, 2010), 'post-welfare' or 'governance' state – a state acting not as provider, but instead as a funder and monitor of educational and social services provided by others. Here an interest in 'youth voice' differs from an interest in young people as cultural actors (as in the early Cultural Studies approaches discussed elsewhere in this volume), or even in youth as explicitly political agents, as Lukose describes. Instead, 'youth' can be seen as a form of technical expertise or capital that can be exploited in particular circumstances, and for particular purposes. It may represent an identity that can be professionalized or utilized in the interests of transparency and increased efficiency. Thus this new attention to youth voice can be seen to represent the rise of new forms of knowledge production and nodes of expertise – most dramatically represented in this volume by Carles Feixa who finds himself conversing with British Prime Minister David Cameron on the subject of gangs, but also in Lissa Soep's work with and for Youth Radio. It can be linked to the ascendance of evidence-based policymaking as a dominant model for policy deliberation, which increasingly calls upon activist and non-governmental organizations to research the populations they 'represent' in order to produce credible knowledge that will further their goals, sway policymakers and gain media credibility. Within evidence-based policymaking, as Grundy and Smith (2007) remark, social science research methods are valorized as the pre-eminent form of knowledge production: they are able to claim legitimacy and render the worlds of hitherto marginalized groups visible in the policy process.

Many scholars have pointed out the political pitfalls of the evidence-based approach: it is often seen as symptomatic of the depoliticizing and managerialist dynamics of neoliberal governance, deflecting notions of politics defined as distributions of power, force and agency. There is an ontological politics at stake here, as research and knowledge production are inevitably bound up with struggles over which kinds of 'youth' realities are to be made real within policy deliberation. We might well argue that the emphasis on youth voice serves as a means of 'enrolling' young people 'into the architectures of governing' (in John Clarke's term, 2010); or that voice can serve as merely a form of 'vernacular ventriloquism', affirming an official and pre-existing position or managerial purpose, and that it is in a sense already 'scripted'.

Yet this would be to underestimate the possibilities here. Youth voice also has a performative function, inspiring changes through moral force rather than more legislative, top-down methods (Bragg and Manchester, 2011, 2012). However constraining and even patronizing they may find it, young people can and do self-consciously mobilize voice – and speak as 'young people' – in their efforts to alter the balance of power. It can also provide an opportunity to make a positive difference, not merely to the position of young people, but in other respects as well. Youth-oriented groups, organizations and individual young people are not simply the victims of a process of manipulation: they are not only what they are constructed to be. Rather, they may be able to employ the social constructions that are available to them, in knowing and self-reflexive (not to mention cynical and even deliberately deceitful) ways, in order to achieve real, material outcomes that are not necessarily foreseen by institutions – although we should beware of assuming that these outcomes will necessarily and inevitably prove to be politically progressive or even democratic.

Nonetheless, in this situation, it becomes difficult to regard 'youth voice' as a straightforward matter of 'empowerment'. This view will do little to explain David Cameron's interest in Carles Feixa's research, or the funding for Rupa Huq's work from a government initiative on Preventing Violent Extremism. Rather, we need to be asking reflexive questions about how 'youth voice' is enacted within and through specific sites and practices, and the positions, capacities and narratives it offers to those involved (Barnett et al., 2011). These all require careful, situated interpretation if we are to understand their meanings and effects. Any youth voice is largely what we – as adults, researchers, educators, policy-makers and practitioners – make it: it has no prior existence and it cannot 'act' alone, whether to improve services, offer emancipation or any of the other virtuous aims with which it has been tasked. On one level, we would agree that youth voice represents a political opportunity – albeit one that, like all political opportunities, is highly contingent and almost inevitably compromised. In such situations, young people cannot be seen simply to 'speak for themselves'. However, they can consciously *use* the imperative for youth voice for their own purposes: they can knowingly construct themselves as 'youth', bearing witness to the imperatives of those who invite them to speak, yet they can also negotiate with the positions that are available to them, and thereby use the political opportunity for their own purposes.

Different youths? – studying youth enactments

What principles for future research and practice might respect the constructed nature of youth, for which our contributors have collectively argued, whilst responding theoretically, politically and methodologically to the demand for 'youth voice'? By way of answer, let us step away from the life-affirming and regenerative notion of 'youth' and briefly enter instead the realm of disease. In *The body multiple* Annemarie Mol (2002) presents us with an exemplary approach to making sense of the complexities of the social world. Her examination of medical practices was carried out using very detailed observations, a kind of multiple ethnography that attempts to examine the object in question – the disease atherosclerosis – and the things that make it: language, spaces, pathogens, texts, interactions, professions, medical devices. Whilst these accrete to construct what is then treated as a *singular* concept, when studied in practice the objects of atherosclerosis are multiple and not co-terminous. Most strikingly, for example, the atherosclerosis identified in an amputated limb by means of a microscope in a lab is not the same as – but is made to cohere with – the atherosclerosis of the consulting room, where it is diagnosed through different procedures with living patients.

Mol's book invokes these disjunctures formally, through juxtaposing different kinds of text on each page to replicate in a small way the complexities of the social world, whilst acknowledging that the book itself is only a partial reproduction of a small part of that world. It shows us that to really get to grips with what surrounds us, we need to listen very carefully to all the voices and discourses at play, and look very closely at the practices that are enacted. Without this we will follow a reductionist path that reduces social objects to single points of 'understanding' and 'explanation', and lose sight of the specificity of cases by grouping together things that have, at best, a passing resemblance to one another. It is only through this detailed and nuanced ethnographic approach that Mol is able to reveal the intricacies of the social construction of complex objects like diseases.

We need to recognize that a disease, in all its complexities and with all its precedents, antecedents and attendants, is a simple object compared to the subject matter of this book – 'youth'. Yet ultimately, we need to do something similar: to trace the proliferation of the concept of youth, the sites in which it circulates or has currency and the different social actors who use it. In the process, we need to consider how it functions, how we come to know what we think we know of 'youth' and the social practices from which the concept emerges. We need to produce complex ways of seeing the specific practices, processes and contexts through which what comes to be recognized as 'youth' is produced.

In her chapter, Lukose discusses how in anthropology the concept of culture gradually changed from being a noun to an adjective. Likewise,

Steve Woolgar (2012) has argued that we should treat reified, revered and standardized ideas like 'childhood' (and by extension, youth) as gerunds in order to convert them into objects of analysis, studying 'youthing', or how youth is produced, assembled and rendered in different contexts. He suggests we might think of 'child' and 'youth' as analogous to notions like 'social' or 'natural' or 'modern': as Bruno Latour and others working within the Science and Technology Studies paradigm have argued, these are not givens, but made and sustained through considerable and significant work, albeit involving mundane devices, ordinary technologies and unremarkable objects. Neither 'youth' nor 'culture' pre-exists their enactment in practices – in social, political, cultural and symbolic acts of making (Isin, 2008). Ontological enactment brings into being the nature and existence of relevant objects and entities. The being engaged in cultural consumption is being enacted (constituted) as youthful or young, as the same time as the texts are being constituted as youth culture. In this way, as Woolgar argues, we can show how these entrenched conceptual entities are not natural and inevitable but could be otherwise.

Some of the challenges of this kind of approach are captured in the work of Dan Cook. In relation to commercial culture's construction of 'childhood' and 'youth', for example, he has shown how the market becomes embedded in how we come to know these concepts and how children and young people might come to identify and understand themselves and others as a result (Cook, 2003). For example, he describes how one kind of 'mundane device' – department store layout plans – offer young people 'ways of locating, materially and bodily, their position with regard to key social indices like age and gender ... social class and ethnicity' (p. 165). As he argues, if commercial interests commodify youth, they do so not by manipulating consumers but by respecting them and taking them seriously, legitimating the' child's perspective' – whether actual or ascribed – as a source of authority and acting upon it. Whilst definitions of what is 'authentic' and 'cultural' in youth terms have often hinged on what can be seen as untainted by commerce, such work contributes to undermining such conventional oppositions (see also Steiner, 2013, Zelizer, 1985). It also shows how agency can arise from our social positioning and construction within discourse, rather than simply being repressed or denied by it. This paradox is also suggested by Koffman and Gill's allusion to the many parodic videos that the official 'Girl Effect' production has spawned, showing how young people can take the terms within which they are constructed in order to speak back in sometimes surprising or unexpected ways.

We also need to attend more critically to what has been termed 'the social life of methods'. John Law in *After method* (2004) argues that 'Method is not ... a set of more or less successful procedures for reporting on a given reality. Rather it is performative. It helps to produce realities ... [it] is not, and never could be, innocent or purely technical.' He goes on to state that 'presence' also makes 'absence' – an idea that we can apply in this context to 'youth' itself. Lukose makes a similar point when she argues that 'youth is often mobilized to mask other matrices of social difference'. Celebrating 'youth' rebellion in the Arab Spring obscures other questions of class, gender and rural–urban divisions. Making youth more visible can often mean making gender less so: the term 'youth' invokes a generational narrative around age differences where feminist slogans referring to 'girls and women' draw forth more solidaristic narratives of what women might share or what kinds of intergenerational relations are possible. As Patrick Alexander's chapter shows, such generational discourses also influence how teachers and students relate to each other, conjuring barriers between and across ages, even as their experiences speak of commonality as much as difference. And as Mary Kearney shows, the endlessly renewing concept of youth – and its all-too-frequent identification with technological novelty – may obscure commonalities with earlier cultural forms and practices.

The ontological politics here extend to the kinds of persons who inhabit the world – how we ourselves have contributed to making young people researchable subjects and offered categories through which they may think of themselves. In their genealogical study Osborne and Rose (1999) claim that as the knowledge practices, scientific devices and research technologies of the social sciences – such as consumer surveys, opinion polls and census techniques – have seeped out into the world, people have increasingly come to 'fit' the demands of the research. They have internalized the phenomena and become 'researchable' from the perspective of the devices and techniques formally created to 'discover' them – as the quote right at the start of this chapter illustrates. The nature of the kinds of identities we attribute to ourselves and the forms of life we have come to lead have, therefore, been shaped at least in part by the methods and analyses of the social sciences themselves. These norms are being embedded in institutional practices, and are coming to set the horizons of how young people can account for themselves as learners and individuals. As researchers, we cannot stand outside this process. Our own methods also enact youth and render them knowable to different groups, from prime ministers and media companies to educators and activists. Acknowledging how we create social realities and social worlds might enable us to attend more closely to the potential and the ambiguities of research processes, to their productive and performative elements, their capacity to produce knowledges about areas of life that might otherwise remain invisible, and to locate what is unexpected and truly creative in what young people do and say.

Perhaps it is on these kinds of theoretical grounds that we might begin to combine, or at least to understand the relations between, the two seemingly incompatible perspectives with which we began. Accumulating yet more data about the diverse manifestations of youth culture is a necessary and important process. Creating the possibility for – and intervening in – forms of youth politics and practice remains an important imperative. Yet there is an urgent need here for much more theoretical and methodological reflexivity, and for moving beyond the rather parochial confines of previous youth research. Despite the historical developments in the field, we would argue that critical questions remain to be addressed. We hope that this volume has provided some diverse indications of how this might be done.

References

Barnett, C., Cloke, P., Clarke, N. and Malpass, A. (2011). *Globalizing responsibility: The political rationalities of ethical consumption*. Chichester: Wiley-Blackwell.

Bragg, S. and Manchester, H. (2011). Doing it differently: Youth leadership and the arts in a creative learning programme. *UNESCO Observatory Multi-Disciplinary Research in the Arts. Special Youth Participation Issue, 2*(2).

Bragg, S. and Manchester, H. (2012). Pedagogies of student voice (Pedagogías de la voz del alumnado). *Revista de Educacion. Special Issue on Student Voice, 359*(September–December), 143–163.

Buckingham, D. and Bragg, S. (2004). *Young people, sex and the media: The facts of life?* Basingstoke: Palgrave Macmillan.

Clarke, J. (2010). Enrolling ordinary people: Governmental strategies and the avoidance of politics? *Citizenship Studies, 14*(6), 637–650. doi: 10.1080/13621025.2010.522349

Cohen, P. (2003). Mods and shockers: Youth cultural studies in Britain. In A. Bennett, M. Cieslik and S. Miles (eds). *Researching youth* (pp. 13–28). New York: Palgrave Macmillan.

Cook, D. T. (2003). Spatial biographies of children's consumption: Market places and spaces of childhood in the 1930s and beyond. *Journal of Consumer Culture, 3*(2),147–169.

Grundy, J. and Smith, M. (2007). Activist knowledges in queer politics 1. *Economy and Society, 36*(2), 294–317.

Hacking, I. (1999). *The social construction of what?* Cambridge, MA: Harvard University Press.

Harris, A. (2004). *Future girl: Young women in twenty-first century*. London and New York: Routledge.

Harris, A. (2006). Introduction: Critical perspectives on child and youth participation in Australia and New Zealand/Aotearoa. *Children, Youth and Environments, 16*(2), 220–230.

Isin, E. F. (2008). Theorizing acts of citizenship. In E. F. Isin and G. M. Nielsen (eds), *Acts of Citizenship* (pp. 15–43). London: Palgrave Macmillan.

James, A., Jenks, C. and Prout, A. (1999). *Theorising childhood*. London: Polity Press.

Jeffrey, C. (2010). Geographies of children and youth I: Eroding maps of life. *Progress in Human Geography, 34*(4), 496–505.

Law, J. (2004). *After method: Mess in social science research*. London: Routledge.

Lesko, N. (2001). *Act Your Age! A cultural construction of adolescence*. New York: Routledge.

Lynch, M. (2001). The contingencies of social construction. *Economy and Society, 30*(2), 240–254. doi: 10.1080/03085140120042307

Meyer, A. (2007). The moral rhetoric of childhood. *Childhood – a Global Journal of Child Research, 14*(1), 85–104. doi: 10.1177/0907568207072532

Mol, A. (2002). *The body multiple: Ontology in medical practice*. Durham and London: Duke University Press.

Osborne, T. and Rose, N. (1999). Do the social sciences create phenomena?: The example of public opinion research. *British Journal of Sociology, 50*(3), 367–396.

Pykett, J. (2010). Introduction: The pedagogical state: education, citizenship, governing. *Citizenship Studies, 14*(6), 617–619.

Rose, N. (1999). *Governing the soul: The shaping of the private self* (2nd ed.). London and New York: Free Association Books.

Steiner, P. (2013). Markets and culture: Viviana Zelizer's Economic Lives. *Economy and Society, 42*(2), 322–333.

Woolgar, S. (2012). Ontological child consumption. In A. Sparrman, B. Sandin and J. Sjöberg (eds). *Situating child consumption: Rethinking values and notions of children, childhood and consumption* (pp. 33–52). Lund: Nordic Academic Press.

Zelizer, V. (1985). *Pricing the priceless child*. Princeton, NJ: Princeton University Press.

Index